MY WAY HOME

MY WAY HOME
Growing Up Homeless in America

A Memoir

Michael Gaulden

WiDō Publishing
Salt Lake City

WiDō Publishing
Salt Lake City, Utah
widopublishing.com

Cover design by Steven Novak
Book design by Marny K. Parkin

ISBN: 978-1-937178-94-9

Printed in the United States of America

Contents

Preface

FOR MORE THAN ELEVEN YEARS, FROM JUNE OF 1998 until July of 2009, I was homeless. Most people view homelessness as a permanent handicap or an unfortunate disability, but I used the circumstances of my world as the fuel for my success.

Allow this memoir to serve as a window into my soul. This is my true story. Feel my grief, feel my hunger, and feel my sorrow—but then, feel my success. This memoir covers the latter part of my homeless journey, ranging from age fourteen to seventeen, predominately my high school years. The horror of my homelessness is what I call it. Allow me to take you down my path and to walk in my footsteps along my own hellacious underground railroad. If you are reading this in the midst of your own overwhelmingly challenging journey, it is you for whom I write. If people laugh at you, tell them my story and let them laugh at me. If they point at you, show them my face and let them point at me—let them martyr me. I will embrace the shame of homelessness and endure the pain of poverty, in order to give someone else the courage to persevere through their own life. It is you whom I urge not to quit. I know your pain and through my pain, I wish to give you strength. For everyone else reading this, please understand my story is only one of millions of other homeless people.

To keep the identities of those involved private, certain names have been altered.

1. A Homeless Boy: Age Fourteen

2005-2006 School Year

"CAN YOU SPARE ANY CHANGE?"

"Not today."

"Can you spare any change?"

"Sorry I can't."

"Ma'am, can you spare any change?"

"No . . . Please get away!"

Aimlessly, I wandered down a busy street of downtown San Diego. Early September embraced me with an icy chill. I had a tattered black backpack on my back and a melted stolen Snickers bar tucked in my right pocket for dinner.

"Sir, can you spare any change?" I asked once more as I pressed forward. A slim man in a business suit smiled with pity as he dug deep into his pockets and handed me four quarters. "Thank you, sir, God bless." He didn't respond. He kept walking as if we had no interaction at all—but being ignored is normal for me.

The night air whipped under my thin black shirt. My master showed little remorse as it subdued me. I had no jacket, no sleeping bag, nothing—except the clothes on my frail body. Transparent to the naked eye, I moved as a ghost. When I walked, no one noticed me. Maybe because my clothes were dirty. Maybe because my shoes were from a donation box. Or maybe because I embodied poverty. Whatever the reason, it made me invisible to everyone around me, except when my silhouette flickered from panhandling, frightening people.

I moved along the street headed toward a part of downtown where the homeless lined up close to the Twelfth and Imperial trolley station. I knew a guy, named Rudy, who usually had a small tent set up outside and—if I was lucky, if he was still alive— I could crash there. I shivered from the wind. All of my panhandling efforts had made me only two dollars and forty-five cents. I could not bring scraps back to my mom and sister.

"Spare any change?"

"Get a job!"

"Ma'am. I'm fourteen," I said back, but it didn't matter. She deleted me from her memory as soon as her eyesight left me.

"Spare any change?" I asked another woman.

"Mike G?"

To my left came my friend, Ray, up the sidewalk. He had overheard me panhandling. The lady I had asked for money had stopped to dig in her purse.

"Keep going lady," Ray shooed her away. "Don't be out here begging these rich jerks for money," he scolded.

I knew Ray from around town. Being sixteen years old, he thought he had some authority over me.

"I have to eat." I shrugged.

Ray eyed me and shook his head. "You won't eat like that. Where you going?"

"I have no clue, bro. You know how it is."

"Yeah . . . I was leaving but come with me."

"To where?"

"Get you some money."

"From where?"

He trekked back down the street. I followed close behind. He turned down an alley and stood beside to hooded figures who shook his hand tossing up their gang sign. I walked next to Ray blowing on my hands for warmth waiting for money to magically appear. After a few minutes, a thin man in a tank top, faded blue jeans, and a mouth with sporadically missing, yellow teeth came up to us. He handed Ray twenty dollars, and Ray placed a sandwich bag containing a crystalline white substance on the ground. I watched the entire transaction. The drug addict illuminated as he reached for the product. Then he disappeared out of the alley as quickly as he had appeared.

"Hell no!" I moved away in a huff. Ray raced in front of me, cutting me off.

"Where you think you're going?"

"I'm out of here," I said. "If the police don't get us, we're going to get robbed or worse."

"Calm down." Ray revealed the barrel to the .38 caliber pistol he had stuffed in his waist belt. "Nobody's robbing me. And I'm just trying to help your bum ass."

"I don't need this kind of help," I said.

"The hell you don't! I can see your ribs, bro. You're like one of those xylophones," Ray exclaimed.

"Whatever man. I'm not selling drugs. I keep telling you and Jason that I'll figure something out," I said.

"You mean you'll die. Right now, you don't have to sell anything. Just be the lookout. I'll make a few more transactions and give you food money. Relax bro, it's easy money," Ray declared.

I deeply inhaled then exhaled. Crack cocaine hit America hard and swept through the inner city crippling most of the minority families before my birth. I had seen it my entire life and wanted no part of it. The nationwide epidemic was just another means to an end; crazy. I brushed past Ray and marched to the end of the alley. "Just whistle if you see something." Ray chuckled.

I leaned against the alley wall—on patrol. The promise of food lured me and stopped me from leaving. I knew it was wrong, but if I left, where would I go? There's no telling whether Rudy and his tent were still there. After about an hour—and endless foot traffic from the alley—I grew impatient. By now, Ray had to have made enough money for me to at least go to McDonald's. I followed another addict into the alley as he strolled up to Ray. Ray slyly flashed a small stack of cash he reserved for me. He gave a head nod acknowledging the time came to go, as the addict limped over toward Ray's friends, and Ray began walking toward me. The addict handed one of Ray's friends money, and Ray's friend directly handed the addict a sack of crack-cocaine.

"Police! Freeze!" The addict grabbed Ray's friend's wrist as he flashed a badge. Two police cars abruptly blockaded the alley entrance.

"Shit!" I said. Ray, his other friend, and I darted toward the opposite end of the alleyway. I sped past the undercover officer as he wrestled with a boy trying to handcuff him.

"Freeze!" yelled the officers behind us with enough confidence to convince me they had their guns drawn. I sprinted with all my might. Ray and the other boy were in front of me—they were a little faster and reached the end of the alley before me. Blue and red lights flashed upon exiting. Two more police cars were parked at this end as well. Two officers tried to restrain Ray as he fought back. A separate officer had his friend already restrained on the ground with a bloody nose. Catching the officers off guard, I sped past the scene. One of them left Ray's friend and chased after me. My heart crashed into my chest. My legs began to quiver as I focused my feet step by step, one fall would be the end of me. He quickly approached. Adrenaline coursed through me like I overdosed on caffeine, tirelessly propelling me forward. I normally saw beer bellied police officers, but not him. He gained on me like he ran track for a living.

"Freeze!" he yelled again which made me run faster. I couldn't stop to explain why I stood in a crack alley. There wouldn't be a point. He saw me there which meant I dealt drugs. I sped down the sidewalk, weaving in between people trying to shake him. I zigzagged across downtown. Most people stumbled out of my way. A few onlookers encouraged my getaway.

I panicked. If caught, I would be going away for a long time, but a part of me wanted to get caught. At least I would have shelter. I turned back to see if I had lost him.

"Aaah!" I girlishly squealed, surprised to see him just a few feet behind me. I dropped my backpack in some bushes so I could pick up speed. I turned left down the street trying to find my way closer to Rudy and his tent, but far enough to shake the pursuing cop. I jolted between two buildings, sprinted across the street, and darted into a corner store. I was breathing heavily and sweat poured down my face. I could not get my heart to stop racing.

"Do you have a bathroom?" I asked the clerk, periodically glancing through the store glass windows.

"Customers only," he replied. I rolled my eyes handing him a dollar for a pack of gum. "It's a dollar fifteen."

"You're kidding me?" I replied.

"One-fifteen," he said in the same monotone. I peered through the window to see the cop across the street scanning the area.

"Whatever." I handed him a quarter and hid in the restroom for about fifteen minutes until another customer began banging on the door.

I opened it to see a heavyset man sweating, holding his stomach. He pushed past me and slammed the door releasing loud gaseous noises before it even closed. I hesitantly tiptoed outside the store and glanced around. The coast seemed clear. I stood by Horton Plaza Mall and knew it would still be about a thirty-minute walk to get to Rudy. Unforgiving cold swept through the night. The police caught Ray, which meant they found his gun. I wouldn't be seeing him for a while.

"Hey!" shouted a voice. I froze in place. I didn't have enough energy to run again. I dropped my head in submission. "Hey! Boy!" it shouted again. I regained my motion when I realized the voice didn't sound authoritative. The declaration sounded too light and high-pitched. The last lady I had asked for money stood behind me. She strolled up with her hand on her hip. "Now I shouldn't even be doing this because of how rude that thug-of-a-friend of yours was to me, but you had manners and seemed worth it. Here!" The lady handed me a single crisp one dollar bill. "Hope this helps." Her eyes beamed with service as if she expected me to leap for joy.

"Stop!" An officer jumped out of the passenger side of the police car as his partner barely managed to halt the car in time. The cop whom chased me pointed at me as he approached. He forcefully grabbed my hands and wrapped them around my back, tightening on handcuffs.

"What are you doing!" shrieked the woman in complete shock.

"He's a suspect, ma'am step back," the officer commanded.

"This is harassment!" she yelled. "I won't stand for this. The boy's already on the streets."

"Streets?" questioned the cop spinning me around facing him. "Weren't you the one I was just chasing?"

"Chasing?" I gasped. "Sir, you must have me confused. We do all resemble each other. I'm just searching for food."

"This will not be another Rodney King moment!" she shouted.

The cop left me standing there as he reached into the car retrieving my abandoned backpack. He opened it, displaying its contents.

"I found this backpack tossed by one of the assailants. There's a toothbrush, some deodorant, a bar of soap, a pack of animal crackers—"

"There's animal crackers?" I blurted out, upset I had not seen them. My outburst almost gave me away as the officer squinted his eyes at me. "Who eats those?" I tried to recover.

"A few black socks and some underwear," he continued. "Is this yours?"

"I've never seen it before in my life," I swore.

"You know him?" he asked the woman.

"I was just about to give him some money. He couldn't have possibly done whatever you're arresting him for. You're racial profiling. He's just a homeless boy. These people have a right to exist too."

People had stopped, and the officer didn't want a scene. He eyed me up and down and reluctantly removed the handcuffs. "You wouldn't lie to me, would you?" he asked me.

"No sir."

"Of course not," he said. "Good day, ma'am."

"Good day, sir!" she remarked. He returned to the police car and drove away.

"What a jerk." The woman stuck out the single dollar bill. I stared at it with a lack of enthusiasm. For some reason her previous words repeated over and over in my head. She had my whole life summed up so meaningless in a few short words: "Just a homeless boy." I mean I existed as a homeless boy . . . but did that tell you my character? Was my circumstance my entire identity? I took the dollar and politely thanked the woman. I meant it for her heroic contribution to my life. She thought my gratitude was for the dollar. She eagerly acknowledged my gratitude and rubbed me on my head, almost petting me.

"Take care, hun." She stepped away, leaving me, the homeless boy to his homeless business. Her words had an emptiness about them, which just didn't sit well with me. I didn't understand why it bothered me as I had been called so many names, but she spoke of me as if my existence wasn't equivalent to hers. Most people insulted me on purpose. I had defenses set up for insults. The problem was she didn't ridicule me on purpose, which was worse.

I headed toward Rudy and his tent, traversing under the night sky. Ray was in real trouble but I couldn't do anything. He tried to help but he almost caused my arrest too. After all of my effort, I gained nothing. I landed right back where I started. I folded my arms into my shirt to generate warmth.

At least I would be safe with Rudy; he was just a homeless man who didn't matter. A ghost only police could see. He sat at the bottom of America with no hope of ever progressing. His moral compass lost on the underside of capitalism. I fit well with Rudy: a mundane homeless man and a mundane homeless boy. I had a name—Michael Gaulden—but my name was irrelevant. I clenched the money the woman gave me tightly in my hand until my fingernails cut into my skin. My life was barely worth a dollar.

2. Walking Alone

I MOVED CLOSER AND CLOSER TO THE STREET WHERE the homeless congregated—where I'd find Rudy. I knew I had arrived by the "smell of homelessness." Loud commotion stirred up ahead. A small crowd of teenagers had gathered around someone. They were yelling at a homeless man.

"Why don't you get a job, you lazy bum!" a girl screamed, pushing the man's chest. Another boy pushed him to the ground.

"You fucking stink!" yelled a boy, plugging his nose as a girl sprayed the man with some of her perfume.

Two others stood in front of the man holding cheeseburgers.

"You want some?" mocked the first girl stuffing a big bite of the cheeseburger in her mouth, chewing it very slowly, and opening her mouth so he could see the food inside. "It's sooo good," she continued, taking another bite.

The second person, a boy, handed his burger over to the man. "Here, take it, you're hungry," he said. The homeless man glanced up at him not sure what to do, but slowly reached out a quivering hand to take the half-eaten burger. Then the boy dropped it on the ground in front of him and stomped down as hard as he could. The boy's tantalizing received a roar of applause as the crowd of teenagers shouted insults at the homeless man. Some threw crumpled pieces of paper, others spat at him. My heart cried for him as no person deserved to be humiliated.

As I neared, the crowd grew more belligerent. I searched around for Rudy's signature green tent. I hoped to find it before I had to pass the ridiculed man and teenagers or froze to death—whichever occurred first. The group of teenagers started shoving the man more violently, spitting long wads of saliva on him, but he didn't fight back. They pulled his clothes, ripping them. The man just sat still taking the abuse. I knew firsthand how mean kids could be. At twelve years old, a bunch of kids caught me washing my body in a bathroom sink at school and told everyone they could. Younger people seemed to thrive on the misfortune of others. I approached close enough to get a side view of the man. He had stubby legs with a large beer belly and mangled hair that looked like it had once been wavy. He actually looked a lot like. . . .

"Rudy?" I shouted, catching his attention and running to his aid. The group of teens suddenly took off running in the opposite direction, all the while laughing. I didn't get a good picture of them. They left Rudy sitting on the ground with a glob of spit hanging on his shoulder. "Damn! That was you? Are you okay? I saw what happened."

"Hey, Mike G! Long time no see man." Rudy was Native American. He always smiled although every tooth in his mouth was either colored yellow-brown or missing. He wore an old gray sweatshirt now torn at the collar and faded blue jeans. He wore sandals displaying his cracked and crusted feet with brown toenails. Doctors diagnosed him terminal with liver failure, but he was such a nice guy.

Wiping hamburger meat from his tangled hair, I inquired, "How've you been?"

"I've been fine, just . . . living," Rudy began eating small chunks of burger from the pavement.

I exclaimed, "Why'd you let those people do that to you? Don't let them do that! We have to protect ourselves. People are going to trample all over us if we don't."

"Mike G, it's the same old, same old. And I'm not young like you. I can't go running after them every time someone does this. I've accepted this. I'm dying anyway. It doesn't matter," Rudy said.

"Don't talk like that," I said. "This type of thing happens all the time, nothing new. Like when we had to go chase those girls away who were messing with your sister. You remember that?"

Rudy responded, "When we were all sleeping at that one place? Yeah, thanks for that by the way. What brings you away from your fancy shelters and down here with us common folk anyway?"

I replied, "Time ran out."

"Hate when that happens," Rudy said. "Where are you going?"

"That's what I came to talk to you about," I said.

Rudy quickly offered, "Well, of course you can stay with me." He wiped off the dangling glob of saliva with his bare fingers and stood. "Follow me. I have an old jacket you can wear; we don't need you getting sick."

"Thanks, Rudy," I replied gratefully.

I followed Rudy to his small green tent perched against a metal fence. Rows of homeless people lined the sidewalk. Some slept in boxes, some in sleeping bags, and the unfortunate just in the clothes on their back. So many displaced people from all walks of life. They appeared savage, almost animalistic, and they definitely smelled like it. I guessed that's what my image reflected to everyone else. Rudy kept his tent away from the main population. One of the few lucky enough to own a tent. Rudy showed me inside, which wasn't even big enough for him, let alone the two of us. He then handed me the jacket along with a can of beans. Rudy didn't even have to inquire whether I had eaten. He just handed me the sealed can of beans and a spoon requesting I save half the can for him. I showed him the Snickers bar. Rudy refused it, stating he watched his calories.

"Hey, you wouldn't happen to have a can opener would you?" I asked.

"No, why?"

"Just wondering," I said. I sat the can and spoon beside me. I rushed to eat the Snickers bar but decided against it, thinking breakfast might be more important than dinner. Outside cold seeped through the slits in the tent, but under shelter comforted me. I curled up in a ball and tried to drift to sleep.

Before I could fall asleep I heard whispering mixed with a lot of snickering. I sat up glancing around. Rudy still snored so I laid back down. A switchblade knife suddenly burst through the tent's wall and sliced up and down letting in the crisp sting of cold air. Another appeared on the other side of the tent and sliced a long opening into it.

"Bum!" yelled an array of voices, followed by the entrance of a multitude of hands holding open bottles and cartons. Cold water and juice flooded the entire tent splashing all over Rudy and me. Rudy abruptly woke in a panic but then, upon realizing what happened, sat still, calm and collected in some weird inner trance of peace. The crowd roared with laughter, pleased with themselves.

I erupted through the ruined tent as juice dripped off my face and shrieked, "Leave us alone!" Teenagers surrounded the tent howling with maniacal laughter. They sounded like hyenas after a kill. I couldn't take it. My life might barely be worth a dollar but I owned that dollar, I had to protect it. I charged one of the laughing boys and tackled him to the ground. I was quickly pulled off him but I broke loose. I swung at the boy who pulled me off and hit him on his right cheek, causing him to stumble backwards. I would fight them all if I could. They picked the wrong homeless people to mess with. Another one attacked me, and I managed to put him in a headlock trying to strangle every happy breath from his body.

"Michael?" A girl from the crowd gasped.

I glanced in her direction and froze. I recognized her. I let the boy go and scanned the kids around me, recognizing most of them. We weren't best friends, but I saw them around school. The girl's name was Brittany; the girlfriend of my friend Carlos.

"Gaulden?" asked another girl staring at me questionably. She continued, "What the hell? What were you doing in there?" I recognized her, too; her name was Jessica. Just a few days ago, she said she liked my smile. She inspected my clothes. She observed the environment. Then she gazed past me as if I turned transparent before her very eyes.

"That's the boy you said you liked?" One of Jessica's friends gazed at me as the eagle gazes upon its prey. The scowl forming on Jessica's face made it clear she didn't like me or my smile anymore. I embarrassed her. Everyone stopped murmuring and, slowly and awkwardly, left me there.

"Wait!" I called out. "Brittany! . . . Jessica!" But no one turned around. Everyone silently faded into the distance. I knew at school there would be no more talking. From then on, I could no longer be one of them. To them I was now like Rudy. I was *now* homeless, and they could not associate with me. Little did they know I had *always* been homeless. I wasn't like Rudy as he became homeless only three years ago. Rudy was, in fact, *now* like me.

I resigned in my mind it was fine. I grew tired of pretending I lived like everyone else anyway. I knew they were going to go tell everyone they could. I didn't really care anymore. They wouldn't be lying when they called me the sewage of society. I burdened the government. Poor and dirty, I exemplified everything their parents warned them would happen to them if they didn't stay in school. I agreed with everything they were going to say. How could I be angry with them if they spoke the truth? As they walked down the street full of homeless people, I could only hope they understood being a "bum" wasn't my fault. I did not chose my birth. In their blessed world, they traveled together—beyond the homeless road in which I traversed alone. If I could, I would join them strolling in bliss. As they traveled beyond our ghostly realm, I could not follow. I was chained to my homelessness. The world of poverty rested on my shoulders as if I became the Greek Titan, Atlas. There was no bliss along my path.

I returned to the cut-up tent to find Rudy lying amidst the flood of water and juice. I guess he used his inner peaceful trance to put himself back to sleep. He snored loudly. The empty can of beans floated in the tent next to the empty Snickers wrapper. Rudy must have eaten it when I left the tent. I laid down in the great flood, coming to peace with it just as Noah did when he built his ark—except "my ark" wasn't water-proof and would not save me. When all the liquid dried, it would leave me sticky and smelly. I couldn't even locate where I could take my next shower. I took out the pack of gum from my pocket. It cost one dollar and fifteen cents—worth more than me. I chewed half the pack, only half because I could save the rest for tomorrow in case I didn't find food. I knew I could have spent more time wallowing, but my mind drifted. I pondered if I should have shown more remorse for Ray, but my mind could not focus. Each thought growing more obsessed with the emptiness of my belly. Saturday's were typically hungry. I hadn't eaten the entire weekend and at least Ray would get fed in jail. I didn't get fed until school breakfast Monday morning—if I made it there on time. I listened as my stomach rumbled, begging for any morsel of food, hoping with each chew the gum would magically turn into food—any type of food. God, I was so hungry.

3. Hunger

MY STOMACH GROWLED, ROARING LIKE THE MIGHTY king of the jungle. Someone had dropped a burning match down my throat, setting my insides afire. Dinner, or what shelter staff called dinner, began at five o'clock; unfortunately, by the time my sister and I returned back from school, and my mom came back from work, not even scraps remained. Missing dinner at the shelter was bittersweet. Bitter, because I would starve until the miniscule breakfast served at school; but sweet, because I was sure the grotesque food would kill me.

I sat on the bed holding my stomach in agony. The shelter room was small—an oversized closet where they herded the three of us. It had a bunk bed and a separate twin-sized bed, plus a sink. There wasn't a television, radio, fridge, or microwave, and hot water was unthinkable. But the cold, dirty, bug-infested, place beat the alternative. We'd lived the alternative, so we were content to live there. Mid-October had come. We had been in the shelter for about five weeks. The only things growling louder than my stomach were my mom's and sister's stomachs. My sister—we called her Pooh Bear—and I ate lunch at school so we were "fortunate"; my mom had it the worst. She's sick. She didn't want us to find out. She didn't think we knew, but how could we not? Despite her sickness, she woke up early every morning and rode the bus two hours to work, where she stood on her feet all day and then returned to the shelter and went without eating. I didn't understand how she did it, but she did. Was it all in vain? The meager minimum-wage checks she made disappeared to taxes, washing our clothes and for her bus pass. Every payday, she would buy us food, but she received paychecks every two weeks and the food depleted in three days. We used to have food stamps, but Uncle Sam kept randomly and "accidentally" cutting us off until we could come into the welfare office and re-prove we were homeless.

We would lay in our beds, incapable of doing anything else. We couldn't go out because of the curfew. The shelter didn't want us wandering. If we did, they would make us leave. So, we sat in a dark closet—our room—trapped within our reality, tortured by our hunger.

The shelter received food from other shelters in San Diego. If we made it to dinner, we would be eating *leftover* leftovers, which had been transported around downtown San Diego for so long that by the time it fell to us, we played the guessing game trying to figure out exactly what we were eating. Of course, beggars can't be choosers, but a little humor helped soothe the pain. Whether being good food or bad food, food was food. The food might not have been pretty, but it kept us alive. Sustenance was the most important part because homeless people like us died daily, and nobody ever noticed or cared.

Late at night, I tossed and turned. Hunger pains were like I had been shot in my abdomen, I gripped my belly in pure agony. I wanted to scream for God but the shelter would kick us out for breaking noise compliance. None of us were asleep, but we all remained quiet; we didn't have any words to speak. I would have eaten a rat if I saw it. My mom told me to try to keep my mind off eating, but how could I when my stomach kept digesting itself? It gurgled louder than any other thought I could think. It prickled the inside of my stomach like a cactus scraping against me. The hunger so painful I couldn't stand it, I couldn't do anything but lie there and take it. I would have snuck out to find some food, but security caught the last family and they had to leave the next day. Not fair, but nobody cared about being fair to us. I just laid there depressed, thinking about how many other people in the world who were hungry. Bottom line, whether it is Africa or America, starving is starving.

My life. I should have been used to the hunger, but I wasn't. I didn't think I could ever get used to it. I wanted to tell somebody, but who really cared enough to listen to the voice of a homeless boy? The shelter staff made us talk to counselors, and we were supposed to talk about how being homeless made us feel. How the hell did they think it made us feel?

They told my sister and me that we should smile more. I told them that they should switch places with us, and we'd see how much they smiled. They said we should open up so they could understand us better, but they would never understand us better. One time, we sat together at a round table in metal folded chairs in a small room of the shelter. The counselor sat across from me scribbling and analyzing everything I did on a yellow notepad.

"You seem angry," the counselor said with her hair slicked back into a secretarial bun, peering through thin reading glasses.

"I'm not angry. I just don't want to talk to you," I said.

"Why not? I want you to be able to trust me." She folded her hands over the notepad.

"Trust you? Lady, I don't know you," I said. "I'll be out of this shelter in three months, and I'll never see you again. Let's not act like you don't get paid to be here. Let's not act like they don't make me do these little sessions. This isn't friendship."

"Yes, this is my job. While you're here, we might as well talk. You've been resistant this whole time." She desperately tried to break through to me. "We can't leave until the hour is up." Her eyes fell on me with a sense of intrigue, mixed with confusion; like a zookeeper interacting with an animal. I fascinated her.

I responded, "Talk about what?"

"How does being homeless make you feel? Angry for certain," She inquired.

I exclaimed, "It makes me feel like shit, honestly. Hell, yeah, I'm angry! Am I supposed to leap for joy waking up in a shelter every day?" I rose out of my chair to stretch, and she jumped back, frightened. I paused at her reaction, then slowly sat back down crossing my arms.

"Help me understand." She regained her composure.

"Understand me?" I said. "Go on a fast and lay outside of your house and sleep there for a few days if you want to understand me. Or spend a night in this hellhole. You'll never understand me."

She replied, "Empathy is being able to—"

"Don't talk to me about empathy. Talk to me about apathy. Or antipathy. That's all I see," I shared.

"Ah, okay, I see you have some vocabulary. I'm impressed. How old are you?"

"Fourteen."

"You're very mature for a fourteen-year-old."

"You got to be. Homeless years are like dog years. You age really fast."

"Well, you seem really smart. Stay in school. You think you have what it takes to pass the General Educational Development test when you're a senior?" she inquired.

"My GED? Are you kidding?" I said.

"Not at all. I believe in you. You can do it," she stated.

"No duh, I can do it. More like I'm getting my diploma," I responded.

"Oh . . ." she said, "I see . . ." She picked up her pen scribbling in her notebook. "Do you know anyone who's graduated from high school with their diploma?"

"No," I honestly replied trying to think of someone.

"Right . . ." She continued to scribble. "Do you think it's your fault that you're homeless?"

"Hell, no," I said. "It's not like I committed a crime or something, and this was my punishment. But this is just how it is;

I don't think it's any one person's fault. Most people who are homeless don't deserve to be, but we still are."

She checked her watch and scribbled something final in her notepad. The hour ended. "Can I ask you one more question?" she said.

"I guess so," I replied.

"How much do you think we—the counselors—care about you?" she asked.

"Not at all," I said without having to ponder.

"No?" she sounded defensive. "And why is that?"

"Because, like I said, this is your job. Listening to our home-less problems is your job and when your shift is over, you go back home to your normal life, in your warm bed, with all your fancy things, and PlayStation, and food in your stomach. But I'm still here clenching my stomach. I can't run away from this. And when you return, you want to talk about how my night was. Is it your fault I'm here? No. Like I said, it's not my fault either. But that's where we are." She let me leave without any further questions.

I closed my eyes and imagined having a plate in front of me. A big white ceramic plate with a blue trim. Stacked on top with ribs, cornbread, two California burritos, macaroni and cheese, jelly-filled donuts, collard and mustard greens, some tacos, carne asada, Brussels sprouts, and a large side order of Reese's Puffs cereal. I wasn't sure how good so much stuff tasted together, but damn it, I was hungry. Maybe I would throw in a steak, filet mignon; I heard it's the good steak. I braced myself to engulf all of it. I reached out my hands to grab the food, but my fingertips passed right through the plate, the price of being a phantom. I abruptly sat up with my eyes open clutching my belly. I had had enough.

I climbed down from the top bunk and sluggishly made way to my new backpack given to me during shelter intake along with a bag of toiletries. I just knew I forgot some hidden food. I unzipped my backpack. I usually stashed some extra food from school. I searched thoroughly, but I couldn't find anything.

"You just have to go to sleep." My sister sat up in her bed watching me. "You can't feel your stomach when you're asleep."

"I'm so damn hungry, it's not letting me go to sleep," I said.

"Think about it this way. The faster you go to sleep, the faster you wake up, and the closer you are to eating," she preached.

"It's not just me that I'm worried about; it's mama." My mother was sound asleep. "I don't want her going back to the hospital."

"Me neither," Pooh said.

"The hell with this." I slid on my donated shoes.

"Where are you going?" Pooh asked.

"I'm about to get us some food." I put on my newly donated hooded sweatshirt, in stride toward the door.

"What if you get caught? They'll kick us out," Pooh said.

"I got to do something." I silently opened the door so I wouldn't wake my mother. Cold air kissed my face. The shelter used to be an old outdoor motel, and we resided on the second floor. I snuck downstairs and tiptoed passed the security booth, and blended well into the night. The guard had his face down, eyeballs glued to his flip phone. I reached the nearby Shell gas station and tiptoed to the candy aisle. The clerk eyed me suspiciously. He must have heard my stomach. I quickly stuffed three honey buns in my sweatshirt and then grabbed a bag of chips. I brought the chips to the counter and handed them to the man.

"One dollar and fifty cents," he said.

"I only have a dollar." I displayed the dollar I had found earlier that day. He took the dollar and waved me away. I made my way back to the shelter eating the chips on the way. I tiptoed passed the empty security booth.

"Don't move." The security guard on duty flashed his flashlight. He stood right behind me.

"Damn." I turned to face a bigger guy, black, with a beanie covering his bald head. He had a cup of coffee in his hands. "Please, man, just let me go."

"What were you doing out past curfew? I have to report you," he said.

I revealed the honey buns in my pocket. "We're hungry. I had to do something. You would've done the same thing," I offered.

Taking a sip of coffee, he warned, "Bro, don't let me catch you out here again, okay? There are cameras. I can lose my job if I don't report you."

"Trust me, you won't catch me again," I assured.

"Get to your room. Stay out of trouble," he said.

"I will." I shook his hand, returning to my room.

"Oh my God, I thought you got caught!" My sister still sat up in bed.

"I was," I said, giving her a honey bun. I set my mom's by her bed not daring to wake her.

My sister and I devoured our honey buns in a matter of seconds, failing to quell the fire torturing our stomachs, rendering vain my entire trip.

"Pooh, I'm so tired of this." I climbed back on my bunk in defeat.

"Maybe we should pray. I see Mama praying all the time. If we pray too, maybe God will hear us," she said with hope.

I stated, "Do you think he's even listening?"

"I think so. C'mon bow your head and close your eyes. Ready?"

"Sure." I kept my eyes wide open.

"Dear God, we come before you as humble as we know how, grateful for everything you've done for us. But right now, Lord, we're hungry—"

"We're always hungry," I scorned.

My sister added, ". . . And it hurts so badly. Please help us. Heal my mom. Please send a miracle. Fast, God. And please give us a TV or something. Amen."

"Amen." My stomach roared. Sure, tap water would shave off some hunger but we didn't have any fountains in our room, water bottles were hard to steal, and I wondered how much water a human could possibly drink—or according to Ray, how much a xylophone could drink. After years of being homeless, my body couldn't adapt to hunger anymore. You don't get less hungry, you just digest your own body into thinking otherwise. "What do we do now?"

"I guess we just wait," she said.

"What do we do while we're waiting?"

"Same thing we've been doing," she said.

"What? Starve?" I declared. "Hungry in America."

"So much for the American Dream," she added.

"I don't think it was meant for us." I tossed on my side.

"Do you think mama's going to be all right?" she asked.

"I hope so," I said. "I really, really hope so. She's strong. She's a survivor."

"I wish we had family to turn to for some form of support. Why do we have to be alone?"

"Our family?" I almost gasped.

The truth: I had never met most of my family. They were either dead, drug addicts, drug dealers, were never told I existed, or just didn't give a damn. When the few pretended to give a damn, we ended up back on the streets in worse positions than we were before. Living with them always turned so horrid I preferred they didn't give a damn. I would rather be alone than with enemies under the guise of family. Family who knew I starved. Some of them who were, for some reason, glad I starved. Even my own grandmother laughed and hung up when I told her my sister and I had nowhere to go. She said we deserved it . . . but why should any child deserve to be homeless?

Homelessness and hunger, the siblings of poverty, were the only things to ever embrace us. Homelessness and hunger always stuck together. I never understood why my family couldn't do the same. I figured we would be okay though; my mom and sister were the only family I needed. I just had to keep us healthy. I needed to keep us alive. Those homelessness success stories were unrealistic. None of those people were raised homeless in the inner city. No homeless person I knew ever made it to success. No one I knew from the inner city did either. Reaching success meant hitting the lottery. Homelessness is a beast, which feeds off the impoverished, beating them into the sewers of life. And when you are born at the bottom, nine times out of ten, you die at the bottom. I just needed to make sure we didn't die while down there.

I wasn't convinced it was possible though. Three days before, an ambulance carried this homeless lady away. She had a heart attack in the parking lot in front of her kids. I saw the whole thing as they screamed and cried. Yesterday I overheard two staff members saying she had died and her children were taken to Child Protective Services. Six months ago, gangsters shot my friend Taylor in the face. He wasn't homeless but from the inner city, just like me. They stepped up to him, and shot him in the face. They killed his girlfriend, too. Like I said, I never met anyone homeless, or from the inner city, who had ever made it out; and I qualified for both. But I wasn't worried about me. Statistics said being an impoverished, male minority made my life expectancy short anyway. I just needed my sister to survive. I heard a grunt beneath my bunk. My mom breathed congested as if her chest slowly caved in. She sounded in chronic pain even while she slept. I worried about her. I just hoped she would live.

4. Dear Mama

WE STOOD WITH BLACK GARBAGE BAGS AT OUR FEET filled with every possession we owned. I had January 15, 2006, circled on my calendar. Our three-month time limit at the shelter had expired, and we had nowhere to go. We moved out the day before; everyone wished us good luck. Good luck couldn't do anything for us. We had no car, no money, nothing except those garbage bags. We were supposed to roam around until we found somewhere—if we found somewhere. I carried my bag along with my mother's. Pain radiated from her discolored face, she kept uncontrollably sweating, holding her stomach, and breathing as if she had an asthma attack. We stopped at the corner so she could catch her breath. Somehow, my mom found a night shelter we were able to squeeze our way in. Come morning, everyone in the shelter had to pack what little they owned and leave. At seven o'clock in the evening, homeless people lined up to enter for another night. Beds in the shelter could not be saved or reserved. If you missed out, you missed out.

The time was six forty-five, and the shelter was still thirty minutes away on foot. We hadn't eaten all day, but what else was new? If we ran, we could make it. But we couldn't run. Both bags weighed me down. My mom's health weighed her down, and we both weighed down my sister. I wanted her to run ahead and wait in line but holding a spot wouldn't have worked. All three of us had to be present in line at the same time when entering.

I was fine. I could go sleep back in the tent with Rudy, but my mom and sister couldn't. With each step my mother took, she grew worse and worse. I had never seen her so bad before. She tried to appear strong for us. She was the matriarch, the provider, but we were not fools. We knew trouble engulfed her. I wished I could reach out my hand and heal her, but I wasn't a prophet. No, just another boy lost in the inner city. I needed someone to reach out their hands to heal me. Disease and poverty plagued from an early age. Hereditary in its nature, passing down from my grandparents to my parents, and from my parents to me. I never had a choice. I never had the chance to screw up in life. I started at the bottom. At ten years old, I stared up at the heavens for a cure to the homeless disease—our impoverished plague. At thirteen, I brought my gaze back to earth thinking there wasn't a cure from above.

Lost in the shadows, no one knew I existed. One of many silhouettes. When the impoverished are together no one can see individuals. All they see is darkness. All they say is, "the homeless." I grew up in that darkness.

I froze outside in the cold. I gave the jacket from Rudy to my sister who gave it to my mom. I then gave my sister my hoodie leaving me in a T-shirt. Thick gray storm clouds loomed above. I heaved both bags onto my back, and we began our journey toward the night-by-night shelter. We all knew we would not get in, but we headed there anyway. What else could we do?

"Argh!" squealed my mom, folding over with her hands on her knees.

"Mom!" yelled my sister, dropping her bag rushing to her side. "Are you okay?"

She didn't respond. Her eyes seemed to roll to the back of her head. Tears streamed down her cheeks. I didn't drop my bags, as every time I had to raise them it drained my energy. I waited for my mom to gather herself and bounce back like she always did.

Her right knee buckled and she dropped to the ground.

"Mom!" I yelled, dropping the bags. She gripped her stomach, twitching on the ground. She began vomiting blood. I dropped to my knees, my nose dripped from the cold and from my own tears.

"Shit!" yelled my sister, shooing me away. "Go get help! Call for help!"

I stood frozen, staring at my mom. Pain emitted from her.

"Go call for help, stupid!" she yelled again, snapping me out of my trance.

I glanced around in a panic. My mom had a cell phone but she only made enough to keep it on every other month. We were in one of the off months. Some people questioned why we might have a family cell phone instead of spending every dime on food. It's simple really. If you didn't have a phone, shelters couldn't contact you when your enrollment came. No one could contact you. Opportunities for food were scarce, but came a lot sooner than they did for housing. The phone's a necessary evil. An evil I wished I had working right then.

I saw the Shell gas station up the street and sprinted for it. Passersby stopped and watched my mom as I ran. They crowded around her, turning our misfortune into a scene of entertainment. I crashed through the gas station door and rushed to the service attendant.

"Call 911!" I screamed, breathing deeply. "Something's happening to my mom!"

"The telephone is not for customers," The attendant noted the line of customers I cut in front of. "Hey, I recognize you! Cameras caught you stealing! Get out of here!"

"My mom is outside on the ground dying," I yelled, pointing outside. A small crowd gathered around her. The clerk from the same night of those starvation-killing honey buns eyed me suspiciously. He glanced out the window and then back at me. "Please!" I begged.

He slowly reached for the phone and dialed 911. The rest of the customers turned to observe as I dashed back out the door. I ran toward my mom with the miniscule amount of energy I had. My body possessed no food to fuel it. I reached her to see my sister without the hoodie I gave her. She had used it to wipe my mom's face. My mom unconsciously rested her head in my sister's lap.

"She okay?" I asked.

"I'm not sure." My sister shivered from the icy wind.

I tried not to panic. God, do not take my mom—please! We need her! People were staring at us, but I didn't care. Tears rolled down my cheeks. I knew a boy wasn't supposed to cry, but mothers are an exception. A few minutes passed, and ambulance sirens grew near. They arrived, and paramedics rushed from the vehicle. They pulled out a stretcher and one told us to back away from our mother.

"What happened?" one asked me.

"We're not sure," my sister said. "She kept clutching her stomach."

They wheeled her to the ambulance. They placed an oxygen mask on her and climbed in. My sister and I quickly followed. But as I placed my foot on the ambulance, and the paramedic who had spoken to me placed a hand on my shoulder stopping me.

"What are you doing? That's my mom!" I yelled.

"Only one," he said. "Where's your dad? He can follow us to the hospital."

"He's in prison," I said. "I don't have a way there. I'm on foot."

"Do you have a family contact to bring you? Are you unaccompanied? I can't just leave you on the streets. I have to call Child Protective Services to bring you."

"Oh, no, that father, oh yeah he can take me," I said. Growing up in the inner city you learn Child Protective Services did only two things: break up families, and lose children in its system. I was better off on the streets.

"Well, go home. Have your dad bring you immediately," he said. "Someone needs to pick up your sister. I doubt your mom is leaving any time soon."

"I'll go with him," Pooh said.

"One of you should ride with your mother." The driver honked.

My sister glanced at my unconscious mom and then toward me. She cried more than me.

"Go," I said. "I'll be all right."

"Dad will take us. It's fine." She jumped from the ambulance and they sped off, sirens blaring.

"I said go!" I shrieked. "What the hell is wrong with you?"

"If CPS catches us, we're done. We have to stay together. Don't worry, we'll visit her."

Thunder crackled overhead and rain began to pour. The crowd started dispersing. I sighed, placing my arm around my sister. "C'mon," I said as the rain began to soak us.

Everything happened so quickly. My mom's worse than I could've fathomed. I picked up my bag and then my mother's. Water soaked through my donated shoes. Somehow, my health ashamed me; as if my mother fell ill because of me. I should've been able to do something. In life, I only had my family to cherish. What good was I in the world if I couldn't even protect them? My sister lifted her bag and we continued our journey. Not toward the shelter, though. Just aimlessly, wishing we could go to the hospital. If Pooh turned eighteen, CPS wouldn't have been a problem. But, her at fifteen and me being fourteen years old, everything was out of our control.

We waited under a sheltered bus stop until the rain finally lightened and made our way to a bench on a small grassy area on the backside of Petco Park where the San Diego Padres just moved in to play baseball in their new $400 million stadium. We sat on the wet bench and huddled together for warmth. We'd run into a nearby public bathroom if the rain picked up again. I used to think God cried for us when it rained. At least someone cared for our well-being. But it wasn't—it's just recycled water spilling out onto the street over and over again . . . sort of like us.

I thought God sent guardian angels to shelter you. Do they not protect the poor? Do miracles not apply to us? Tears streamed down my sister's face. My mom's well-being weighed heavily on her conscience.

She turned to me with somber eyes and questioned, "You think she'll be okay?"

My mom's the only angel God sent us. The only light we had in our world. Her comfort, her strength, gave us courage. She wanted us to be better off than our forefathers. I lowered my head and didn't say anything because I wasn't sure. I couldn't imagine our angel leaving us. However, the truth of it all, angels returned to heaven all the time, especially when they had no home on earth.

5. To Kill an Angel

S HE'S DEAD?" I SCREAMED AT THE TOP OF MY LUNGS.
"No." My sister wiped tears away from her face, handing a
worried stranger back her phone. She waited for her to continue
past. A few days had passed and we were getting by the best way
we could. We hadn't been to school since my mom had to go to
the hospital. We had called a few times but still hadn't been to
see her. Partly because we had wandered too far and needed bus
fare, partly because we still feared CPS. "They said she lost too
much blood."

"Too much blood? *Too much blood?* They're supposed to be
saving her, not killing her!"

"Yeah . . . I know."

"Is she going to make it?"

"I hope so."

"She can't die!"

"She's too strong. . . ."

"What are we going to do?"

". . . Why are you asking me?"

We sat on the curb in grief, mourning the possibility of
our mom being dead. She's the only one fighting the system
to keep us three together. After I turned twelve two years ago,
I had complicated things for us. Most family shelters said they
couldn't take boys twelve and over. They said we would harass
the women or whatever. So most times, shelters wouldn't take
me and we were forced to go somewhere else. We tried to split
up a few times, them in one shelter, me in another close by, but

after I turned twelve no one would take me, so I ended up alone on the street. Family is sacred for my mom; big for me too. My mom and my sister were the only people I had. With her, we were able to sleep in day-to-day shelters but still all in vain.

We realized at any given moment my mom would have to go to the hospital. We knew she was sick but we didn't understand exactly how bad. I don't even think she knew, she had a high tolerance for pain. Now she lost so much blood and I couldn't do anything about it. If she died, my sister and I would float around. Eventually CPS would catch my sister and have the court issue a warrant for me for being a runaway. If she died, in a way, we all died.

Mom lay in the hospital as we sat there with nowhere to go. She had an appendectomy and total hysterectomy. They said there was a nine-centimeter tumor in her right ovary which had to be removed, too. The thought of them cutting into her body scared me. I never imagined cutting into her body to save her life might possibly kill her, too. Lately it seemed like I had been more wrong than right, like finding places for me and my sister to sleep. With my mom in there we tried to get by the best way we could. A friend of my mom's named Lisa said we could stay with her a couple of nights but we would be better off outside. The three of us briefly stayed with her a few years back and not much had changed there since then.

Always the same type of people around, the same type of thugs, the same type of drugs, the same type of chaos and violence I saw back then. The lady's nice but her place wasn't an environment for anyone to try and live. Her own kids stayed with her only for the weekends but we all understood it was better for them to live there part-time. She wasn't a bad person. Just a reflection of the environment we all were raised, therefore entrapped, in. There were too many problems in her house. We had enough problems. However, it seemed like it might be our only salvation on that night. I didn't want to sleep outside.

Someone was always home because her boyfriend sold dope out of the house.

Our cousin Romel, from our first set of cousins, just got hired at Subway which meant we knew where we could get something to eat. It's nice to see him out of juvenile hall and doing okay. Since Lisa lived nearby we made our way to Subway where he stood preparing a customer's order. I love all my cousins. They didn't have it any better than we did. We grew up homeless and they grew up in foster care and the two are pretty much the same. I always thought foster kids had more opportunities than we did, but whatever. My mom's sister, my Aunt Lynn, lost all five of my cousins to Child Protective Services. Growing up we didn't really see her, but we always heard stories of her getting arrested. My cousins were running around in the streets from an early age, and had to grow up quick just like we did, so we understood each other's position.

I wished I could help them, but then again I couldn't even help myself. Romel saw us come in and told us to wait a minute. After the customer left, he came and sat next to us.

"What's up, you guys?"

"Nothing really, just hungry," I said.

"Y'all want a sandwich?"

"No money," Pooh said.

"I didn't ask that, Winnie the Pooh Bear."

"Shut up," she said.

"If you insist." I knew he would make us free sandwiches.

"All right." He stood and slid behind the sandwich counter. "What you want?"

"I want the Spicy Italian."

"On what bread?"

"Uhh . . . Honey Oat."

"Pooh Bear?"

"Give me the Cold Cut Combo on Italian Herbs and Cheese."

He sliced open the bread and began fixing the sandwiches. "How's Auntie?"

"We don't really know," Pooh said. "I talked to the doctor, he said she lost a lot of blood. He said she was still in surgery."

"Damn, that's messed up. How long has she been in surgery?"

"She still has Nana listed as her emergency contact. Michael borrowed this lady's cell phone and I called the hospital pretending to be Nana. They had said for a couple of hours now. They're still not done," Pooh said. "They said they'll be done by tonight and to go visit her tomorrow but she might not be conscious. They also asked about her kids."

"Yeah, shouldn't y'all be down at the Bollensky Center or something?"

"Shut up," I said. "We're being serious."

"Are you going to go visit her?"

"Yeah," I said.

"Where are you guys living?"

"Couch-ish surfing," I said.

"I'd let you stay with me if I had a place."

"Right . . ." I said. "I'd probably get a place before you did."

"Ha, ha, ha. Shut up, Mike. I'm really about to get one. I just got to save up. I'm getting a car, too. If Auntie gets better maybe we can room together or something."

Romel rang us up. He opened the cash register, fidgeted around with his back to the camera and closed it. He gave us our sandwiches and we sat and ate as more people came in.

"Hi, welcome to Subway!" Romel said, all cheerful and bubbly.

I laughed at his professional voice. He sounded so corny. He laughed a little too, as he listened to another order. I didn't want to go to Lisa's but I really didn't want to sleep outside. Come to think of it, her place really wasn't bad. It would probably be only a few strangers, a couple of drug sales here and there, which wasn't a big deal, and we could take a shower. She had a soft couch too and it beat another park bench. We just needed somewhere to stay until my mom left the hospital . . . Why would she push herself past her limits? I knew we had to survive but trying to survive slowly killed her. We didn't even know she needed surgery. If my mom died, then life would end. I would quit if she died. What kind of story would that be? A woman born into poverty, grew up in poverty, had kids and became sick, which made her have to fight to keep her family together. She did everything she could to get us a home, yet we remained homeless, and then she died. No. She's a fighter. A little blood loss wouldn't stop her. She knew how much we needed her. She knew we're hanging in limbo out here while she's hanging in limbo in there.

Right then I wished I was older, less terrified, and able to do something. I wished I could take care of my family and save my mom. She really could die at any moment. Thousands of homeless mothers and fathers did. If she died, my sister and I would hang around for a while but then we would eventually fade away like most homeless do.

I prayed for her life, but then again, I prayed for a lot of things. All I knew was if God took my mother, my angel, away from me, I would be surrounded by demons. As we ate I became certain of two things, neither being the future. The first, if anything went tragically bad at Lisa's, there's an escape route around back that led to the main street. And second, somehow some way we were going to find a way to the hospital to see our mother tomorrow. It'd be easy to slip in and out without revealing our age and relation. My sister appeared grown enough to be her sister. CPS would never find out. I guess first we needed to get to Lisa's.

We finished up the sandwiches and told Romel we would see him later, whenever later turned out to be. We reached Lisa's house and knocked on the door. The door swung open and Calvin stood holding an eighth of an ounce of marijuana wrapped in clear plastic wrap.

"Oh, I thought you were someone else." Calvin turned back inside. We followed him in where the doorway opened up to the living room. Calvin's a bigger guy, with tattoos and cornrow braids in his hair. He's a cool dude if you were on his good side but Calvin didn't really have a good side. "Lisa, Monice's kids are here," he yelled disappearing into the back of the house.

I set my backpack down and sat on the long couch in the living room. My sister sat on the shorter two-seat couch and laid down. Lisa hurried into the living room, smoking a cigarette. She was a slender woman with her hair pulled back into a ponytail.

"How's your mom?" She exhaled a puff of smoke.

I shrugged. "We're going to find out tomorrow."

"Well all right. Tell her I said hi. Sorry there's no extra blankets."

"It's cool." I lied down as well. "Thanks."

"Yup." She disappeared back into her room until she heard a faint knock at the door. She returned to the front and opened the door letting a tall man in. She returned to the back of the house leaving the man up there with us.

Calvin emerged shaking the man's hand and passing him a sandwich bag full of marijuana. The man handed him forty dollars and left. There wasn't much to talk about. This happened over and over again throughout the night. I could tell it made my sister uncomfortable, but I had a lot of troubled friends. I'd rather her be uncomfortable in a house than uncomfortable on the streets. Another knock banged on the door, this one louder than the rest had been. Calvin stood in the kitchen making a bowl of cereal when he heard the loud knocks. He cautiously opened the door.

"Killah Cal, what's up my man?" asked a hunched over man with a backwards baseball cap, stepping into the living room. His clothes were faded and he brought a foul odor with him.

"Hell no, get the fuck out of here!" He pushed the man toward the door.

"Be cool man, be cool." He held up a few crumpled dollars. "I got money this time."

Calvin snatched the money out of his hand counting it. "Three dollars?" He balled it up throwing it at him. "Get out my house."

"Just give me some of that white stuff man. Anything three dollars will get me."

"I'm not selling your crackhead ass nothing, Ezekiel, get out." He pushed him a little bit more aggressively.

"Wait man, be cool, be cool!" He struggled to hold his ground, but lost. He quickly reached into his pocket and pulled out a small switchblade knife, swinging it at Calvin who lifted him up and slammed him on the porch.

"Young Mike G, ride with me," Calvin yelled forcing me to rise. I ran outside to see him pinned on top of the man. "Grab the knife!"

I picked up the dropped knife and folded it into my pocket as Calvin punched the guy in the face. I grabbed the man's arms as Calvin grabbed his legs. He squirmed as we carried him to the street and tossed him on it. Lisa stood in the doorway smoking another cigarette.

"Come back to my house again and you're gone, done." Calvin pointed at him. Ezekiel slowly picked himself up spitting out blood from a busted lip. "I'm cool man." He tip-toed away. Calvin shook my hand as we watched Ezekiel leave before we returned back inside where he handed me twenty dollars. "Good shit." He closed the door. My sister still had her eyes tightly shut on the couch but I knew she wasn't sleep. How could she have been? I sat back down as Calvin and Lisa walked to their room like nothing had just transpired. I put the new bus money in my pocket and laid back down. Another knock hit the door but I didn't bother to move. Whoever knocked didn't come for me. The knocks thudded louder and louder, so loud it sounded as if someone were trying to break the door down, and Calvin came storming back into the living room.

"What, y'all don't hear the door?" He swung it open. Two hooded figures emerged and entered the living room. I paused, not sure what would happen next. I saw one reach into his pockets. I tensed up ready to grab my sister and run. I didn't like being there, anything happened at any moment without warning and it happened all the time. I waited to hear the gunshots ripping away Calvin's life, then mine, then my sister's. The man traded him money for the sack and shook Calvin's right hand by tossing up their gang sign.

"I needed this," the other hooded figure said. "Two little homies got shot dead earlier today at the Four Corners of Death. They caught them coming out of Green Cat Market. One of them wasn't even from the turf. I think he was about to graduate. . . ."

I turned on my side and stopped listening to the conversation, drowning out the sound with my inner thoughts. I had heard it too many times. I needed to get away from the South East community of San Diego. Too many kids die young there. If I stayed too long, I probably wouldn't make it out alive, like one kid I heard about, Willie James Jones. They named the street where he died after him. Gangsters murdered him in a drive-by shooting at his high school graduation party the day after graduation. He was the valedictorian and I heard even going all the way to college or something big. If they killed the valedictorian, what hope was there for a homeless kid? If my mom stayed unconscious for too long, what hope was there for a homeless woman? In the end, we would both be angels going to heaven, just like Willie. But I couldn't be too pessimistic. I had to take it one step at a time, run if someone kicked Lisa and Calvin's door in, the next day go see my mom; and after, just try and make it to the next holiday.

6. Thanks(for)giving: Age Fifteen

I HATED HOLIDAYS IN SHELTERS. THE SHELTER ATMO-sphere always seemed to drain every ounce of holiday spirit from me. Every holiday, we had to sit in a room full of strangers and put on fake smiles pretending to be happy. Thanksgiving had rolled around and the only thing I was thankful for was my mother was still alive. I was thankful for my legs too. The day before we had to scrape together quarters and carry bags of clothes all around downtown trying to wash. We went to high school downtown so I always hated running into my peers while they shopped around the Gaslamp District and grilled me with a thousand questions about why I dress the way I dressed and why I carried bags around like a vagabond. The scene embarrassed me, but I had to do what I had to do.

The good thing about Thanksgiving is food is usually more abundant. Not in our current shelter, though. We had to travel down to another sister shelter nearby along with other homeless families, stand outside like a herd of sheep, and wait for them to let us in as everybody drove past and stared at us. Standing there wasn't ideal, but we didn't have another choice. We drug our feet to the shelter and stood in line by the door. I hadn't eaten since school lunch so I became a little anxious. My mom leaned against the wall, trying to keep standing. She slowly regained her strength but she shouldn't have been out there. The doctors told her to be on bed rest for a few weeks; an impossible task when you're homeless and therefore bed-less, too.

After a while, the double doors swung open and a middle-aged lady with a big smile ushered us all inside. We entered a Thanksgiving-themed auditorium and were instructed to get into the food line. Servers, all with big smiles, stood waiting to fill our plates. I pushed past a few families and brought my mom and sister to the front of the line. Everyone rushed to eat because they were so hungry. Probably a little rude, I will admit, but I had learned if we were not aggressive, we might not get a plate.

It had happened to us before when I was younger but it wouldn't happen again. I wished good luck to the family who didn't get to eat because I knew the struggle, but we would happily eat. I stood behind my mom and sister, making sure they grabbed their plates. A row of large aluminum containers filled with assorted food sat on tables in front of us. It actually smelled okay. I could tell the dry cuts of turkey were actually turkey and the macaroni and cheese actually resembled macaroni and cheese, to some degree. The cheese just needed to be a little less on the brown side. I went down the line and filled my plate. I filled it with more than I needed so I could take the rest back to our shelter room later. I sat and apparently should have waited for everyone to get their food so whoever was in charge could say grace, but I started eating anyway. They frowned at me but at that point I didn't have control. I was starving.

After they finished serving food and drinks, the servers came and sat amongst us which I thought odd because of the usual invisible wall between them and us. They filled their plates with the same food and began to chat as everyone officially waited for grace. After grace, a woman skipped onto the festive stage and stepped up to the microphone.

"How is everyone tonight? How's the food? Is it good?" she seemed undeterred by all of our lack of enthusiasm. "We'd like to welcome you all here tonight. Every staff member you see has volunteered their night to give back to the community and help you all. Let's give them a round of applause . . . Now I realize this isn't anyone's ideal place to spend their holidays, but trust God has a plan for you. Now enough of my babbling, please enjoy."

I sat and stuffed my face not really saying anything to anyone. One of the servers had sat next to me and tried to make polite conversation. She appeared to be in her early twenties and appeared to mean well, but I didn't really want to talk. I wanted to eat.

"How's the food?" she asked.

"Fine," I said, as polite as I could.

"My family and I always volunteer to serve the homeless every Thanksgiving. Christmas sometimes, too."

"That's um . . . cool."

"Yeah, it makes us feel like we're doing the right thing."

"How nice for you." I slurped the last of the liquefied cranberry sauce.

"How do you spend your free time?"

"Panhandling. . . ."

"Oh . . . I always try and give what I can."

"Can I have twenty dollars?"

"Well . . . I don't have any money on me right now. But, um, do you like sports?"

"Yes."

"What's your favorite team?"

"Lakers . . . Chargers . . . Padres . . ."

"Oh cool. I'm a Charger's girl myself. LaDainian Tomlinson is too good."

"Yeah, he's my favorite player."

"Mine too!" she said, happy we found something in common. "Hey, if I may ask, how'd you and your family end up homeless? You seem like a sweet boy. You don't seem like other homeless people I've met."

"Actually, I don't really remember exactly. We weren't always homeless. When I turned seven is when things became hard, my mom got really sick, and no one was there to help us."

"No one?"

"We had a fairy godmother in the beginning. Her name was Mamma D. She used to let us live with her in her bedroom. She cared for the elderly, and she lived in a home with a lot of old people. She could have got fired but she didn't care. She was the only one who I'd say really loved us."

"What happened?"

"She caught lung cancer, it spread to her brain, and she died." I completed the last of my macaroni and brown-cheese.

"Oh! I'm sorry."

"Me too. Next thing I remember I'm bouncing around in shelters explaining to random people how I got here."

"Well, that's why we come, to help people like you. I mean people in your situation."

"Well, with all due respect, how do you help me? Or people in my situation?"

"What do you mean?"

"You said you volunteer to help us? How do you help us?"

"We help give you something to eat."

"You place food on our trays and I appreciate it, believe me, I do, but this food you serve only stops my hunger now. In two hours what will I do? Sure, you'll feel better about yourself doing this great justice, but my life doesn't change. This meal lets you see my world then you go home to your normal life just like those stupid counselors."

"Counselors?"

"I still have to deal with this when I go to sleep. I'll still be homeless tomorrow when I wake up. I appreciate it, I'm glad this food is available, but it changes nothing, I don't receive any help, just someone scooping food on my plate; which I can do myself if you hand me the utensil."

"But then what would us volunteers do?"

"I'm not saying don't. But it doesn't heal my mom or give us a house. It just tricks us into thinking for a moment we're not homeless. Even though we're surrounded by complete strangers, we can enjoy Thanksgiving like everyone else . . . then tomorrow when all the smiles and holiday spirit goes away, we're still homeless."

"I mean, well, what are we supposed to do? Give you a home? We're doing the best we can. We can't snap our fingers and fix everything."

"No I don't expect you to give me a home. I don't expect anything. I'm just telling you how it is."

We sat in silence for a while as she nibbled on her food. "How's the food?" she said.

"You asked me that," I said.

"Oh, right. Christmas coming up. Do you have any plans?"

"Probably roam around, be cold, and shiver a little."

"What about gifts, do you want any?"

"Yeah, a PlayStation 2."

"You have a TV?"

"Hmm . . . good point," I said.

 What games do you like?"

"Well I'm not sure. I never really got to play video games but my friends always play basketball and football games and it looks fun."

"Do you have a lot of friends?"

"This is a lot of questions." I took a sip of water. "I feel like this is a job interview."

"I like meeting new people. Some small talk won't hurt anyone. I could be an elf. And hey, Santa might even bring a gift this Christmas."

"Santa just brings me socks," I said.

 She sort of laughed and mixed her food around with her fork. "How's the food?" I asked.

"Fine." She shrugged. "I bet it's scary."

"No, I've eaten way worse, believe me."

"I meant being homeless."

"Oh . . . yeah . . . I'd say so. Never knowing what's going to happen next or which homies are going to disappear. Right now I'm talking to you, tomorrow is a coin flip on where I'll be or what I'll be doing. And then you have to watch out for the gangsters."

"Gangsters?"

"Yeah man, homelessness puts you out on the streets where all the gangsters hang out. The gangs try and jump me because I'm not one of them. The police won't me help because they think I'm one of them.

"Oh, my. Well I hope everything will be all right. That's intense. I'll have my church pray for you and your family if that's okay?"

"Sure. Pray for us. Please do. The more the merrier. My mom prays for us all the time."

"It must be hard to hear, but things will get better. If you have heart and persevere, you'll win eventually."

"Allen Iverson had heart and persevered but he didn't win, he never beat Kobe or Shaq."

"You just have to believe."

"That's what they keep telling me." I took another bite of food, cautious to save some.

"You shouldn't sound so bitter. It's hard, but try to be optimistic, at least for tonight. It doesn't seem like you're really enjoying this Thanksgiving."

"What do you mean?" I questioned with a mouthful. "It's the best Thanksgiving I've had in years."

7. Houston, I Am Your Problem

2006-2007

I LAID ON MY BACK, EYES CLOSED WITH MY HANDS propped behind my head. I inhaled deeply bringing in the stale air. The type of air you only smell in places I lived. Late July, a year had passed and we were back where we were a year ago, in a shelter. I swore time in shelters slowed down when you wanted to move out and sped up when you wanted to stay. We had reached the last day in the shelter we were in. We wanted to stay for a while, get ourselves together, but our time had come to an end and we would leave the next day. We had our few belongings already packed up and we would be forced to carry them all across town until we could find somewhere else, if we could find somewhere else, again. We'd cycled around the city so many times through the years, over and over. The insane cycle always had the same results: nothing.

I hated roaming around like transients, it was even worse the time we moved to Houston, Texas, back in the seventh grade. I remember not wanting to go there, but also curious about living in a new place at the same time. My mom's old time friend Easy had invited us to come stay with him. We didn't have anywhere else to go so we rode the bus all the way there. We were searching for a new life. Back then I was guilty of being hopelessly optimistic. In my mind, we were going to go there, stay with her friend for a month or two until we could move out and get our own place. Texas's cost of living is way cheaper than most places. It seemed really feasible at the time.

When we arrived, however, everything changed. Easy arrived at the bus station to pick us up but his disturbed expression alarmed me. He motioned my mom to go to the car and she told us to wait. Inside the car she began exhaling deeply and talking in frustration. Whatever they were saying, I knew it would be a bad outcome for us. It always turned out that way, and in Houston everyone was strangers besides Easy. We had never been there before and wouldn't have gone if he didn't invite my mom.

Without turning around, because she knew we were watching, my mom motioned us to come to the car. She stepped out as the trunk popped open.

"Oh cool, for a second I thought there was a problem." I loaded up the trunk with our luggage.

"There is a problem," she said.

"What?" Pooh said.

"We can't stay with him."

"What?" I said. "That was the whole reason for coming here in the first place!"

"Just come on." She slammed the trunk closed and we entered his car.

Easy had simply changed his mind. He said another friend came to stay with him plus he lived with another woman. He nonchalantly told this to Pooh Bear and me as we rode quietly in the back seat. We pulled up in front of a social services building and he parked along the curb, popped the trunk, but kept the engine running.

"Why are we here?" Pooh asked.

"They have resources to help you guys." Easy turned toward us.

"That's messed up," Pooh said. "We came all the way here to get dropped off at a social services building? We could have stayed where we were!"

Easy didn't respond. He casually turned back around in his seat. He didn't give a damn about me and my sister.

"Can I take you out somewhere once you get situated?" he asked my mom.

My sister opened the car door and slammed it behind her. I opened my door, too.

"Mom, let's go," I said.

"Where are you in a rush to?" Easy said.

I stared at him and laughed. He's lucky I wasn't older or I would have dragged him out of the car and beat his ass. But I wasn't, so I slammed the door louder than my sister did and helped unload everything out of the trunk. My mom stepped out and closed his door gently. She grabbed her backpack of clothes and Easy wasted no time in speeding away back to his happy little home.

We entered the social service building and waited for about two hours until they called my mom's name. We followed a caseworker into a back office and sat with her. At first, she asked us preliminary questions like if we were on drugs, were alcoholics, or if we had gambling problems among other things. When she found out we were from California, she asked why we had come to Texas. She asked as if she wanted to know, but the real question was why become a part of Texas's homeless population. Why become Houston's problem? We explained our situation and told her as of right now we would be sleeping in a park or wherever we could find. She pulled out a list of shelters and began calling them, seeing if they had room. She assured us we wouldn't be sleeping outside, but she couldn't quote how long it would take to locate a shelter with room for the three of us. She called place after place as we sat in front of her blankly staring, waiting for any smidgen of good news.

" . . .Monice King, she has a family of three . . ." she said into the umpteenth phone call. "They need to move in immediately . . . they don't have any alternative . . . no vehicle they're on foot . . . sounds great thank you so much . . . all right have a nice day." She hung up the phone and scribbled an address on a piece of paper. "That was the Beacon of Hope shelter. They have a space available for you."

We cheered, feeling as relieved as we could be under the circumstances.

"Now you have to meet them at this address and a van will bring you there."

My mom blankly read the address and stared up at the case-worker. "Where is this, exactly?"

"It's simple: just hit the main road and keep going straight for about three blocks until you reach the corner of Magnolia Avenue. They'll pick you up from the corner."

"Thank you so much." My mom shook her hand.

"My pleasure. Hang in there, things will get better."

Back then I actually believed it when people told me it would get better. I believed in a lot of fairy tales in the seventh grade. We left the social service building and carried our possessions seven blocks instead of three until we reached Magnolia. The sun died and we were exhausted from carrying everything. There were other people waiting by the corner. They watched us as we approached.

"Can you spare any change?" A woman held her little boy by the hand, expecting us to snobbishly brush past. Her clothes were tattered and so were his. They had an unpleasant smell emitting from them, but so did everyone else around. My mom said no as we sat our bags down on the corner. The woman gazed at us confused.

"Can you spare any change?" I stuck out my hand.

"This is a line to go to a homeless shelter," she said.

"Really? I thought all these homeless people were waiting for the ice cream man," I glanced at all our bags.

"Oh wow, I'm so sorry. You didn't look homeless. I thought you were going to keep walking by."

"I wish we could." I observed the group of broken people in front of us. "I really wish we could."

We rode the van to the Beacon of Hope. It had the spherical shape of a baseball stadium. Inside consisted of one large open space with individual rooms cut into the circling walls. A section of empty space had been reserved for the cafeteria. We sat through intake listening to the rules and regulations of the shelter, then we were escorted to our room. Although smaller than a lot of other shelter rooms I had lived in, we took what we could get.

A mixture of people lived there. The most interesting people I met were the Katrina "refugees." Not so much the adults but the children. They were regular kids just like me, but no one else saw them as normal. To the world, we all were outcasts, me for living homeless, them for being refugees. Every day they woke up remembering everything they lost, including people they cared about. I saw the girls cry. I saw the boys cry.

"It just feels so bad," Cornell said. He was my age but his physique far bigger. Whatever they fed to those kids down in Louisiana to get them so big, I wanted some. "One minute everything's fine, the next everything's gone. They're calling us refugees like we're AIDS babies from Africa. Or like were from Pakistan or wherever the Middle East is. I'm American!"

"Yeah, me too," I said.

"My friends died in those waters, man. I lost everything. I don't deserve this, bro. I didn't do anything wrong."

"I get it, man. It's not fair, but at least you're alive. A lot of people died."

"How do you seem so cool with this? We're all like homeless now. You remember teasing those guys on the corner? That's us now, bro. I had it all. All the new Jordans, clothes, man. I had game systems, at least three girlfriends."

"Three?"

"Yeah man, my mom's friend Tina, my teacher Mrs. Louensky, and this hot high school girl across the street."

"Like you kissed her?"

"All the time, bro. Best kisser she ever kissed."

"You had it all," I said.

His face grew dark and still. A silence swept over his spirit bringing remorse. "I lost it all. We lost it all. You're okay with this? Being in here with all of these homeless people? Some mystery lady named Fema said I can't go back home, the place I was born and raised for twelve years. I'm not cool with this. You're cool with all of this?"

"Well . . . I'm not from Louisiana."

"You're not?"

"Nah, bro," I said, almost amused.

"Well, where you from?"

"I'm from California."

"Cali? What you doing in Texas? In a shelter?"

I hesitated before speaking. Hurricane Katrina didn't make me homeless. "I'm not cool with it," I said. "I've just never had anything to lose. I don't understand how losing stuff feels. I don't remember how having stuff feels."

My life had not been great. When I searched back through my memories I only saw being homeless. I had always been at the bottom. He's fortunate enough to have had a middle-class experience. He would always have those memories from before he became homeless. I would never have those memories to put my mind at ease. Homelessness was all I knew.

The staff didn't allow seasoning on the bland food unless we put it there ourselves from little salt and pepper packets. They cooked the food bland because everyone couldn't eat seasoned food without having a bad reaction so they decided to keep everything seasoning-free. At first, I thought the rule was stupid. Who didn't like seasoned food? But I remember going to dinner one night sitting across from a lady with her three children and watched as they ate their food. The lady had befriended my mom so most nights our families ate together. The lady sprinkled salt over her food then added some more. She seemed to enjoy it until she started holding her chest in a panic. Her children screamed as she fell over to the floor. Too much salt had caused her to have a heart attack. The paramedics came and rushed her to the hospital but her children couldn't go with her. Social workers came the same night and escorted her children away. I never saw them again. The next morning staff emptied their room and filled it with new occupants by noon.

Life at the Beacon of Hope wasn't bad. They fed us three square meals every day plus a snack. They gave us soap, shampoo, new toothbrushes, and kept the community bathroom clean. After ten, nine for children, we all had to go to our rooms but the beds were softer than a lot I had slept on so I didn't really mind. An ex-body builder guy lived there who would cut my hair (horribly) for free. I was bald most of the time, but it did the job. We were even able to wash our clothes every week; yeah life was pretty good there.

The Beacon's one of those shelters where I thought back, like, man I had it all living there. Living there we were in a dream, but like all dreams, we had to wake up. It happened when we were told about a new hurricane, Hurricane Rita, whose trajectory headed straight for us. The Beacon of Hope evacuated all of its residents and sent us to different places. We were sent to a church a few cities away to be sheltered until we could return. But we couldn't return due to wind and rain damage and at the same time our time living there had come up.

We asked what we were supposed to do but no one had an answer. No one ever had an answer. They asked where we were from, and told us at best they could help get traveling vouchers to take us back there. Otherwise we'd be headed right back to the social services building. We took the vouchers and went back to San Diego. I'd rather be homeless in familiar settings, the lesser of two evils.

I sat up in my bed and held my head in my hand thinking of the journey ahead. I wished we could go back to the Beacon of Hope, or somewhere close. Living there we had the good life. I really wished we could, but the truth of the matter is we wouldn't. Our Beacon shined in Houston and we were no longer their problem. We were San Diego's. There was no sign of hope there.

8. Traveling Circus

I WANTED TO GO BACK TO THE LAST SHELTER. THE LAST half of July didn't treat us too well. The beginning of August wasn't treating us any better. Those last few shelters had been horrendous. I had to panhandle every day to ride the bus two hours to and from school to get all the way to my current shelter. I would rather stay on the bus. We lived in the type of shelter known as a rotating shelter. I didn't hate the people who operated the rotating shelters, because I appreciated their service. But I hated rotating shelters themselves or what I called "traveling circuses." The concept was for different organizations, community centers, and churches to come together and allow an assorted group of homeless people to alternate occupying an empty room for a one- to two-week basis and then "rotate" somewhere else. These centers were spread throughout the city, some were even in a different city, like the Helping Hands community center, the one I stayed in.

We had to sleep in a small room with a large group of strangers, all there for different reasons, and get along. We were monitored very closely and we could not leave the room. It was prison. We had to ask for permission to do everything. Can I use the bathroom, can I go get some water, can I have a snack to eat, and we had better get everything out of our system before ten o'clock hits. Staff strictly enforced the eight p.m. curfew. At ten p.m., they turned off the lights and we were imprisoned within the room.

Our particular room was very small and circular. There were about fifteen of us all together and the time read nine-fifty p.m.

A nice strong musk floated through the air. Some people in there had not washed in weeks. I leaned against the wall sulking as my mom and sister lay in their cots.

One of the circus freaks stumbled up to me. She dressed in a tattered blouse, short black skirt, and black high heels. Makeup and red lipstick covered her face and she only carried a backpack and a purse. She looked like an older woman, late thirties. Her nose shone red and she kept scratching her flesh from years of drug abuse. She seemed exhausted from her life full of what I deduced to be prostitution.

"Hey big daddy," she said. "You're kind of cute."

I pitied the woman. She probably started off young, as a fast way to get money. It must have been fun back then. She had made poor choice after poor choice but still never learned to do better. Her face showed sadness. Behind all of the makeup twinkled a deep sense of sorrow she compensated with heavy drugs. Most of those types of women ended up just like her. All fun and games when they are young but youth fades and habits don't, they get stronger.

"How old are you? Probably my son's age."

"Michael! Come here!" my mom said, glancing up to see the woman talking to me. I brushed past the woman as all of the lights were shut off. I laid in my cot but the woman had positioned herself right behind mine. My mom noticed her staring at me and immediately switched me positions.

"Sun, I better not ever catch you dipping into something like that," she whispered. She made it a point to tell me when she called me her "son," she meant S-U-N, because I was the brightest star in her universe. "That's nasty. I raised you better than that."

She turned on her side and shut her eyes. I knew she wasn't about to go to sleep. The guy across from us reeked from his skin to his clothes. Already asleep, he snored loudly. Everyone had shifted their cots away from him making space even tighter. Some people didn't smell too much better, but even his stench proved too much for them. My mom had always taught us to wash ourselves. Even when we had to sleep at rest areas, we made way to the bathroom and washed ourselves. She taught us the importance of good hygiene early, but not everyone learned the same lesson.

I hated when they said there wasn't any way to wash themselves unless it rained; which was a lie. They knew it, I knew it, we all knew it. They were just being lazy. You might not always be able to wash your clothes but you can always clean yourself. It could be in public restrooms, in the library, or anywhere with a sink and running water. Again, embarrassing, but you have to do what you have to do. Soap is abundant, too. Everyone always handed out bags of soap and shampoo everywhere we turned. They could at least take the soap and use it. No, they didn't wash themselves because they had quit. They had accepted a homeless life. Most people did. Fighting homelessness was hard. If you don't have anything to work with, it is hard to build off nothing.

I pulled my shirt over my nose trying to filter the air. Our last night couldn't have come quicker. Thursday nights were usually our last night at most places. Tomorrow, Friday, we'd pack up and be shipped somewhere else with mostly a new group of circus acts. I couldn't wait. I hoped there would be a clown.

After school, my sister and I slowly made our way to the bus stop. We had to ride the bus back to Helping Hands and by the time we journeyed there, it should be time for them to let us in. We finally arrived and my mom already awaited us. We grabbed our bags, sat alongside the building, and waited the rest of the day to be transported to another circus tent with the rest of the show. No matter how much we complained, we knew we were not going to get any food until we reached the new place. Too much complaining would only upset the volunteers and get us kicked out.

One guy, however, apparently wanted to be kicked out. Tired and hungry, he belligerently screamed at the mother of his kids. But acting out wouldn't help. He jerked as if he was about to strike her. Domestic violence was a big mistake. Those homeless places didn't tolerate domestic violence or any type of spousal abuse at all. The ringleader and his henchmen appeared out of thin air. They grabbed the man and forcefully pushed him away in front of his three crying children and wife; who all remained behind.

Three large vans slowly pulled up and they piled us all inside and then drove off in different directions. We rode in silence. The driver appeared more agitated than we were. He was young, probably twenty or twenty-one. I could tell he didn't want to chauffeur us. His parents were probably forcing him. I unfortunately sat in the front seat next to him.

"Why don't you just get a job?" He didn't bother to look up at me. "And stop having other people take care of you. Wasting people's time. I'm just saying." I didn't respond. If I said something he didn't like, he could lie to his parents and get us kicked out. His voice permanently stained snobbish from a life of pampering. "The government just needs to come and round all of you up, and take y'all away. The cities would be so much safer and cleaner. People would be much happier."

"We're people, too." I stared out of the window.

"You guys? You guys don't count."

We drove across town and pulled up in front of a large church named Victory Baptist. We were led into a back room of the church where dinner awaited to be served. We sat at a table and staff brought food to us. The tables were draped with decorative tablecloths and the food smelled decent. The only bad thing, there were a lot of other people already present when we arrived. Decent smelling food meant they had put all of their efforts and resources into one thing which didn't leave much resources for anything else. And resources were very limited.

There were about forty homeless people in there all together. We all sat and ate with the volunteers hovering around, asking if we wanted more food, more to drink, and how we were enjoying them. They didn't sit with us, though. They all stood and stared, intently watching us with giant smiles fixated on their faces. Definitely odd seeing so many people awkwardly smiling, but they were just trying to be friendly and pleasant. I'd rather see awkward smiles and overt friendliness than attitudes and evil glares. An older woman stepped forward and asked for our attention.

"Good evening, ladies and gentlemen," she softly said. "I'm glad our last group could finally join us. Welcome to Victory Baptist Church. It is open to everyone whether you share our denomination or not. You'll be staying here for about a week. You have to be out every morning by nine and can return at six—this includes weekends. Curfew is at eight."

"Where do we go if we don't have anywhere to go at nine?" someone asked.

"There's a park nearby. I'm sorry for those who have no place to go, but these are the rules and they will be enforced. There is no fighting, no alcohol, and absolutely no drugs. Once everyone is done eating, we'll head to the room where you can leave your belongings. Lights out is normally at ten, but since it's the first night of this cycle, we've pushed it back to eleven-thirty so you can all finish eating. I hope you enjoy your stay here. We'll all be taking shifts supervising you throughout the week, so feel free to talk to us if there's any problems. We're all ecstatic to have you here. Enjoy the food!"

I didn't stop eating to listen to her speech. I heard it everywhere we ended up; the same speech just in a different place with a different voice. It became way too repetitive. Everyone finished eating and we were guided to one room much bigger than the last place we were at, but not big enough to fit all of us as we piled in like clowns in a clown car. Blue sleeping mats were spread all over the floor. Helping Hands gave us army cots but mats were fine, too. Over time, I had learned to adjust to everything in order to find sleep. Once you adjusted, you didn't toss and turn anymore. My mom and I secured our three mats. We grouped them together and sat while everyone scrambled to secure their own mats.

Multiple odors polluted the air. We all laid head to foot, foot to side, side to head, scattered all over the floor across the room. Everyone around me coughed and sniffed. I covered my head not sure what good it would do but it made me feel better. The last thing I needed was for any of us to get sick. We laid still surrounded by strangers. The mix of so many different body odors nauseated me, becoming almost unbearable.

They turned the lights off but everyone around us kept talking. It didn't bother me, though. I had learned to tune most sounds out when I needed to. Being homeless, going mentally deaf is the only way I would sleep, or study, or do my homework. Wherever we went, noise greeted us. Usually there were too many people with too much to say.

The cold room lacked blankets. I curled up in a ball and began to drift asleep. A sudden quiver of grief swept over me like a chill down my spine. I opened my eyes and observed my grim surroundings. I hated having to sleep in shelters every night. Extreme poverty turned people to crime, so they wouldn't have to suffer. I thought about all the people at home, lying tucked in their warm beds and I lay there, cold on a mat on the floor. Sometimes I wanted to cry like I saw those refugees cry. But crying wouldn't change anything so I never saw the point. I held my head up to make sure some creeper wasn't trying to sneak a feel on my mom or sister, then I laid back down. I figured I should really go to sleep. I had to wake up soon and perform in this circus all over again.

I started to get used to Victory Baptist already. The food hadn't been anywhere near as good as on the first day but at least the portions were consistent. It had been three days since we first arrived and today started the school week. We sat on the bus riding back to the church from school. It had been a long day and I just wanted to sleep. We rode back, met up with my mom, and stood in line outside the church waiting until they let us in. I placed my backpack inside the giant room and joined my mom and sister in the food line. The extra hospitality shown to us in the beginning had dwindled into a regular volunteer-recipient interaction. We grabbed our food and sat.

The worst part about dinner was it being so early. We ate at six or six-thirty and were not expected to get hungry again until dinner the next night—if you weren't in school. They offered a late-night snack, but a small bag of apple slices or animal crackers did very little once our six o'clock dinner digested by seven. Sometimes I would play with the animal crackers. I pretended the crackers represented the people around me. I would spread them out on my mat, representing how we were all huddled in one room. I created imaginary hoops they all had to jump through, just like we did. I made myself the tiger. I would eat every animal cracker, except the tiger. The tiger wouldn't be swallowed like the rest of the circuses' animals. The tiger's strength couldn't be destroyed.

We ate and made our way to the bathrooms. My mom and sister had their own Ziploc bags of soap and so did I. I stood at the sink inside of the men's restroom. Someone talked to themselves in a stall while taking a crap, stinking up the entire bathroom. I tried to hold my breath as the stench of burnt eggs mixed with sewage vomit floated through the air. The way his feces sounded as it squirted from his anus into the toilet bowl gave away he had the runs. It sounded like he had a dirty orchestra in the stall and I purchased the only ticket to the concert.

I ran the sink water and took off my shirt. My mom told me if you couldn't wash anything else, clean under your arms and your privates. We didn't always get to take showers or a bath, but all we needed was a sink. I pulled my washcloth out of my bag and lathered it up. I washed my upper body and under my arms. I went into an empty stall and scrubbed my privates. The guy in the stall came out of it and left the bathroom. He didn't flush the toilet, he didn't wash his hands, he reeked, and we would be sleeping in the same room.

I finished up and exited the bathroom to see some guy pushed up against my sister. He stunk and smelled drunk. My mother still washed up in the bathroom. My sister tried to push him away as he pressed his chest up against her. Instantaneously, I was next to them and grabbed the guy from behind, pulling him away from her. He's a little bigger than me, heavier due to his beer belly, but I didn't care. I pinned my forearm to his throat.

"Touch her again and I'll kill you!" He didn't seem threatened. He tried to push me away from him, but I slammed him back into the wall. I pulled out the small switchblade I still had from staying with Lisa and Calvin. I held it at his neck as well. If anyone saw me with the knife, we would get kicked out but I cared less in the moment. I had to send a message.

"I was just talking to her. I'm married. I swear."

I let the weasel up and pushed him away. He stumbled back into the large room where we would be seeing him again.

"Fucking creep!" my sister yelled after him. She gave me a hug whispering thanks as we awaited my mom to come out. I tried not to leave them by themselves ever. There's always someone around trying to harass women. We met women all the time who have been raped and assaulted because they were left alone in a homeless world. We had had close encounters, very close encounters. I remember living in Sacramento when this woman tried to rape my sister after she had befriended our family. I had learned everyone smiled, but you couldn't trust any one of them, which kept my eyes glued to my mom and sister at all times. There would be no more close encounters as long as I lived and breathed. If anyone wanted to harm my mom and sister, they would have to kill me first.

When my mom exited the bathroom, we didn't mention anything to her about it. She had enough to worry about; plus, as the man of the family, I handled it. We walked back to the room and sat on our mats smelling like the fresh scent of soap. Normally, smelling like soap would be a good thing but our soapy aroma mixed with the stench, body odor, and filth circulating around the room made the overall smell even worse.

One room along with a foul smell is where we would stay, along with everyone else until lights out. We couldn't wander around the church due to the curfew they took extremely serious. Last night, a family had been put out for missing curfew; and staff shipped another family in and filled their spot immediately. No questions were asked about what the other family would do now and no questions would be asked. The clear message that every single one of us was expendable.

I conversed with my family for a while before I reached into my backpack and pulled out my homework. I had only two hours to get all of it done before they hit the light switch and I would have to work in the dark. I had to get all of my homework done. I hadn't told anyone, but I'd been having problems at school. Some teachers had this ugly way of being assholes.

I could smell a substantial amount of alcohol, which meant a lot of people were drunk. I hoped they didn't cause any problems, although drunk people usually did. I wondered where they were getting this money to keep buying alcohol. Everyone claimed they didn't have money, yet kept magically getting drunk. I heard yelling and turned around. Some woman accused another woman of stealing her things. They both were intoxicated and shouted louder at each other. Everyone watched them and they were putting on a show. They stood in each other's face and started waving their hands around, cursing each other out. They were two circus acts eager to perform. They began swinging and a brawl broke out. The bigger girl picked the other one up and slammed her on the floor like a wrestling move. She leaped on top of her trying to force her to submit.

The dinner volunteers hadn't left yet and those lion tamers all came flooding into the room. They pulled the women apart and told them to immediately grab their belongings. They tried to explain but were wasting their breath. They didn't care what happened between circus freaks and they kicked them both out. They searched through the rest of us; pulling aside those who smelled of excessive alcohol. I whispered for one of them to check the guy I had the encounter with and they kicked him out, as well. He told them I had a knife and they searched me thoroughly for it, but I had already hid it under my sister's mat. A few more people were forced to grab their belongings and the rest of us laid back down on our mats like nothing happened.

Due to the fight, they turned the lights off an hour early and I tried to read my math book in the dark. I pressed the page up close against my eyeball but it changed nothing. I still couldn't see. I put my book away and lay down. I wasn't tired so I lay there, once again trapped within my own thoughts. I thought a lot. Most nights I thought of a better life. What it must feel like to go inside of a restaurant and order anything I want to. Or to go into the mall and buy something nice for my mom. To open a refrigerator in my own home and see it filled with food. Not having to switch back and forth between my only two pairs of jeans. Or wash my clothes when they get dirty. What a life being housed would be. Thoughts of it tortured me. After a while, I tried to clear my mind so I could fall asleep. I had to wake up early and perform all over again.

Friday had come and we waited for the van to transport us away. We had been assured we would be staying for a little over two weeks at our next destination. A longer stay was good because we had a little stability now. Bad because it could only mean one thing: the end of the program cycle. It would be the last stop for the circus. After those last two weeks, everything would just kind of stop and we would be in the same position we were in before we joined the rotating cycle, but we knew our results going in. It wasn't our first time traveling with a circus. The structure of the circus wasn't designed to cure homelessness, but only to hide its symptoms for a brief period of time.

They split everyone into separate groups, keeping all families together. They also filled in single persons where they could fit and sent people every which way across the city. I gladly couldn't wait to distance myself from some of those other people. We loaded into the third van and it took us back across town to God's Grace, another church much smaller than the last. Seven of us rode in the van and when we entered the church there were four more sitting down eating cold cut sandwiches. We sat and joined the dining. An assortment of people ate there: another family, a married couple, and a few single men and women. I'd never seen a place that blatantly welcomed single men alongside single women. Volunteers stood around us, but it didn't seem like they had intentions on eating. There were five of them and they were a bit older than all of us. They seemed nice enough. A woman stepped forward and greeted us with a smile.

"Welcome to God's Grace. It's open to everyone regardless of their religion. You'll be staying with us for about two weeks and we're happy to have you. A few rules, there's no smoking or drinking on the premises. We have a nine o'clock curfew and we'll come by to do a room check every night. You all have your own rooms which is always nice to have a little privacy in your own space. You have to be out by ten every morning except weekends and can re-enter at seven. Dinner is at eight. You are allowed to have food in your rooms so if you have food stamps you can stock up. Do so at your own risk because bugs are an issue. We'll stay every night until eleven where we lock the main door and no one is permitted to enter or leave. We'll try to make your stay here as pleasant as possible and hope you can get back on your feet as soon as possible. Enjoy the food. There's plenty. Beverages are in the cooler."

We ate and staff escorted everyone to their rooms. Each family or individual received their own room. Families received the bigger rooms. All of the rooms were lined down a dormitory styled corridor. The rooms were luxurious in comparison to sleeping on the mats. There were three beds in our room. Two were twin bunk beds, and one a single twin. I took the top bunk, my sister the bottom, and my mom claimed the single. The room's single small window brought in a cool breeze so we closed it because we were already too cold and there wasn't a heater in there. The beds even came with sheets and a pillow. God's Grace didn't seem too bad. The quietness of our own space was the best part. The bathrooms were right down the hall and they came with full showers so now we thought we were really living luxurious. The only major fault I could find with God's Grace turned out to be the man living two doors down from us in a single. I didn't like the way he stared at my mom at dinner. I didn't like how she smiled at him. I heard a tap on the door and I hopped off the top bunk and beat my mother to it. I barely cracked the door open to see the man standing and smiling. He asked for my mom and I told him she was sleeping. He asked me to tell her he stopped by and would try again when she awoke. I closed the door and my mom asked who knocked.

"Just a homeless guy," I said.

"That's mean," Mom said.

"It's honest, Mom," I said. "He can't do nothing for you."

"He's trying like the rest of us."

"Is he?" Pooh asked. "Because not everybody's trying."

Sunday afternoon came and they had just served brunch. We sat in our room bored out of our minds. Again, there was no television, no radio, no game system, no books, nothing, never. We talked about anything we could think of. Moments like those, I valued my mom's immense, never-ending conversation. It kept us entertained. She talked mostly about when we were little kids, and how we acted. My sister used to punch me right in the gut every time she became mad and thought no one looked. My mom said I would fold over like a chair, grabbing my stomach and hit the ground screaming. She would come running toward me and spank my sister who would yell she always kept getting hit for no reason, and she only gets hit because my mom liked me more. She always seemed to forget pummeling me in the stomach.

Pooh Bear didn't like the stories of how she would beat me up. As we grew older, our love for each other had become unbreakable. She didn't play around when it came to me. All my fights or problems were her fights and problems. And she didn't allow anyone to talk bad about me. She wanted to protect her baby brother, her only brother. Although she was older, I saw myself as the big brother, the protector, and I didn't let anyone mess with my little sister. At times we thought we were fraternal twins, too.

We all sat cooped up in the room reminiscing about better times. We weren't always homeless. When we were toddlers, my mom always took good care of us. The good times made living homeless even worse for her because she knew what it's like to not be, just like the refugees. I barely remembered though, living in a homeless world can consume all of your memories.

Unluckily for us, in a couple of days, when the rotating cycle stopped, when the circus closed, we'd have another unwanted memory. I wasn't sure how many more of those memories we could take.

9. Breakdown: Part I

"MONICE KING. YOU CALLED ME YESTERDAY AND scheduled an appointment for today."

"How many kids?" asked the caseworker behind the clear glass window in the front lobby of St. De Paul's, one of the biggest shelters downtown.

"Two," Mom said.

The caseworker scrolled down a piece of paper attached to a clipboard, "Yes, for one p.m."

"Yes."

"We're are you currently staying?"

"Day shelters."

"Well, I think we have a room available for you to move in today, actually."

"Really? Girl, don't play."

"Mmhm, Just take a seat and someone will be right with you for intake."

"Oh my God, thank you so much." She led us to the lobby chairs.

We had hoped September would be kind to us. About time we caught some form of a lucky break. The rotating cycle of the shelters had ended two weeks ago. It had been day by day ever since.

St. De Paul's was supposed to be one of the better shelters, like the Beacon of Hope. The residents we saw going in and out didn't appear too happy, though. I wondered if the unhappy expressions were because of the conditions there, or because of their homeless state in general.

Moving into new shelters was always bittersweet. On one hand, we were ecstatic about having a place to exist, on the other it was still a shelter, we were still homeless, and we were treated accordingly. Yes, I was happy we were able to get in there, but I didn't want to be there.

"Monice?" A woman burst through the back door holding a folder full of our entire identity. My mother stood and professionally greeted her, shaking her hand.

"Hi, I'm Elena, your caseworker here. I'll be doing your intake as well as giving you a tour."

"Sounds great," Mom said.

We followed Elena into the back of the shelter. The large building had multiple floors and housed multitudes of San Diego's homeless. With so many homeless people all in one place, we lost our individuality and became numbers for their population statistics. They stopped focusing on individual families and instead focused on the population as a whole; which translated to them caring about *all* of us, but they didn't care about any *one* of us.

Elena stopped in front of a cafeteria. "This is where you'll be eating most of your meals. They serve breakfast, lunch, and dinner and you wait outside in the line. I'd advise you to get to the line early because once the cafeteria fills up, they don't let anyone inside until space clears. If you're still in line when breakfast ends, you don't eat. Now as part of your stay here, you have to take shifts serving in the cafeteria."

"Can my son take some shifts for me? The doctors told me I'm not supposed to be standing on my feet for long periods of time," Mom said.

"How old are you?" Elena asked me.

"Fifteen. I'm almost sixteen, though."

"I'm sorry, he's too young. But if you have a doctor's note confirming your health issues, there shouldn't be a problem bypassing service."

She led us past the laundry room. The washing machine took quarters, which I considered strange because most of us couldn't afford enough quarters to wash. Probably why the laundry room was empty. She brought us upstairs to the third floor and gave us tours of the communal bathrooms. The boys' and girls' bathrooms were on opposite ends. She led my sister and mom into the girls' and I escorted myself into the boys'. There were shower stalls lined across the wall and urinals lined across the opposite wall. The bottom of the shower where people stepped had been stained black. I approached one of the toilets to find it caked full of feces and with tissue paper dumped inside. The horrible stench made me plug up my nose, but I had smelled people who reeked worse. The spacious bathroom seemed capable of holding a large capacity of men.

I met them back in the hallway and Elena took us to our cramped room with small bunk beds inside.

"This is your room. There's absolutely no food inside. You don't want to have a bug problem and bugs usually come with food. You can stay here for six months. You have two months to obtain employment. Failure to do so is grounds for the immediate termination of your stay."

We set our bags down and followed her back to the front lobby to complete the last of our paperwork. My mom handed me our family's prepaid cell phone to hold as she disappeared into a back office with Elena. Luckily for us they didn't reach out last month or we would have missed St. De Paul's call.

I slipped outside for some fresh air. I never knew how long those meetings could take. I was happy but unhappy. I thought about what I would have given to be a normal kid. I didn't even like normal kids. They didn't understand me. Foster kids were cool, they knew the struggle. A lot of them spent days homeless.

They didn't ask obvious questions like why I always tried to eat, how come I missed so many school days, or why'd I be randomly standing on the corner in front of a shelter.

"Michael G?" Christine said, a girl I met in the eighth grade in San Diego. Christine's a nice girl but on intake days I never feel like talking to anyone; especially normal kids.

"Why are you standing in front of this shelter?"

"I don't think you'd get it," I said.

"Hmm," she said. "How're you? Long time. What's up?"

"I could complain," I said.

We stood awkwardly. I wanted her to keep going so I could go back inside. She stared at me very strangely. Like she wanted to laugh.

"Going home?" I said.

"Yeah," she said. "You?"

"Just chillin'."

My sister pushed open the glass doors and called, "Michael, mama said come on."

"I'll see you later." I gave her a side hug. I headed back inside. Christine followed me into the lobby.

"I completely understand." She embraced me again, wiping her eyes.

Elena returned to the lobby. "Hey Christine, is your dad feeling any better?"

"He's doing all right."

"That's good to hear. I have to steal these two away from you to sign some paperwork. I want to see you and your sister both at dinner tonight, okay?"

"Okay." She glanced back at me. "I'll see you there."

Living at St. De Paul's over the next month had its ups and down. My mom had to pay a high percentage of the low wages she made from her new security job to the shelter every paycheck. They said it would help us save up to move out. They said upon completion of the six-month program they give all the money back. The keywords were "upon completion," meaning if we didn't complete it, we did not get the money back. Giving up most of her paycheck left us with little money to do anything else besides wash clothes and put a few minutes on the family cell phone; which wasn't new. We had gone without buying them before so it wasn't an immediate problem. Sickness once again had found us, but it wasn't my mom; it had attacked my sister.

At first, she didn't say anything, and I blamed my mom. Watching her, we had learned how to cover up our pain in order to keep moving forward. Most of the time we figured it to be little things like getting sick from the common cold which turned out to really be the flu, or in my sister's case, her minor stomach pains turned out to be her gall bladder. My sister underwent surgery at the hospital to get it removed. They caught it just in time before it ruptured. Frightening though, because of her being only sixteen. I wondered if I'd be next to have surgery.

A shelter wasn't a place to recover properly, but it had to do. We were going to catch the bus to the hospital tomorrow to escort her back to St. De Paul's. She would miss a week or two of school and should be back to normal. When she first found out her stomach pains were actually her gall bladder and she needed immediate surgery, my sister sort of slumped into a mini depression. On top of homelessness, the weight of any other bad news multiplied tenfold. I hoped she would turn out okay. The doctors said her surgery went well, she hadn't lost much blood, no major complications, and we shouldn't worry. But I worried.

We rode the bus silently from the hospital. I had my arm tightly wrapped around my sister as she rested her head on my shoulder. The pain medication they gave her made her drowsy. We reached the bus stop in front of St. De Paul's and exited the bus. I helped my sister step by step to our room with my mom right behind us. It took us a while to get there but I didn't mind. My sister had always been so strong, weird seeing her so feeble. I had seen my mom undergo different surgeries but my sister was different. She's young like me. I could've easily been sick. We were supposed to be too young for those types of health problems. If her gall bladder had erupted, she would have died right in St. De Paul's. The ferociousness I usually saw in her eyes had gone. She didn't say much but when we reached the room, tears streamed down her face.

"This is so messed up." She sat on her bottom bunk.

"Always is," I said.

"It's just one thing after another. I'm sick of it. I'm done. I quit."

"You can't quit." I tried to sound strong.

"I quit. Screw school, screw trying to make it big, what's the point?"

"The point is to get out of this, Pooh. Quitting is only going to make it worse."

"Trying isn't making it better. Nothing makes it better. No matter what we do, something goes wrong everywhere we go. I can't do this anymore."

"You have a bright future ahead of you sweetheart." My mom lied on her own bed. The trip to the hospital physically exhausted her more than it should have.

"It's dark and gloomy from where I'm standing," Pooh replied. "We're all alone in this world."

"We have each other." I glanced around the shelter room, its confined walls constricting our existence.

"Yeah, well, we're alone together. Nobody cares about mama except us, and nobody cares about us except mama. Right now, I'm feeling like screw everybody. And triple screw this shelter."

"I think right now everybody around us or who knows us is probably waiting to hear the inevitable bad news about us," I said. "They're waiting for mama to die, you to prostitute or something, and me, I'll be dead too. Or like dad. They think it's only a matter of time."

"Yeah, they're right," she said.

"Yeah, maybe, but maybe not. I don't like people just telling me how my life is going to end. They just write us off. It's not fair. Why do we have to stay homeless?"

"That's how the world works, little brother. Some people are on top, some are on the bottom, and the rest of us aren't counted. It's been like that since before we were born, it'll be like that after we're dead."

"Yeah, and that upset me. Why are we even in this shelter? Is my spleen going to pop open next? We're already down here at the bottom; I don't want to stay here. Do you want to stay here, mom?"

"Hell, no." She turned over on her side. I wasn't sure if she really listened.

"Oh, so you can get us out of these shelters? You're going to fix mama? You're going to stop something else from going wrong with me? What if your spleen pops out? Huh? Then whatchu gonna do?"

"I'm just saying. Maybe I can't actually do anything . . . but I can't give up."

"We're too young to work. Oh, what you're going to hustle? Murder someone? End up like dad? What's up? Let me in on the plan."

"I don't really know anything right now. I'm trying to figure it out. All we can do is keep going. Every hit we take, we just have to keep going. Eventually, we'll be able to fight back. Like Rocky."

"Who? And that's not for certain. What if mama really dies next time or something happens to you? What if something happens to me? Something just happened to me."

She was right. Life had made me just as sad as her. But I just aspired for more. "I'm just trying to be hopeful. What else do we have?"

"Take a look around, we don't have nothing to be hopeful for! Do you understand how other people view us? Do you see how they stare when they see us enter and exit here?"

"Yeah, I'm not blind."

My mom murmured something I couldn't comprehend; she drifted to sleep. I sat on the floor next to my sister's bed.

"Can you imagine how hard it's been for her?" I said.

"It's been hard for us."

"Yeah, but we're young. I'm fifteen. We can bounce back from this."

"You don't sound sure."

"I'm not sure. But mama's been through the abusive childhood, abusive relationships, rape, and that's all before we were born. She survived that. She's surviving now we're homeless too. We're tough. Like Wolverine."

"Who's that?"

"He's a superhero . . . he has metal claws. He can heal. You can heal from this too. We all can heal from this."

Pooh stared at our mom for a while but didn't speak. I understood her emotions, anger, sadness, and others she couldn't possibly describe. Living as we did made you go a little crazy. Some people go completely bonkers, but no one's the same after they're homeless.

"I feel like three-quarters of a person," she said. "Everywhere we go they make sure to tell us we're homeless. We were told to be grateful for this, and to be grateful for that."

"But that's what I'm saying. I'm tired of being grateful. I just want to be normal. It drives me crazy. I want to be free. I want a PlayStation. If something happened again, you at least deserve a bed. If we quit, none of that is possible. We won't have any money. As long as mama keeps going, we don't have an excuse to stop. We need to do this for her."

"Do what for her? Everything's out of our control."

"I agree," I said. We sat for a moment.

"You think we'll live like this forever?"

"Probably," I teased. "But honestly, if we try it's a fifty-fifty chance. But if we quit then we will fail for sure. I need you with me if we're going to do something about this, though. You feel me, ride in limos and stuff. Eat at fancy restaurants. One day we'll go to a new city and won't have to map out where all the shelters are."

"I'm with you. It's just a lot sometimes, like why'd I have to get surgery? But I'm with you. One day we'll look back on all of this and laugh."

"Hahaha, will we? It doesn't seem too funny right now."

"Hey, I said 'one day'!"

"Hahaha, probably not, though. I'm sure mama doesn't look back and laugh at none of that stuff."

"I probably won't be laughing because it's funny," she said. "I'll be laughing because it's not."

10. Merry Christmas!

TOMORROW'S CHRISTMAS AT ST. DE PAUL'S AND WE
couldn't be more unenthusiastic. I learned Santa Claus
wasn't real at an early age, around seven. My mom couldn't pretend Santa Claus brought gifts when we woke up with without
presents or a tree. She had always given us what she could and
we her, which usually involved scraping together some change
and shopping around at the ninety-nine-cent store. Not exactly
much, but it made us happy.

At shelters, they always tried to be festive and promote holiday cheer but it's hard to be cheerful. Christmas, like Thanksgiving, like my birthday, I considered just another day. I couldn't
tell the difference between Christmas and a regular Monday.
I wasn't talking about the religious aspect, I meant the actual
day as it pertained to my life. However, I could say Christmas
resembled Thanksgiving because of the extreme influx of food.
Food's always good.

My mom finally turned our food stamps back on so I didn't
really starve anymore. We could go right into a grocery store
and buy anything to eat. Virtually heaven. I didn't care what
anyone said about food stamps, I appreciated them. Some people were too embarrassed to get them but we didn't care. People
can talk about entitlement, people can talk about government
handouts, and people can talk about whatever else they wanted
to talk about. I really, honestly, didn't care. They had never been
where I stood, trapped at the bottom, gazing up at them. I didn't
care what they said; they couldn't comprehend the desolation of
having to go without. They want to talk about entitlement? No,

they were entitled. What am I entitled to? Food? Is it a human right or an entitlement? I have heard people say, "You have to pull yourself up from your bootstraps." But you could not pull yourself up from your bootstraps if you didn't have any boots.

Those people were crazy because they were so entitled they thought everyone had a pair of boots. You can't create something out of nothing. It sounded good in theory saying you did, but in this real world we live in, if you don't have anything, you do not get anything. I remembered all those hungry nights without food stamps, we would be fools not to get them. The Bible says foolish pride is a sin and now we had food to eat. I was happy for food stamps; whatever people said, they couldn't say we were starving.

Elena had told us St. De Paul's, like most, didn't allow food into the rooms but of course we snuck it in. They should expect us to. They served us three meals in the cafeteria at set times during the day. They were decent meals. The lines were long, but I didn't mind because St. De Paul's didn't really run out of food, but with the set meal periods, it's best to be on time. Toward the end of the meal period, the food became a little distasteful and once it ended, no more for the day. If you missed dinner for work, or could not make it for whatever reason, it's nice to have food in the room you could go to and eat. Or else you didn't. Everyone snuck in food.

On Christmas Eve, they were offering a free photo service for families to take a professional portrait. My mom signed us up to take our picture. A family picture would be nice, I couldn't remember the last time we had one taken. I might have been five or six. I could barely remember the moment. My mom said Rod Luck, a locally famous San Diego news anchor, had showed up to our apartment with cameras and presents for us. Our very own miracle and we were so happy. Although the vague memory flickered in my mind, I held on to it for dear life as we sat and waited for them to call us back to the photography room.

After our Rod Luck Christmas, presents just sort of stopped, so did food, so did all income, and Christmas cheer turned into a simplistic "Merry Christmas." Then it turned from "Hooray, it's Christmas!" to "Oh . . . it's Christmas?" and then to "Screw Christmas."

A man called us back to take our picture. The photographer positioned us and told us to smile on three. He counted to three and we smiled big and bright. He took multiple pictures telling us how good they were turning out. We couldn't see the pictures he took but he told us we could go back the next day and pick it up. We thanked him for his time and went back to our room where I ran into Christine.

Weird we both ended up there in the same place. In a way, her being there comforted me. It's easier to talk to someone who is where you are or who has been where you are. We could vent to each other, it made time go by a little faster. Her family and my family grew pretty close; well, as close as we could be. You never wanted to get too close with anyone because at any moment somebody could just disappear. You didn't want to be too hurt if someone you befriended vanished. You had to constantly remind yourself it could happen any day. If they did vanish, and most times they would, it would not leave a giant void because you were prepared for it.

"Hey, are you guys eating with us tonight?" I asked her as my mom and sister entered our room.

"No, I'm not really in the mood."

"Starving yourself again?"

"Shut up. I'm not in the mood."

"Not in the mood to eat?"

"Nah, not really. The paramedics came and took my dad to the hospital."

"Damn. . . ." I thought back to when they carried my mom away. "Again?"

"Yup."

"How is he?"

"I think he's bad."

"He'll pull through. He's strong. He reminds me of my mom."

"Yeah, he told me about all the surgeries she had. That's crazy. What did you do when your mom was in the hospital?"

"Well, I ate."

"I'm serious."

"I tried to visit her. There's not much you can do. We just have to wait it out . . . pray I guess . . . and keep waiting. Keep telling yourself he'll be all right."

"But what if he's not?"

"He might not be and be ready for that if it happens. Right now, convince yourself he will be. I mean that's all you can do."

"Well, that sucks."

"Yeah, it does."

"Is it enough?"

"It's enough to get you through the day. That's all you need, for now." All the advice I had to give. I gave her a hug and entered my room. I decided to take a nap until dinnertime.

Thirty minutes before dinner, my sister woke me up to stand in that food line. With all of those people there, the lines were long and the cafeteria could fill up quick. Some people were already waiting when we arrived. They finally opened the doors and the line began to move. We reached the food and the servers piled small portions of food on our plates. The servers were the other residents living in the shelter. My mom bypassed serving thanks to her doctor's note, which we were happy about. None of the servers acted happy to serve, and being there, happiness was crucial.

Different Christmas paraphernalia decorated the cafeteria. We sat at an empty table and started eating. A mother with three little children came and sat next to us. Two girls and one boy all under twelve. My mom, always the chatterbox, started talking and found out they had to leave St. De Paul's in four days. The mother seemed discombobulated, anxious like she recently just became homeless when she moved into there. She said she was lost. She started crying and my mom tried to console her.

"I couldn't take it anymore, I just had to get away from him," she said.

"A man should never put his hands on a woman," my mom said. "I was in an abusive relationship when I was younger. You see this brown mark on my eye? It'll never go away. Don't put yourself through this."

"I'm not. That's why I ran away. I took the kids and we left while he was at work. It was the best decision I ever made."

My sister and I stared at the mother and her children. Her voice quivered when she said, "it was the best decision she had ever made." The uncomfortablity of living in a shelter evident form her loss of hair. Her right eye still had faint traces of black around it from when her husband punched her in her face. The black mixed with heavy bags under eyes. She reeked of bug repellent. Her long hair fell out. Her clothes were name brand. She held her head high. The woman said she left him for good, but a shelter is not a home. Her children never looked up from their plates. They weren't laughing or joking around like kids are supposed to do. I couldn't say anything to comfort them because nothing anyone said comforted me at that young age. They left a middle-class lifestyle for a lifestyle below poverty; a drastic change for them. Honestly, the fact she had lasted so long surprised me. She would most likely go back to him in four days when her times up, maybe in five days if she had any strength left.

We told her about some of the other shelters we had been in and where to find them. Her three kids were still little so she shouldn't run into too many rejections or waitlists. She acted as if she listened but the more shelters my mom listed, the vaguer the interest in the woman's eyes became. My mom probably wasted her voice, but I was glad she told her. She should subconsciously remember what steps to take if she ever did decide to leave him for good, at least I hoped.

I had seen a lot of women in shelters who went through abuse. I witnessed the same continuous cycle over and over again just with different faces. My mom had been through it, she told me that a self-realization had to occur. Only they could save themselves. Not saying they would not need help, but for the most part, salvation's all up to them. Still, the cycle's tough to see.

We finished eating dinner and said our goodbyes. Before we left, she asked my mom for her number which she gave. We knew we would never see or hear from them again but sometimes people just needed to see any type of support system no matter how big or small. I wished them the best, though. Homelessness or abuse . . . sometimes it wasn't possible to win no matter what you do.

We headed back to our room with our stomachs full. My mom roamed to the bathroom to take a shower and we used her absence as an opportunity to wrap her Christmas presents. We bought her a box of Fiddle Faddle Butter Toffee Popcorn, and it cost every penny we had. We wrapped the box in an old newspaper and hid it. My mom re-entered the room and we acted like nothing happened. She would be so surprised. She didn't expect anything. She never did.

I knew she went and somehow bought us a gift too, which I appreciated. The thought is what counted. It's always a nice feeling going to sleep Christmas Eve knowing you had something awaiting you in the morning, even if it wasn't really anything. Last Christmas, my mom gave me a small pack of donuts and a root beer, my first favorite soda, and I rated it the best root beer I'd ever tasted.

Christmas morning came sneaking in quietly like it always did. My sister and I pulled my mom's gift from under the bed and tiptoed over to her bed since she still slept. We counted to three and screamed, "Merry Christmas!"

My mom jumped up startled and gazed at us confused. Then she began to blush and sit up as we handed her the present. She opened it and became teary-eyed, giving us both long hugs and offering to share her Fiddle Faddle, which we declined. She then rummaged through her things and emerged with gifts of her own. My sister had more gifts than me but she always did because her birthday landed two days after Christmas. I unwrapped my present, also wrapped in newspaper, and it pleasantly surprised me. I had a new pack of black socks. There's nothing like a nice pair of black socks. A PlayStation or Xbox would have been nice, but I liked gifts I could actually use. My sister only opened one of her two gifts saving the other for her birthday. A new hair comb.

We ate breakfast, and my mom reminded us we had to pick up our family picture. On the way to pick up the picture, we saw paramedics wheeling a woman on a stretcher out of the door. The paramedics were there pretty often—like most shelters. A lot of people in shelters were sick or became sick. Not the common cold sick, well, that too, but sick like my mom and Christine's dad.

Our Christmas celebration then concluded. The end. We exchanged gifts, exchanged good will, done; back to the rest of my homeless day. Like I said, I hated holidays in shelters. It beats holidays outside, but it wasn't much better. Everyone acted glad to be there, but nobody really wanted to be there. We had no power there. We had no voice. We had to do whatever they said, and they talked to everyone like we were little children. Like they were so much better than us. I hated it, especially on holidays when all the staff loved to say, "Cheer up, it's Thanksgiving," "Cheer up, it's Easter," or "Cheer up, it's Christmas."

How could they expect us to be so cheerful? There's nothing cheerful about living in shelters. We would be back on the streets anyway. Nothing magical happened on holidays. Santa didn't bring us money. The Easter bunny never left us quarters to wash our clothes. As far as Thanksgiving, well, the Europeans came over and slaughtered all the Native Americans, so why did we celebrate genocide? I didn't have anything against holiday spirit. I just didn't have any and neither did any non-staff around me.

We waited in line to pick up our picture and finally received it. The more time went by with us staying in shelters, the grimmer and grimmer we became—especially me. Nothing mattered, just our time limit. I grew older each day. Life started to weigh heavier on me.

We pulled the picture out of the manila envelope containing it and stared. I loved it. We smiled so bright and beautiful. We looked so happy. Happiness was the allure. As long as you smiled, you were happy. We appeared so happy in that picture when in all truth, we couldn't have been sadder.

11. The Pursuit of Happiness

EARLY JANUARY, I WANDERED THROUGH THE HORTON Plaza mall. Everyone shopped, searching for the after-Christmas specials. To not have anything and be surrounded by people who had everything killed me. I saw it everywhere in school. Everyone had to have the newest shoes, clothes, accessories, and all of their luxurious possessions. Living downtown materialism emitted everywhere, rich people driving around in their fancy cars, eating at their fancy restaurants, shopping until their hearts were content.

I strolled to the Foot Locker to see boys around my age buying Nike, Adidas, and Jordans, smiling and joking with one another. My own two feet had a regular pair of cheap black shoes. They didn't even have a brand. I used to own a white pair of Shaq's shoe brand. He sold them at Payless and I hustled enough money until I bought them. At least Shaq cared about the kids who wanted a name brand but couldn't afford it. Some kids teased me about buying from Payless but Shaq was Shaq. I wore them down until my mom and sister finally sat me down in an intervention and told me I had been basically walking barefoot.

I stood next to the jewelry store. Everything inside it glistened, including the people in business suits. A man waited outside of the door, greeting people as they strolled by, inviting them inside. His smile faded when he saw me. I must have just resembled poverty. I had on an oversized black T-shirt and some baggy blue jeans with the black shoes. Nothing fancy about me. He glanced beyond me and resumed his duties as the next person walked by. I stopped and stared through the jewelry store window. I'd never owned real jewelry. I wanted some. It was beautiful. I stared in awe.

"Keep moving," a mall security guard said as I turned around to see him behind me. The man at the door had called him on me. I wanted to ask what I did but I already knew. I lowered my head and dragged my feet away.

I ghostly roamed into Macy's, seen but unnoticed. I walked through the perfume department smelling every scent I wish I could buy my mom. All of the clothes were expensive. I walked through the women's aisle. I picked up a nice sleek black dress made of quality fabric. I roamed to the men's section. The business suits were crisp. The business shoes were polished to a nice shine. I wanted to try on a pair but I refrained. Usually I did, but right then it was more pointless than ever.

Everywhere I looked constantly reminded of everything I didn't have on a material basis. I didn't need materialistic things to survive, but honestly who didn't want some of them? Especially as a child?

I left the mall and dragged my feet along the street. Night fell. Hooded men up to no good lurked in the corners glaring at me as I passed. Classy people with bright smiles and nice cars stampeded the main streets glaring at me as my appearance flickered past. I glanced away when I saw the hooded men. I smiled at the classy people. I drifted lost somewhere in between their worlds. Police cars crept around corners, evading the light of the classy people, and searching through the shadows for the hooded men.

I was desperate. Something had to change. No telling how long I could keep living hand to mouth. Especially since I got older. I tried to live right, tried to do it the right way. I stayed in school, I didn't gangbang, I wasn't out committing felonies, but all my efforts gave me nothing in return. All I had was nothing. I crossed the street headed back to St. De Paul's. I passed a few local drug dealers parked, just sitting in their glistening Beamers. They had wads of cash in their pockets. They weren't living right but they sure weren't homeless either.

I stopped believing in fairy tales long ago, maybe in Houston. I wasn't going to magically wake up middle class tomorrow.

Sure, we could keep pushing; keep moving forward, but I wondered how long we could keep actually going. Surviving is like running a race, eventually we were going to get tired and have to stop. Only if you're homeless, when you stop, you die. Dying is what society would want, what society predicted would happen to me.

I heard a whistle then saw a group of black teens standing at the following corner. I had to cross the street in order to get to St. De Paul's which was still about ten minutes away. One of them threw up a gang sign at me. I shook my head no to signal I didn't bang as the walk sign came on. I didn't want to tread through them so I stayed on the street and stepped along the curb instead of getting on the sidewalk. One, two, three of them began following me, then the rest of the entire group.

"I think he's a Crip, they think they own downtown," one of them said. "Fuck crabs." Crabs, of course, is the term Bloods use to diss Crips.

"What set you from?" I heard again, not bothering to turn around.

"I know you hear us," another said.

Two of them jogged ahead of me, cutting me off. They didn't care if I gangbanged or not. They were just waiting for something to do.

"I said where you from, Blood."

I always thought putting "Blood" or "Cuz" for Crips at the end of every sentence sounded stupid. It made them sound illiterate and they probably were. I kept my feelings to myself, however.

"I don't gangbang."

"Blood's lying," the other one said. One of their friends bumped into the back of me. They had me surrounded. They saw me by myself and jumped to attack. But I wasn't about to deal with it.

"Where you from?" asked another.

"Just get Blood, already," said a voice.

"Beat Blood ass."

"Take off on Blood."

They all sounded stupid. The two boys in front of me fidgeted. They were getting ready to try and do something. The first boy lunged at me with a haymaker and I ducked under it. The second caught me on my chin with a jab. I returned with a jab of my own, hitting him right above his left eye, and then everyone rushed in all around me swinging wildly. A few punches stung but my adrenaline kept me going. I started throwing random punches at anything moving around me, trying to create space. Without a second thought, I took off running when a small opening in the fracas emerged, pushing past two of them.

They all chased after me. Some of them were fast, really fast. I ran across the street through open traffic closer toward St. De Paul's. Cars swerved around me honking their horns. The gangbangers followed. I zigzagged around corners trying to lose them. I saw a flash of police sirens and we really started running as they chased all of us. I slipped away from the commotion and started jogging toward a few residences in the dirtier part of downtown. My tongue licked my busted lip as I caught my breath from running. Even my blood tasted poor, bland, deprived of nutrients. I tiptoed down the street toward the shelter. I didn't feel like going back with a busted lip just yet. I entered an ally and leaned against the fence of an empty lot. If the police or gangsters caught me, they would have just caught me.

Two men in tattered clothes plus a smell entered the ally carrying a black grocery bag. The shorter one squinted his eyes at me. I didn't glance away. He reached into his bag and pulled out a forty-ounce beer bottle and offered it to me. I took it and he smiled a toothless grin. They sat next to me.

"You been fighting?" asked the shorter man.

"I don't really want to talk about it," I said.

"Well duck next time someone swings at your face." The two of them start laughing. I laughed too. Life up until then was just so funny.

I took a long swig of beer letting its effect numb my busted lip. Letting it numb me through another hard time. They always came when we were about to leave a shelter. Our stay at St. De Paul's ended in one week. Timing out of shelters was like speeding down a raceway and running out of road. We knew the edge neared, we could see it, but had no way to slow down. We didn't have a parachute so no matter what we did; crashing is all we could do, which was what was so sad. We worked so hard for so much more and still had nothing. We lived the right way and still had nothing.

I pulled and unfolded the family picture from out of my pocket. I had borrowed it without asking my mom. I stared at the family picture a little longer. It came out really nice. I chugged half of the bottle of beer, letting the carelessness overtake me. What a happy family.

12. The Walk of Shame

THE FIRST OF MARCH ROLLED AROUND AND THE INEVI-
table time had come and we were forced to move shelters.
We used the money we had saved from St. De Paul's to stay in
motel rooms for two weeks until the money ran out. Before it
did, my mom found us a new shelter. St. De Paul's was the cream
of the crop, everywhere else drastically worsened. Decent shelters were like a lottery pick. The odds of finding a good one
were slim to none. We were currently in a new temporary shelter. We had about three weeks there; enough time for us to
apply to another shelter. Applying didn't mean we would get
into another shelter, but we would have time to search for them.
Shelter waitlists are often extensive and the list of shelters taking
older boys became shorter and shorter from an already short list.

The next shelter operated under a church. They sectioned off
a large room into smaller spaces with blue tarps hanging from
feeble rails serving as walls to separate each space. Different
families occupied these spaces and each space had army cots for
us to sleep on. The temperature's generally cold in there so we
stayed layered up with jackets. We all lived in a room right beside
the church. They welcomed us to the deserted early morning
service but nothing else. We were under strict orders not to talk
to the congregation. We weren't allowed to interact. In fact, we
had to stay as far away from them as possible, especially during
service. They were afraid of us. They were afraid of a bunch of
homeless people wandering around their church. It made them
nervous. They couldn't tell the homeless people there were all

families. They couldn't distinguish between us and dirty vaga-
bonds on the corner drinking and swearing.

Being on the other side of town gave us a nice break from
downtown; which made me glad. We would be headed back
there sooner or later because it had the most resources, but for
then I enjoyed the break from there. We could only come on the
church premises after six. They were really strict about us keeping away. We couldn't wait in line to enter until six; we had to
be completely off the premises until exactly six. Any infractions
and they kicked us out, no exceptions for any reason.

The minuscule food tasted awful but you get what you pay
for. They fed us dinner but it wasn't really dinner. They gave us
some concoction of peanut butter and jelly sandwiches mostly,
maybe some fruit. We filled up bottles at the sole water foun-
tain so we could have something to drink. It didn't feel welcom-
ing there either. Some of the staff frowned at the fact we were
even there. It didn't bother my family as much as it bothered
some of the other families. They kept complaining about staff
members but complaining would only make the living situation worse. In circumstances like those we had to play our cards
right. The staff directly controlled our lives. If we pissed them
off, they could make our lives hell. They could skip giving us
food, not give us supplies, knock down the tarp walls, or could
lie on us about breaking rules, and have us immediately kicked
out. A lot of those other families didn't understand the dynamic.
They believed someone owed them something. Like people had
to help them. But no one had to do anything for us. If anything,
we were at their mercy.

The army cot beneath me was hard and very uncomfortable,
but of course, it wouldn't stop me from sleeping. Before we
drifted to sleep, we wanted to shower. I liked the families there
because most of them showered. The little kids cried too much
but understandably so. When I first became homeless as a little
kid, I cried a lot too. The family designated to shower before us

returned signaling our shower time, so we braced ourselves. I took off my shirt, letting the cold stale air of the room ram into my chest. I had my back turned so my mom and sister wouldn't see me completely naked. I took off my tattered jeans, then my underwear, allowing my privates to freeze over. I removed my socks, stepping on the icy tile floor. I grabbed the short towel the staff had given me and wrapped it around me. My mom and sister, who had their backs to me as well, did the same.

We all simultaneously changed in our tarp section. The shower wasn't in the building where we slept, though. Some genius put it across the parking lot. We could only take showers at designated intervals, those slots mainly around service times where more staff could monitor us. To take a shower, we had to strip down to meager towels and walk across the parking lot to the shower building with everyone around watching. Without a doubt one of the most embarrassing things I had ever done. I couldn't begin to describe the humiliation all those cold eyes feeling sympathetic toward us, glad we were unfortunate and not them, it made me feel so bad. It didn't make sense to me why we had to strip down to our bare essentials. I think they said an incident had happened which made them have to create such an embarrassing ordeal.

We grabbed our cleaning supplies and headed out into a busy parking lot. People were just arriving for evening service and lingered in the parking lot as they met up with family and friends. We started inching toward the small building consisting of the shower stall and could hear as the noise level slowly dropped. I saw a few teenagers pointing their fingers, snickering at us. One of them ate a hamburger but hid it around her back when she noticed me staring at it. Heads turned as they watched us move half naked. I tried to avoid eye contact as all of them stared at us. I held my head down so they couldn't see my face. I passed a little boy staring at me with big bright eyes. He couldn't have been any older than five. He smiled and I smiled back.

"Hi!" He waved as he started taking off his shirt like me. His mother quickly ran around the front of the car and yanked him so hard by his arm I thought she pulled it out of socket.

"Don't talk to him!" she scolded as she quickly grabbed his arm and drug him toward the church.

"But I want to go swimming!" he yelled back.

I watched as she dragged him away. He glanced back at me shocked by his mother's reaction. I didn't take it personal. In her perspective, her son had no reason to attempt to befriend a heathen. I understood. I didn't like it, but I understood it. I pressed forward with my mom and sister, careful to keep our heads hung low. As we passed women, they grabbed on tighter to their purses, as if we were about to steal their money with one hand while running away and keeping our towels on with the other hand, and I guess while balancing our cleaning supplies on our head.

They moved out of our path, far enough so we couldn't touch them, but hovered around us close enough to get a good view. They didn't speak but those silent cold eyes said it all. Some people had disdain in their eyes. Some had sympathy. None had true understanding. They made the ordeal even worse. They just kept staring. No smiles, no friendly conversation, just relentless attention. They didn't whisper about us, they just silently watched. I would rather them snicker, I'd rather them whisper, don't just watch me and thank God you're not me. While they were thanking God they weren't me, what did I thank God for? I truly wished they were me and I them. I wished I could stare at them how they were all staring at me.

I wondered what they saw when they stared at me. Did they see a human or did they see something else? Did I lose my humanity when I lost my home? I was the same person, my skin displayed the same color, I had all my limbs, but I must have turned purple with spikes growing out of my head because they stared at me as if watching a spectacle. I wasn't being recognized as human. Right then, I knew they recognized me as something else, something lesser. I thought the Bible said, "Come as you are," but I guess the rules didn't apply to us.

The never ending parking lot disheartened me. I just wished they would stop staring at us. I tightened my towel around me. The bottom of my feet scraped against the tar of the parking lot. The wind blew against my bare chest. We picked up the pace and finally made it to the shower building where a nude line awaited us. There were two families waiting to shower in front of us. We stood outside, blatant in our naked hour for all to see almost every crevice on our bodies on full display to those who placed immediate judgment. Behind us, they still stared.

When you were ahead in line, no one could see you waiting because you waited near the front of the building, but when you were last in line like us, nothing hid you. You stuck out like a sore thumb and everyone watched you like a sea of endless eyes. Their cold sea of eyes stripped me of all dignity, all humanity, all in the name of one shower—a daily occurrence for all of those eyes, but a once or twice a week event for us. We moved up in line and finally entered the building as the line grew behind us with other naked families. The crowd had died down due to the start of service. With only one shower stall, we had to take turns. A staff member sat in the building monitoring us. He checked to make sure we didn't have anything he found suspicious. My mom told my sister to take her shower first and we sat outside the stall waiting.

"I really don't like this place," I said.

"Me either, Sun. We won't be here too long. We just have to stick it out until we can leave."

"Where are we going next? Where've you been searching?"

"I've been to every place they've given me. Everywhere is full and the ones that aren't are not family shelters."

"Is there any group homes open?"

"Nope, not even for your sister."

"What are we going to do?"

"We'll figure it out."

"We have no choice but to figure it out. . . ."

My sister stepped out of the shower and my mother told me to go next. I hopped in the shower. I began to wash myself as I sung. In my mind I sounded like Usher, so I gave it all I could.

Then they started singing, and they could sing louder than me so I stopped. The water wasn't ice cold, but it was far from warm. The old and rusted showerhead hardly had any water pressure. The shower wasn't a comfortable shower, but a shower none-theless. I finished up and my mom stepped in the shower next. I dried off while my sister and I waited for her.

"I'm getting sick," Pooh said.

"It's because people keep on coughing and not covering their mouths."

"Not that type of sick. Really sick."

"What do you mean? You don't have another gallbladder."

"It's a different kind of sick."

"Like you need another surgery sick?"

"I could. They say I have a condition."

"Who's they?"

"The doctors."

"When'd you go see a doctor?"

"That's not the point."

I paused trying to process what she told me. ". . .Well what kind of condition?"

"It's called Polycystic Ovary Syndrome. I don't really under-stand too much about it yet."

"Is it curable?"

"It's treatable. It has something to do with my hormones and stuff."

"Damn. Shit just keeps getting better and better."

"Mama told me not to tell you. She said you get mad at us for being sick."

"No, that's not true. I mean I get mad, but not at you two. I can never get mad at you two for something you can't control. It could easily be me who gets sick next time. I get that. My mad is more of a frustration. I see you getting sick, mama was sick, and I feel so helpless. There's nothing I can do to help. I can't change anything and that's why I get frustrated. I'm healthy for the most part, I just want to give some of it to you and her. It's not your fault. I don't blame either one of you. Nobody's to blame, it's just unfortunate."

"Haha, unfortunate . . . the story of our lives."

My mom turned the shower off, dried off, and stepped out. The staff member checked us again to make sure we didn't have any drugs, drug paraphernalia, alcohol, or anything suspicious. We told him we had the same cleaning supplies we had the last time he checked. He told us he didn't want to check us but he had to, his job required it. Some people have had drugs and overdosed, some people had alcohol poisoning, and now they had to monitor us at all times.

He politely told us our time ended and we were forced back out into the parking lot so the next family could come in. Our showers had made the outside air even colder against our skin. A new line of naked families waited patiently for their turns. The parking lot wasn't as crowded so we scurried across. There were still a few stragglers lingering about, mingling.

"So one of them comes up to me and like begs for fifty cents, harassing me. I thought a skeleton had jumped out in front of me. Thank Jesus I had my pepper spr—" A woman noticed us approaching and let her speech fall into silence. Her and her friend glared at us, and then both glanced away as we passed.

It amused me how conversation always trailed off and died whenever people saw us coming. We kept our heads low and hurried to the building where we slept. We entered and signaled for the next family to take the walk, each terrible step, and stand in line. They were the last family of the day, what horrible attention they would receive. A mother, father, and two children stood nervous. They gathered their belongings and headed to the door with their towels wrapped around them and stared back at us. They weren't familiar, so they must be a new family. It must be their first shower there. Fear emitted from their eyes. I heard loud commotion outside and saw the congregation filing out of the church. It sounded like there were more people outside now than during our turn.

The father, the rock of the family, even seemed disturbed. No one and nothing could prepare a person for the humiliation. Male or female, it would degrade them the same exact way. Actually, it might be worse for men because most women readily do what is necessary for their children, but most men have too much pride. My mom embraced the family and told them to keep their heads down and move quickly. The father grabbed the mother's hand, took a deep breath, and they slowly stepped out with their two children. We listened as the loud commotion quickly died down and all eyes began to watch them as they stepped into shame.

13. Friends

NEAR THE END OF MARCH, I SAT AT THE BUS STOP rubbing my hands together trying to warm them from the crisp night air. I awaited the last bus of the night to take me to my friend David's house. My mom and sister were staying with a different friend who only had room for them. My mom didn't want to go there without me, she wanted to stay together, but I insisted. We tried going back downtown but the only two shelters we found would take us already had waitlists, which we still signed up for. An acquaintance of my mom's then offered to let her and my sister stay with her for a few days but for some reason I couldn't stay there. We tried to get me into a boy's group home in the meantime, but as usual no room meant no room.

The thick clouds invading the sky were gray and dark as the wind jousted through the night, rendering my thin jacket useless. My heavy backpack carried most of everything I owned. I had been waiting on the bus for about forty-five minutes now and I couldn't feel my fingers or my nose. My ears were cold with a constant ringing noise inside them. When the bus finally arrived, it honked at me, waking me up from my cold-induced sleep. I grabbed my backpack and I paid the last of the money I scraped together for bus fare and took a seat at the rear of the mostly empty bus. A guy sat across from me with a bag and a nasty odor. I had seen him on the bus before. I could recognize homelessness and the bus ride was another trick we sometimes used to kill time. A lot of homeless people rode it back and forth all night to nowhere just for temporary shelter. It kept you warm and safe. But when the buses stopped running, you were stuck where you got dropped off until the morning. The guy gave me a head nod of recognition and I returned the gesture. After a forty-minute bus ride, I pulled the cord and exited on my friend's street.

My friends were a little erratic. Not on purpose, just a part of the life they lived. When David told me I could spend a few nights, I already assumed it to be contingent upon if David was still home. David involved himself with a lot of things, gangs, selling drugs, but I wasn't in a place to judge anyone about anything. We were cool, and being cool was as far as I was concerned regarding all my friends. If he answered the door everything would be fine for the night, but only if he answered. I knew his mom, too, but she never stayed around. He practically lived by himself. The last time I talked to David happened earlier in the day when I had first asked to come. If anything, I should have come over right then because I knew he was there, but I had to escort my mom and sister to where they were staying. They couldn't carry everything by themselves.

I slid up to the front door and all of the lights were off. I rang the doorbell a couple of times and banged on the front door. I hopped the side fence and jogged around to his bedroom window. I knocked once again, but he did not reply. I tried to see if he might have left it open but I already knew paranoid David wouldn't leave a window unlocked and open. I didn't have a cell phone, so I couldn't call him . . . or anyone else and the buses had stopped running. I hopped back over the fence and sat in front of the door.

Zeus hurled his thunderbolt overhead which could only mean one thing. Sure enough, droplets of rain began to sprinkle down upon my head. David's house didn't have a porch cover so I stood and walked across the street toward some apartments. There were no trees around big enough to shield the light drizzle so I huddled up on top of a set of small steps on the side of the apartment building. I crouched over hugging my knees as the drizzle picked up, soaking my clothes in a matter of seconds. I kept my head down so my face wouldn't get wet. The wind blew hard against my body as if I turned into a sail and the steps a boat. My hands had turned icily numb and now I could definitely feel my fingers due to the icy chill stabbing at them. I had school in the morning but I would miss it anyway. I probably wouldn't go all week, not until we could find a new shelter and stabilize a little more. I had been told to drop out, but I didn't see the point in dropping out. School wasn't too difficult and it offered somewhere to go. Plus a nice way to kill time . . . and had girls.

The idea of a stable shelter for a few months or even weeks comforted me as I listened to the rain drops splash against my body, I just needed to make it through the next couple of nights. Sleeping in shelters for so long, I started to hate them, I became ungrateful, but when I didn't have one to rest, I remember why we chose to live there in the first place. Anything beats outside. My stomach gurgled as the rain blanketed over me. Each drop hit my head like a frozen dagger.

It wasn't my first time sleeping outside, but my first time sleeping under the rain. Somehow, when we had to sleep outside, my mom always found some form of a shelter. I tip my hat off to her because I couldn't find any shelter out there. I would never forget sleeping in rain. No matter what I did or where I went, it was one of the memories I'd always remember. Hard times like those made a person examine and question their relationship with everyone they had ever known. Situations like sleeping outdoors made a person start to truly dislike people. Isolated pain creates the "me against the world" ideology. In my time of need, I had no one. No shelters, group homes, relatives, friends, nothing besides the steps I sat on and the rain falling over me. The cold stopped me from being too angry. I could either focus on being mad at the world, or focus on trying to stay warm. I unzipped my backpack and took out a thirty-two ounce beer this random guy at the bus stop gave to me earlier. He said I needed it, whatever he meant. I opened the top and chugged as much of it as I could on my empty stomach. Alcohol kept you warm. It would make the night a little easier. I lifted my head up and let the water crash into my face. If I started to cry, anyone who passed by would think it's just the rain.

After a while, the pitter-patter of the rain lured me into a light sleep but I couldn't remain in a continuous slumber because of paranoia. Out in the open, hungry, cold, and constantly on alert, I slept in a semi-conscious state huddled over on top of the steps. The rain finally subsided and I stretched out for more comfort. My clothes stuck to my skin but I didn't fret over it. I would be dry by the time the buses started running again.

"Mike? Mike wake up bro."

I opened my eyes to see another friend of mine, Jason, staring at me as he savagely consumed a bag of Chester's Flamin' Hot Fries, holding a sixteen-ounce can of beer.

"What's up bro . . . what time is it?" I rubbed my eyes, brushing off a few bugs crawling over me.

"It's noon. My dude, why're you sleeping on the steps?"

"I was waiting for David to get back."

"David? David got locked up."

"Locked up?" I sat up in shock. "When? I just talked to him yesterday."

"Yesterday. He left to go make a sell but it was a set up."

"Damn, man."

"Right, and his mom is locked up. She got locked up a week ago."

"Shit."

"Yup. But you know how it goes. I heard the same thing happened to you and Ray?"

"Yeah . . . you know how it goes."

"David owe you money or something?"

"No, he said I could stay with him for a few days."

"You need somewhere to go?"

"Hell, yeah."

"You can come with me and Husky."

"Where's Husky?"

"He's meeting me in front of David's house."

"Where you guys going?"

"Nowhere right now, but the homegirl said she'll sneak us in tonight."

"You got a bus pass?" I stood, stretching my legs.

"Nope, do you?"

"Nope. But let me have some of those hot fries."

"Here, you can have them. This is like my third bag. These things are addictive. It's like they sprinkle crack inside or something."

I downed the rest of the bag in seconds. Jason laughed at me as I wiped the crumbs off my face.

"Shut up, I'm hungry."

"Yeah, I see that." He handed me the beer to wash it down.

We waited on the steps until we saw Husky gangster-limping down the street toward us.

"What's up, Mike G?"

"What's up, Husk?"

"What's up, Jay?"

"Nothing, waiting on you fool. It's like one-thirty. Let's go."

"Where she live anyway?" Husky said.

"In Encanto."

"You're trying to get me shot or something?"

"Calm down, ain't nobody worried about you."

Husky, like most kids I knew, were caught up in gangs. Being homeless, I couldn't afford to get into gangs. Gangs are too territorial and homelessness forced me to roam around too much. Plus, I had seen the outcome of most people who gangbang. I didn't preach to anyone, and like I said I couldn't judge, but I didn't allow myself to get caught up in the violence. But sometimes, living in the neighborhood of Southeast, the violence always seemed inevitable and inescapable.

The three of us trekked to the bus stop where a small crowd of people were waiting. I had met Jason and Husky years ago. Jason always schemed about something. He started figuring out a plan to get us all on the bus because only Husky had a bus pass.

"Okay Husky you go on first in front of the crowd, slip me the bus pass through the back window, then I'll get on and slip it to Mike G."

"That's not going to work twice," I said.

"Yeah it will, trust me," Jason said.

"No, it's not enough people around to slip the same pass twice."

"Yes it is, Mike. I do this all the time."

"Okay, well let Husky slip me the bus pass first."

"No, it was my idea."

"All right, then I'm not doing that."

"What're you going to do? Fly?"

"Are you?"

"Well, how're you getting on the bus?" Husky asked.

"All right, new plan." I said. "Husky you go on first in front of everybody. I'll go in the middle and stall and try to see if he'll just let me on. Jason you'll go on last and Husky will slip you the bus pass."

"That's not a new plan, that's a modified one," Jason said.

"Whatever, it's better than your plan," I said.

"It's like the same plan."

"What if the bus driver don't let you on?" Husky asked.

"Then I guess I'm missing it."

"Then we'll take somebody else's bus pass." Jason glanced around the small crowd.

"We might as well take their whole wallet then," Husky asked. "Why stop at a bus pass?"

The bus pulled up and we set the plan in motion. Husky stepped on before me and rushed to the back to slip the bus pass.

I approached the bus driver, an older guy with short salt-and-pepper hair.

"Excuse me, sir, do you think I can get a ride? I'm just trying to get home."

He examined my worn-out appearance. He glanced up into one of his mirrors staring into the back of the bus. "Yeah, come on."

"Thanks, I really appreciate it." I met Husky in the back.

Jason stepped onto the bus and showed the bus driver Husky's bus pass.

"Nope, get off," the bus driver said.

"What do you mean get off?" Jason said.

"I just saw him drop the bus pass out the window."

"No, you didn't, this is my bus pass."

"Get off my bus or pay the fare."

"What are you talking about? This is my bus pass."

The bus driver glanced in his mirror again, this time directly at Husky. "Come here," he said into the intercom. He turned around and pointed at Husky. "Come here."

Husky stomped to the front of the bus. "What?"

"Show me your bus pass."

"Why? I already showed it to you."

"Show it to me again."

"No, I don't have to show you my bus pass twice. You just saw it."

"I saw you slip it to him. You can either take your bus pass back and have a seat or both of you can get off my bus. Hurry up, you're making me behind schedule."

"I just showed you my bus pass."

"This bus isn't moving until you take back your pass or get off."

I leaped out of my seat and joined them up front.

"Sir, I'm sorry. These are my friends. Me and him don't have bus passes. We're just trying to get home, we've been out all night."

"So instead of trying to run scams, why not ask for a ride like you did?"

"They're idiots, sir. We're trying to get home the best way we can. Can they get on? Please?"

"Well, they insist on lying still, so, no. They can't."

"Yeah, I slipped him my bus pass then," Husky said.

"Of course you did. I used to catch the bus, I'm aware of how it works. Next time just be upfront even if the bus driver says no. Trying to scam us won't get you anywhere. Go sit down."

"Thanks," I said.

"Thanks," Jason said and we went and took a seat laughing amongst ourselves. The plan didn't work, but according to Jason, next time it would.

We rode to the Euclid transit station and lingered all day, drinking to kill time. The girl couldn't sneak us in until later when everyone slept. We saw a couple of fights, drug sales, and police pass until we finally caught the trolley to the Encanto station around ten p.m. We trekked about thirty minutes uphill. The girl planned to meet us halfway on foot and we were going to follow her back. After what seemed like forever, we approached a petite girl sitting on the curb. She stood as she saw us and a wide smile spread across her face.

"Hey, Jason!" she cheerfully exclaimed. "Hey, I remember you, too!" She pointed at Husky.

"Me?" Husky said.

"Yeah, you're Husky, right?"

"Yeah, but who are you?"

"Didn't you go to Warner Elementary?"

"Yeah."

"And you have an older brother."

"Yeah, I do."

"Remember being in Mr. Thomas' class? Remember Tim and Ernie and Rebecca?"

"Oh yeah, you're name's Samantha. You tried to date my brother. I remember you, how've you been?"

"Oh, now you remember!" she scowled. "And I've been whatever. Who is this?" she asked staring at me. "Are you trouble like they are?"

"I wouldn't say that." I followed them down the street toward her house. She opened the door and told us to be quiet as we tiptoed through the living room and into her bedroom. The entire house remained quiet. Her parents and siblings were fast asleep, oblivious to the strangers entering their home. We all sat in the tiny room as Samantha began to tell Jason her long-lost feelings for him, as if Jason hadn't already realized. I asked to be pointed toward the bathroom and stood to use it. I had to urinate since we had first exited the trolley. I opened the bathroom door to see Samantha had closed her room door and Husky moved about in the living room. He had two backpacks in both of his hands and stood with his back toward me facing the television. At his feet were different game systems: a PlayStation 2, a Game Cube, and an Xbox 360. He bent over and proceeded to stuff the PlayStation 2 inside of the first backpack followed by the Game Cube. Next went the Xbox 360 into the second backpack and zipped them up. I didn't even see where the backpacks came from.

"What are you doing?" I asked.

"We're robbing her."

"Right now? I thought we're going to sleep."

"Yeah, right now. Jason's in there distracting her. He's going to meet us outside."

"Where are we going?"

"Shit, wherever."

"Nah bro, put it back."

He laughed at me as he continued stuffing his backpack. I placed my hand over the backpack. "I'm not robbing her."

"Well, I'm robbing her." He snatched the backpack and stepped into my face. "Don't be a little bitch. You're going to try and stop me? Over her?"

Another one of those awkward situations circumstances forced me into. Samantha graciously opened up her home for us, only for them to want to rob her. I just wanted to go to sleep, but if they left, I had to leave. I had remorse, but I didn't know her. I knew them so they were where my loyalty had to lie. If I tried to stop them, they would turn on me for the simple fact we were supposed to be friends and have each other's back no matter what. We were cool. No one ever said the rules in the jungle were fair. Unfortunate, really. I could imagine the conversation between her and her parents in the morning.

I pushed him away from me. "Shut up, man."

Husky slung the backpacks over his back and jetted out of the front door. I reluctantly followed closely behind him. I saw a small silver Razor scooter with blue wheels lying on the sidewalk. I picked it up. We had a long way back to wherever we were going and I didn't feel like wearing my feet down. If they were going to rob her, I would rather it be in the morning after I had slept or at least when the buses were running. The thrill of robbing her excited them, but it blinded them from the aftermath of what could happen. I think they forgot the whole point in going there was for shelter. A few stolen game systems could do nothing for us right then.

Husky and I strolled up the empty street.

"Hey!" Jason yelled behind us, running up to us laughing. Husky joined in on the amusement. "What you get?"

"I got like all her game systems."

"Let me see."

Husky opened the backpacks and Jason observed inside.

"Where's the cords?"

"The what?"

"The cords. And controllers? It can't turn on without the power cords."

"Haha, damn. I forgot them."

"Stupid ass. How do you take the game system but not the cords?"

"All right, well what did you grab?" Husky zipped up the backpacks with a hint of irritation.

"Man, I was the one who had to distract her."

"I could have distracted her."

"You're not me, Husk. She wants me, buddy."

"Yeah, whatever. We can still sell them on the street, though."

"What'd you think we'd do with them? Mike, where the hell you get that scooter from?"

"Right, we're walking and shit. Get off that."

"Hell, nah. I shouldn't be on my feet right now in the first place." I scooted along shamelessly.

The scooter did compensate for me being up and unsheltered. At two-thirty in the morning, we walked without a destination; well, they did, I rode. We were mostly going downhill now so I had an easy ride. However, Husky and Jason had enemies and we were in their enemy territory which made me extremely nervous. Enemies was another reason why I didn't bang. They seemed just as nervous as I did, but tried not to show it. Being on the open streets was dangerous; a common way people got murdered.

A small black car silently drove passed us. Through the car window sat an old Latino couple. About six minutes later another black car drove passed. I couldn't get a good glance inside of it, but I did see hoods and black skin.

"Mike G, stop," whispered Husky as the car made a right turn just up ahead. I turned back to see Jason and Husky had stopped all motion a few feet behind me.

"What happened?" I asked.

"That might have been Mydell and them," Jason said.

"Who?" I asked.

"He's from Eastside," Husky said. "One of those dudes I had beat up." San Diego was divided into different black and Mexican gangs occupying the same space. Eastside housed Bloods. Husky repped the Southside, also Bloods. But they didn't get along. The black car, which had turned right, crept its way back to the corner with its lights off.

"Fuck!" Jason said. "If they come, run."

"Oh, God!" I panicked. "I don't want to die."

"I'm busting back." Husky revealed a battered nine-millimeter Glock pistol from under his shirt. He cocked it back ready for trouble like a western gunslinger. "I got us." The gun was most likely dirty, used for robberies and murder even. Guns get passed around from person to person and always seem available in the inner city. We had no food, no shelter, but guns galore. I stared at the glistening barrel. I was far from a gangster. I didn't want to be Bugsy Siegel. Bugsy Siegel had been shot dead.

"They might not have saw us," Jason said.

The car slammed on the gas pedal and sped our way. I dropped the scooter and we all fled.

Thunderous blasts sounded in the air like an old western. Loud gunshots barked from the car, waking up the entire neighborhood. Husky fired back and glass shattered as we took off running in different directions. I ran for my life in complete terror and still pissed off more than anything else. I just wanted to go to sleep.

The thunderous booms echoed throughout the neighborhood.

The shots sounded closer than ever. I jumped over a fence into a backyard and cut through it. I leaped the fence again exiting it and ran down the side walkway of a house. I slid down in between a trash can and a blue recycle bin as my heart pounded the inside of my chest. I felt pain somewhere. Blood dripped from my hands. I tried not to hyperventilate; too scared to check my body. I didn't want to die. I wasn't sure how much blood I lost so I had to check myself. I touched my torso and shoulders, then my legs and thighs but I seemed fine. I reexamined my hands, confused. I analyzed them as close as I could in the darkness to see them actually bleeding. I must have cut them on the fence. My stomach growled, reminding me the energy I used wasn't going to be replenished.

After about twenty minutes, I cautiously began moving again. I couldn't stay planted because eventually police would show up to check out what happened and do a sweep of the area. I hoped Jason and Husky escaped. A split second's all it took for someone to die. But they were smart—and fast. I made my way back to the main road. Luckily, the streets were clear. I traveled for another thirty minutes and made it back to the deserted trolley station. My body shook from the gunshots, which could have easily hit me for no reason. The trolley should be running in a few hours. I think like at six so I would have to stay put until then.

I sat on the trolley station bench and then lied across it. The icy night air whipped through my clothes, but my flesh had hardened from years of whipping. I hoped my clothes weren't starting to stink from the previous night's rain. They were starting to feel a little itchy. I used my arms as pillows and tried to convince myself the trolley station bench had no difference from one of the many army cots or blue mats I had slept on time and time again. My nerves were shot, but I was so tired, I had no choice but to go to sleep until the first trolley arrived. When it did, I would catch it to who knows where. I'd rather be on my own, though. Jason and Husky were full of too many bad ideas.

14. Breakdown: Part II

I SAT WITH MY MOM AND SISTER RIDING THE BUS WITH all of our possessions toward the City Heights neighborhood. The people on the bus all stared at us funny because our belongings took up many seats, but what could we do? As generous as my mom's acquaintance had been, she only offered temporary shelter. During the second week in April, where we were going was also temporary. Right then we were headed to the home of one of my mom's childhood friends. I guess they ran into each other and she invited us to stay for a while. If she didn't, all three of us would have been sleeping outside.

We struggled off the bus and toward her apartment building. After a brief struggle getting all of our things up the stairs to her apartment, we knocked on the door. Someone approached and waited as they peered through the peephole. The door swung open followed by a, "Hey girl!"

"Hey!" My mom gasped out of breath from climbing the stairs. "This is my son, Michael, and my daughter Pooh Bear. Kids this is Bernadine, we go way back."

"Way back, too far back." Bernadine laughed. "Well, come on in. Mi casa, su casa."

We filed inside the living room and sort of stopped. We had really nowhere else to move. The apartment's a one bedroom and by my count there were already seven people living in there including Bernadine, her son Demarcus, Demarcus' girlfriend, Queenie, their child, Bernadine's other sons Dave and Ryan, and her nephew, Keith. Usually, when people said they didn't have any room, they were usually lying. Bernadine should have told us her place had zero room, too, but in her case, she would be telling the truth. But just from her conversation with my mom, she knew we were in desperate need of somewhere to go, even if it meant squeezing into one space. I appreciated her hospitality though.

Besides being cramped, the dirty apartment barely had any food, and everyone kind of slept everywhere. In the living room sat two sofas across from each other, one with three seats, and the other with two. My mom would be sleeping on the longer one, my sister the shorter, and me on the floor next to Demarcus, Queenie, and their son. The other kids were all younger so they slept in the room with Bernadine unless she had company over at night, in which case they would sleep in the living room.

We couldn't get into another shelter, which disappointed me. I knew one day we would stop being able to, but I didn't think it would be so soon. Usually shelters had only one of two reasons why: either I was too old, or they were too full. Whatever the case was, we still didn't get in. Luckily, my mom ran into Bernadine. I would hate to see my mom outside with me. I could sleep outside—but my mom, or even my sister, I didn't want them to have to again.

We settled in and Bernadine and my mom rushed to Bernadine's room closing the door to chat. I sat on the shorter couch next to my sister and watched the commercial on the television screen. I hadn't seen TV in so long it put me in a trance. My sister had fallen fast asleep. Not too bad of an idea.

"Michael?" Bernadine stepped out of her room. She had a few crumpled up dollar bills in her hand.

"Yes?"

"Go with Demarcus to get some tacos from Jack in the Box on the corner. You hungry, right?"

"Starving."

"Yeah, go with him. Get up, Demarcus. Go get us some tacos."

"What about to drink?" I said.

"You got some drink money?" Bernadine said.

"No."

"Here's ten dollars. Make sure there's enough for everybody." She, waved the money around.

"Can we go later? I don't feel like going." Demarcus undid the long braids in his hair.

"Go now or don't eat," she said, crossing her arms.

Demarcus shrugged his shoulders. "Then we won't eat."

"The hell with that," I said. "Give me the money, I'll go by myself."

About a week later, I arrived to Bernadine's from a long day at school. The bus ride from school there always drained the life out of me. I was hungry; all the food we bought last week with the rest of our food stamps had been depleted in three days. I had nothing to look forward to coming back except the roof over my head. I knocked on the door over the loud noise coming from inside the apartment. I waited a few minutes then knocked again a little harder. The door opened with Bernadine's daughter, Clarissa, Keith's mom, standing in it. She's cool but usually came when Bernadine invited her for some type of social. Bernadine's place didn't have space for a vacuum let alone any type of social gathering; but it wasn't my place to tell her what she should do in her place. A few people I didn't recognize lingered about the apartment with all of the kids running about. I smelled pizza so I headed to the minuscule kitchen to the four pizza boxes sitting on the table. A margarita concoction sat in the blender on the counter. I opened the top box finding it completely empty. Same with the second box, all the boxes were empty.

"Hey, Sun, when'd you get home?" Mom followed into the kitchen behind me.

"Just now. Is there any more pizza?"

"Boy, food goes immediately around here."

"You didn't save me any?"

"Of course I did. It's wrapped on a plate in the microwave."

I opened the microwave touching aluminum foil and a plate, but no pizza. "There's no pizza in here."

"What do you mean?" My mom checked the microwave for herself. She stormed out of the kitchen. "Who ate my son's pizza?" After careful interrogation, the truth came out. Dave and Keith had split my two slices. They already had three a piece but said they were still hungry and considered it extra pizza. Bernadine called them liars because she said my mom announced to everyone she saved the pizza in the microwave for me. They tried to convince me how they didn't realize I wasn't there to eat, but I waved them away. I was pissed. Unless they were going to tell me where some more food could be found, I didn't want to hear anything coming out of their mouths. The fridge was completely empty despite a half empty bottle of cheap tequila.

"Is there any more money?" I asked.

"Everything we had, we all put toward the pizza," my mom said. "I'm so sorry, Sun. I have half a slice left. You will have it."

"No, Mom, go ahead and eat."

"No, I said you *will* have it. You need to eat something." She knew I was completely starving. My mother left and returned with a paper plate holding half a slice of pizza along with a full crust. I didn't like pizza crust but knew bread filled you up. I would have eaten a bowl of yeast or anything to take some of the fire from my belly. It seemed like I swallowed the pizza slice and crust in one small bite. I stared at the empty plate hoping something else would just appear, but it never did. I went and sat on the couch, tired from a long day at school and hanging out after. Too much noise went on around me but I would manage to go to sleep regardless. I imagined how much of a buzz kill I must've seemed to everyone else around me, but I didn't care. They didn't seem to care about me being tired; hungry, and that

I had to wake up early. I could only look forward to breakfast at school in the morning, which I could get to quicker if I fell asleep.

Commotion surrounded me. People socialized, trying to have a nice time. They would have been partying whether I lived there or not, so I just had to find the serenity within me to lure myself to sleep. My sister came and sat beside me, resting her head on my shoulder. She tossed a paper plate with a full slice of pizza on my lap. She always watched out for me. She had the insight to save another slice separate from the ones my mom saved. The slice quelled my stomach enough to ignore. The commotion around me suddenly seemed less bothersome and I found my way to sleep.

A week and a half later, I awoke on the floor to find my mom furiously cleaning around the apartment. She harassed the kitchen floor with the mop. The house, on a Saturday morning, surprisingly emptied leaving only my mom, sister, and me inside. I inched over to her. The smell of water mixed with bleach and ammonia burned in my nose.

"Mom?" Lost in her own thoughts, she didn't notice me. She cleaned as an outlet for her frustration. "Mom!" I surprised her. She didn't see me standing there.

"What, boy?"

"Don't break the mop."

My mom smiled weakly at the mop. Her eyes became watery like the bucket of cleaning solution beside her feet.

"What's wrong, Mom?"

"This isn't what I wanted for you two."

"The mop?" I rubbed my eyes.

"No!" She, set it aside. "Not the mop. This life."

"Yeah, us too, Mom."

"When you guys were little I use to dress you all nice, you had clothes, shoes, food . . . we were good. We had our own place, we had our own things, we were happy."

"I saw the pictures, you took great care of us."

"Do y'all hate me?"

"No, we don't hate you," Pooh chimed in from the living room.

"Sometimes I think y'all hate me."

"No, we love you, Mom," I said. "We hate a lot of things, but not you. You're one of the good things we have."

"Y'all blame me for all of this. For living like this. It's only right."

"We have eyes, we can see what's going on." Pooh arose from the couch and entered the kitchen.

"We blame a lot of people but not you. You're trying to do everything you can, and that's all we can ask. I'd blame you if you were on drugs or an alcoholic, I'd blame you if you were unwilling to work or something. It'd be easier if we could just blame you. But you're doing all you can. We understand that. It's not your fault." I said.

"It's so damn hard out here."

"We get that, Mom. You're not the only parent who has struggled," Pooh said.

"There's like billions of parents out there right now struggling just to make it. I mean everyone doesn't have it as bad as us, but everyone's struggling."

"Not like this." Mom grabbed the mop, stabbing the floor.

"We'll be all right, mom. We've been all right, we'll be all right," Pooh said.

"We have to leave here," Mom said.

"Why?" I said.

"There's no room. There's no food. Sun, you're dropping weight. We're better off on our own."

"Did you get into it with her or something?" Pooh said.

"No, I didn't have to. She has eyes; we can't stay here too much longer. It's not good for any of us. I just wish I had somewhere to take you. I never wanted to fail as a mother."

"Mom!" Pooh made way to the kitchen.

"You didn't fail as a mother," I said. "I mean, if anything, that's where you've excelled. I mean, with everything we've been through, somehow you managed to keep us together. Aunt Lynn lost all five of her kids to social services chasing crack cocaine. Your cousin Casey's kids hate her; she beats Dennis mercilessly. Stephen told me she used to do the same to him. Casey has failed as a mother, a nurturer. You've managed to keep me and Pooh out of social services. You've kept us safe. You've been a super mom."

"Remember that one lady lost all her kids downtown," Pooh waved her finger to make a point.

"Who, Rachel?" I said. "Yeah, when Child Protective Services came and took all of them."

"Well, that's because they were all sleeping in a ditch in some canyon somewhere," Pooh said.

"See, exactly, mom," I reached for the mop, which seemed to symbolize her drowning hopes. My mom pulled it back. "We've never slept in a ditch. Maybe outside when we had to, but nothing like that."

"Plus, she had little kids." Pooh placed her hand on my shoulder, signaling me to relax. "We weren't sleeping in ditches at five."

"I wanted the best for you two." Mom continued mopping. "I wanted you to have everything I didn't have. It hurts as a mother to watch my kids go through such pain. Pain I can't save you from. It's like we're all alone."

"We are alone," I said. "But we're alone together."

"If something ever happens to me, if I ever die—"

"I hate when you start talking like this." Pooh folded her arms.

"It has to be addressed. If something were to happen to mama, if I died or something, you'll be able to claim life insurance." My mom's mopping speed intensified.

"How'd you get life insurance?" I said.

Pooh scratched her head pondering options. "Probably through her security job."

"They take a little out of my check. Just to be sure that in death you'll be taken care of, even if I couldn't do it alive," Mom said.

"I don't want to talk about dying," I said. "Nobody's dying. Not me, not Pooh, and especially not you. I'd rather be poor with you alive than well off with you dead."

"I'm just saying, stick together. Mama loves you guys. We're not going to always be together, but I'll always love you. I'll do anything for you. I'll sacrifice everything for you." She leaned onto the mop in deep thought.

"Same for you, Mom."

Pooh reached toward the mop. "Yeah, we'd do the same. Here, let me help mop."

Mom lifted her hand in refusal. "Sometimes I think it'd be easier if I was dead. You'd get the insurance, wouldn't have to go through this."

"That doesn't make any sense, Mom." I said. "What good would that insurance do for us if you were dead? We don't care about insurance; I'd go crazy without you. If we're poor we're going to be poor together. If we get rich, we'll be rich together, but nothing at anyone's expense."

"You're not suicidal are you?" Pooh said.

"Don't make us call the people on you," I said.

"I'm fine," she said, "Of course I don't want to die, but what kind of a life is this?"

"It's a miserable life." Pooh replaced her hand on my shoulder signaling my support. "Anyone with eyes understands that, but it's our life. If we don't hold high value to it, no one will. As hard as it gets, remember we have to keep going, right Michael?"

"Yeah!" I said. "We just have to keep pressing forward, keep forging our own path. Life will get better eventually, it has to. . . ." I wasn't sure how much of that I even believed.

"No, it doesn't." My mom dipped the mop into the bucket of water. She pressed and pressed it as if drowning its white strands.

"Huh?" I knew exactly what she meant.

"It doesn't have to." She began remopping the same spot. "Life doesn't have to get better. That is a misconception of millions. Life doesn't have to get better, most times it won't. Take me for example. You're aware of what I've been through. Life still isn't shit. It might maintain its course but it doesn't have to get better."

"We're just trying to be optimistic, Mom." I reached for the mop. "What else can we do? Accept the fact that we're going to have a terrible existence? I can't accept that. I want more. There's more out there. There's more to the world. I'm searching beyond the ghetto, beyond poverty, beyond homelessness. I want to reach a level we can't even begin to imagine or understand. It sounds dumb."

"It sounds like a dream." She refused my help.

"You need a dream." I brushed off the counter with my hands, helping regardless. "You have to start somewhere. Bill Gates had a dream; you see how he turned out. I'm sure people thought he was crazy when he tried to explain his concepts. John F. Kennedy had a dream. Oprah had a dream. Martin Luther King Jr. had a dream. I have a dream. Dreams and aspirations are what start everything. You need a dream. Without one there's nothing to inspire you, nothing to make pushing forward worthwhile. As human beings, we need something to believe in. Why not believe in ourselves? Why not believe one day we'll achieve more in life? My dream is to move past my circumstances. To move into a world free from being homeless. To get a good job and have a lot, and I mean a lot, of money one day."

"Well if we're just speaking on dumb dreams," my sister chopped imaginary food with her hands, "I want to become a chef. I want to cook all the fancy food we could never have."

"And if that doesn't work out you can always come work for me." I ate her imaginary food.

"Shut up stupid, nobody's going to work for you. You're going to come work for me!"

"Do you have a dream, Mom?" I reached out for the mop one more time.

"I'm too old for dreams." She stopped mopping.

"You're never too old for a dream," Pooh said. "Hell, it's all we got, Mom, you better have a dream."

My mom stared at my sister and me. She smiled and handed me the mop. I leaned against it. The last thing I wanted to do was mop. "My dream is for my children to realize all of their dreams. As a parent, as a mother, that would make me the happiest."

"We'll try and make that come true," I said.

"Where is everybody?" my sister asked.

Mom lethargically shrugged.

"Why are you cleaning up everything?" I rested the mop against the counter.

"Because it's dirty."

"That's not our dirt," Pooh said. "We always clean up behind ourselves."

"Doesn't matter, it needs to be cleaned and I can't go around living in filth. It's already overcrowded in here; the fire department would go crazy. We don't need black floors and roaches running around. I mean, I'll be okay, Sun, you're the one on the floor."

"Hey, I never said don't clean." I offered her the mop. "I wish a roach would crawl over me in my sleep, I'd wake the whole house up screaming."

"Oh my God, what would you do if you like woke up with a roach on your face or in your mouth?" Pooh said.

"Pooh Bear, that's disgusting," My mom brushed past me. "I don't want to even think about it."

"We've been here longer than I thought," Pooh said. "When do we have to move out?"

"She has two weeks to vacate the apartment before the sheriffs come."

"Two weeks?" Pooh said.

"She actually was evicted months ago, but what can we do?" Mom sat on the couch.

"Aw damn, that sucks. Does she have a place to go after this?" I said.

"Maybe." She rolled her head back against the couch as if to drift to sleep.

"Do we?" Pooh said.

"We'll see," she said.

"Don't worry about it, Mom," I said. "We'll figure it out."

"Duh," Pooh said. "That's the only thing we can do."

I sat in the backseat of a white car with my mom in the driver's seat, and my sister in the passenger's. The small and cramped car had been our first car in forever. It used to be someone else's car but he sold it to my mom for pennies on the dollar. She took all the little money she had been saving for a deposit, asked a few acquaintances for "loans" and bought it for six hundred dollars because we all had to leave Bernadine's, including Bernadine. Bernadine found a place to go, but we couldn't follow and honestly didn't want to follow. We just needed a way to transport all of our possessions, so the car couldn't have come at a better time. The engine had something wrong with it, the old frame wobbled as we drove, but we needed something, we would have rode in anything.

With the purchase of the car, we lost the last few hundred dollars to our name. We filled up the gas tank and aimlessly wandered around. We stopped by a few shelters to make ourselves feel better, but we knew what our end outcome would be. The sun started to slip under the blanket of night and if we didn't stop soon, would eventually run out of gas. The last shelter we visited had us drive forty minutes from downtown. They said they might have had an opening, but when we arrived every space had filled. We questioned why they didn't reserve a bed for us, especially since we had just spoken to them over the phone. They answered they didn't reserve homeless beds and all available space was, of course, first come first serve. We stood in the doorway of the shelter in disbelief.

My mom explained to them we were explicitly told they had room for us. The man told us there had been room for us, but there wasn't any more and to try again tomorrow or the next day. He said the beds open up sporadically and there wasn't a waitlist for this particular shelter. We turned around and started leaving right in the middle of his spiel, which we had heard before from so many others. We piled back into our car and drove away.

After a short while on the freeway, my sister pointed out a rest area sign in two miles. Downtown was just too far right then. Pulling over and trying to sleep was the only thing we could do there anyway so we'd rather sleep where rest was designated. We exited off the rest area exit and pulled up in front of the public bathroom. We grabbed our toiletries and entered the bathroom. I entered the boys' and gave myself a quick wash using the sink out in the open, empty bathroom. With the rest area deserted, I thought safe enough to do so. I finished up and headed back to the car awaiting their return. When they came back, we backed up and pulled to the far left side of the rest area. I could see truckers exiting the freeway making their way to the rest area. I never minded sleeping next to truckers. For them and for us, sleeping in vehicles was normal. Everybody did it so nobody made any comments. The only difference: sleeping in vehicles was a part of their job, but it was a part of my life.

15. Home Is Where the Heart Is

I POURED WATER FROM A WATER BOTTLE ONTO MY toothbrush and began to brush my teeth. I leaned out the back door of our car and spat, rinsing my mouth out with more water. The morning May breeze scratched against my face. I added another jacket on top of my sweater and closed the door. My mother again in the driver seat, my sister the passenger. I sat in the passenger seat last night, so I perched myself in the back seat behind my sister. To the left of me and in the trunk stored all of our belongings. We had just found a place to pull over. There wasn't a lot of foot traffic or parked cars so it was where we would stay.

Last night we pulled over by a park, tonight it was on the side of the road, but we tried to stay as close to downtown as possible. We just finished eating some Vienna sausages and crackers, but the lion in our stomachs still roared, begging for more. The thing about food stamps is they were virtually useless unless you had somewhere to cook and refrigerate the food. We bought a lot of canned foods, Vienna sausages mostly, and some meat spread we put on crackers and bread. We bought some Cheez Whiz for crackers too, but our selection altogether had been extremely limited and very non-satisfying.

I turned on my side trying to get comfortable, waiting for my body to adjust to cramped space. I closed my eyes and told my mother and my sister goodnight. Pooh sat curled up in a fetal position trying to gain some comfort in the tiny white car. My legs were too long for her to comfortably lean the tattered seat back and I couldn't move them because of all of the other things piled up in the car. My mother slowly became sick again. She tried to hide it but I could see the warning signs, her fatigue. I could see her pushing herself past her limits again. She would definitely go back to the hospital, I just didn't know when. I placed a loose shirt over my head so nobody passing by could see my face. I didn't feel uncomfortable anymore which meant I had adjusted. I tried to relax as best as I could and I drifted off to sleep.

My mom's same prepaid cell phone alarm went off and we groggily woke up. I yawned as I stretched out my arms. I opened the car door and brushed my teeth. I poured water on my rag and washed my face. I reached into my backpack and put on my deodorant. I took off my jacket and sweater revealing my clothes for the day. Putting on clothes the night before was easier because we didn't have to hassle with changing in the morning, and it allowed us a chance to wear out the wrinkles since we didn't have an iron. My mother and sister beat me getting ready, and my mom started the car engine. She dropped us off around the corner from school and told us to have a good day. We told her the same and we would see her after work. Traveling to her security job at Sony PlayStation took an hour and thirty minutes but since we had a car those days she could commute with the help of gas vouchers. We watched as she drove off and scratched our heads as we made our way to class.

After school, Pooh and I stumbled around downtown putting in job applications everywhere we could. Our chances of getting a job were slim to none. We were competing with adults with greater availabilities who were applying for the same jobs. Undeterred, we put in more and more applications. My mom had given my sister the EBT card, so we headed into Albertsons to get something to eat. We ate mostly salads because Albertsons has a salad bar we could fill with different square chunks of meats. Not the healthiest salad, but we were eating to get full.

We wandered to the downtown library where we had developed a sort of friendship or understanding with the librarians in the computer lab. We trekked to the library just about every day so eventually they started talking and interacting with us. I thought they knew we were homeless. The library is where a lot of homeless people go during the day to kill time or just to be inside for a change. We came to kill time. We had to linger around until my mom left work to pick us up and then find somewhere to park so we could sleep.

We weren't the only homeless kids who went there during the day. A group of us were there. I had lived in shelters with a lot of them before so we all knew each other and knew why each other were there. I talked to a few of them before I sat and did my homework. Completing homework had always been a fast way to kill time; it wasn't difficult and it only helped me intellectually. Pooh and I sat across the table from each other, half doing homework and half talking. We noticed the clock and realized we had to meet up with our mom, so we packed up and left the library.

The sun went down and we passed by our high school. I had forgotten my jacket in the car and shivered. We sat on the curb and waited until my mom finally pulled up with a smile. She always smiled when she saw us like she had not seen us in a long time. Her friendly face actually refreshed us. We loaded into the car and drove off. My mom instantly began going on a rant about work and about all of the assholes she had to deal with as a security guard. Medical data entry had been her trade, but she took what she could get. She always came back from work irritated because some jerk didn't want to follow the rules.

". . . And I told him, 'Sir, I can't let you through without your ID badge.' He said I just saw him leave, which I did, but the rule is everyone who enters the building has to show their ID to get back in. He said, 'Can't you just let me go?' I told him no and he knew the rules. We'd have to go through protocol if he didn't have one. He started yelling and screaming getting all loud, causing a scene."

"What's the protocol?" I asked.

"So if you forget your badge, I have to call in to dispatch and have them confirm you. It takes like fifteen minutes."

"Fifteen minutes," Pooh said. "That's why he went crazy."

"Do you think I wanted him sitting in my face for fifteen minutes? I could smell his breath from my seat. Whatever he ate for lunch, he should never eat again."

"So what happened?" I asked.

"He started calling me everything except my name, trying to belittle me. He said 'You're just a security guard and you don't understand shit' and blah blah blah . . . 'You're not happy with how your life turned out and I'm so high and mighty,' and this and that. He said, 'You take your crappy job too seriously' and he said, 'women shouldn't even be allowed to be security guards.'"

"Oh, hell no," Pooh said.

"What did you say?" I asked.

"I stood up and told him to sit down and shut up."

"What did he do?" I said.

"He sat down and shut up. My supervisor even had to come over. I guess there's been problems with him before and my supervisor made him wait thirty minutes before he confirmed him."

"That's what he gets," Pooh said. "Oooh, I wish I was there."

"Why so you could get her fired?" I said.

"You can't just let people disrespect you like that."

"If you want to keep your job, you can," my mom said. "Nothing's worth me getting fired over."

"But if we don't stand up for ourselves, people will try and trample all over us," Pooh said. "I'm sick of people stampeding over us."

"Aren't we all," my mom said, as she found a spot to park and pulled over. We sat in the car, changed into our next day outfit, and eventually fell asleep.

Later around three a.m., I heard loud laughing and I strained to open one eye. A group of teenagers, about seven of them, stood outside of our car laughing and pointing at us. They were really loud and drunkenly obnoxious, but I tried to ignore them for the most part. People have teased us before, nothing new. One of them whispered to the other and pointed at our car. They rushed toward our car, chuckling. They placed their hands on our car and began to violently shake us back and forth, laughing. My mother and sister jumped up out of their sleep, half startled, half enraged as the rocking persisted. Pooh and I quickly opened our doors and jumped out as they took off running. I took off running after them, my tired red eyes burning in the cool night air. I briefly chased them a few feet and then turned back to the car. Their laughter echoed as they continued to run away. One noticed I stopped chasing after them.

"Bum!" he yelled, giving his friend a high five before flipping me off.

I jumped back inside the car and slammed the door. We were infuriated—beyond pissed. They came and bothered us for no reason. Sleeping's all we tried to do. I had enough. We had to wake up early, go to work and school, so we just wanted to sleep as peacefully as we could. Now they had ruined our night.

"That's bullcrap!" Pooh said. "Why can't they just leave us alone?"

"Idiots!" my mom said. "Are y'all okay?"

"Yeah, I'm fine," Pooh said.

"That's bull," I said.

"Sun, don't go chasing after them like that."

"What am I supposed to do? Just let them shake the car like that? We were asleep that's not right."

"It was way too many of them, they could have turned and easily jumped you. You're upset, but be smarter than that, Sun."

"What am I supposed to do?"

"The only thing we can do is try and go back to sleep. We still have to wake up in the morning. . . ."

They had made us too paranoid to fall back into a good sleep. We jumped at every noise, ready to strike at the next group who tried to mess with us. They were so inconsiderate. Did it seem like we needed someone to come by and shake us out of our sleep? They thought we were so much different from them, as if our lives were planets apart. They had a home and we didn't; that's the only difference between us. Not even them, but their parents had a home. And if they lost their home tomorrow, they would be just like us. A lot of people thought they were far above us; like they were a lifetime away from living on the streets. But losing a job's all it took, an accident, any misfortune, and then they would be right there with me. It happened in the blink of an eye.

We managed to settle down and relax. I wanted to stretch my legs but then remembered I had no room. I closed my eyes and began drifting asleep. I could still hear them laughing.

We woke up and continued our morning routine, ready to start our day. We stumbled through school and after, we wandered around downtown. We didn't go eat our daily salad at Albertsons right away. Our EBT card balance depleted fast so we needed to start rationing meals. We stashed some extra food from school lunch in our backpacks and we sat at an outside table and ate.

"How long do you think we're going to be in the car this time?" my sister asked as she drank a juice box.

I pulled out four more juice boxes and sat them on the table. "Probably until it breaks down."

The sun went down and we sat around waiting to meet up with our mom again. We reached the rendezvous point around the corner from my school and waited for her to finally pull up.

"Hurry up and get in!" she yelled. "I'm almost out of gas."

We rushed inside.

"How are you going to go to work tomorrow?" I asked. "You don't get paid until next week."

"We need to worry about parking right now," she said.

An ongoing Padres baseball game crowded the streets of downtown. We skipped our daily trip to Albertsons in search of a place to sleep. We raced through congested traffic against our gas tank. The car started slowing down. My mom pressed the gas pedal, but the car stuttered and then shut off.

"Shit!" She hit the steering wheel.

"What do we do now?" Pooh asked.

I opened my car door. Cars were honking behind us. The light had changed green and we blocked the road.

"All right, Mom, put it in neutral," I yelled over the ruckus.

I stood behind the car, pushing it with all of my strength. The car failed to budge. Cars steadily honked.

Two men jogged up to the car. They resembled hillbillies and reeked of cigarettes.

"Push it to the gas station!" one shouted over to me. He had long, straggling blond hair, missed a few teeth, a thinly built frame and appeared to be in his late thirties. Another guy ran up and helped us push the car over to the Shell gas station. My sister stepped out of the car to lighten the load. We inched our way there; still about seven minutes away. Cars were everywhere. I pushed and pushed with the three men in unison. We made it to the gas station and briefly applauded our own success. Cars still honked as they rode by. The men saw all of our possessions in the car. They dug into their pockets and gave me the little change they had.

"This is all I got, dude," the guy with the missing teeth said. "Good luck, man." They walked away. They had handed me two crumpled dollar bills and a bunch of change totaling three dollars and sixteen cents. I handed the money to my mom.

"This isn't going to get us anything." Pooh stood beside me.

"Stay here." I left.

"Where are you going?" my mom asked.

I kept going until I turned the corner. I saw a couple in front of me eating pizza at an outdoor table. Being bothered seemed like the last thing they wanted while enjoying their meal.

"Spare any change?" I asked. The man laughed in discomfort and handed me three dollars.

His girlfriend seemed nice. "Spare any change?"

She blushed and shot a glance over to the guy. She stared at me not sure if I was serious. I stood staring at her with my hand still out. She stopped smiling and rummaged through her purse, handing me two more dollars. I turned and carried on. A woman approached.

"Spare any change?"

"No, thanks," she said.

I saw someone else. "Spare any change?" He kept walking without a reply. It didn't matter, though. I would be out there until we had enough money to go park and get my mom to work, even if it took me all night.

After what seemed like forever, we finally managed to park under a lamppost which shined a bright orange light into our car. A few days later, my mom's coworker had loaned her forty dollars. My mother passed around cleaning wipes so we could all wash ourselves. The wipes would suffice until we could find a suitable shower. We put up newspapers in the windshields so no one could peek inside of our car. The newspaper also blocked out most of the blinding streetlight.

I took my wipes and wiped under my arms and then my privates. Being a boy it's always easier to clean myself. I had extra wipes left over so I wiped down my torso and tied the used wipes in an empty Albertsons bag. We listened to another one of my mom's stories accompanied by my sister's story of the girl who complained about not being able to drive the Mercedes. After a while, we sat in silence ready to fall asleep.

Someone tapped at the window on the driver's side. A light flashed into the car. My mom rolled down the window to see a police officer hunched over, pointing his light inside and taking a look around.

"You can't park here," he said.

"Seriously?" Pooh said.

"I have to leave for work in a few more hours. Can we catch a break? Please?" my mom said.

"You caught a break. You're lucky I didn't give you a ticket."

I rolled down my window. We weren't the only cars parked on the street. The sign in front read: *Two hour parking between eight a.m. and eight p.m.* I glanced back at the officer. "The sign says we can park here."

"Are you getting smart with me, boy?" He stuck his head inside.

"No, sir," I replied.

"You'd best get moving," he instructed my mom. She turned on the car and we pulled away. We barely managed to find that spot close to the freeway. We drove around the quiet streets for about forty-five minutes.

"This is ridiculous," Mom said. We drove up Park Boulevard into an open parking section of Balboa Park, adjacent to the Municipal Gym. My mom turned off the car and leaned against the window. The sun came up.

We drifted to sleep and woke up in what seemed like a few minutes ready to repeat the same cycle. We got ready for school, my mom prepped for work, and we were dropped off. After school, we headed to the library and tried to study for our upcoming tests. I had a math exam coming up and she had a chemistry test. Dark gray clouds filled the sky. I knew the cold wind meant one thing: rain.

We reached the rendezvous point and waited for my mom as the sky began to whimper and sob little droplets. We sat under a bus stop with an overhead cover to shield us from the rain. The wind brought its icy chill and the sprinkles turned into drizzles. We still had about ten minutes until my mother came. I had a love-hate relationship with the rain. I thought it to be naturally wondrous and under the proper conditions, its pitter-patter could lure me to a deep slumber. But it seemed like I never stood in the rain under proper conditions. But it wasn't the rain's fault. It just aimlessly fell on whatever was beneath it. It didn't discriminate on me, by nature it had no choice but to fall, I just happened to always be underneath it. I loved to watch the beautiful rain fall. I just really hated being in it when it fell.

My mom pulled up and waved for us to come get in the car. Now heavily raining, we managed to avoid getting completely soaked by hiding under our drenched backpacks as we ran to the car. We smelled chicken when we hopped in and saw a Popeyes chicken bag.

"Oooh, Popeyes," I said. "What's the occasion?"

"We're the occasion," my mom said. "We deserve some good food every once in a while."

"Hallelujah," my sister said.

We were glad she showed up with chicken. I couldn't keep forcing down those salads forever. After a while they lost their taste and it resembled eating a bunch of leaves, even with the cut-up chunks of turkey. I needed something different. The chicken tasted so good. On top of the chicken, we had biscuits. We loved Popeyes biscuits. We sat in our parked car indulging in the chicken, laughing and joking, drowning out the sound of the pitter-patter of the raindrops splashing against our car. For a second, in the brief moment, life didn't seem too bad. We were happy, eating good food, and enjoying each other's company. The little things in life sometimes made you the happiest. Pooh and I pulled out more juice boxes to drink and we washed down the chicken. I switched my shirt to tomorrow's shirt and shifted my weight to my side. Rain always had a funny way of putting me to sleep.

My home might not have been ideal. Fancy? No. Not luxurious, spacious or comfortable. But it was ours. We didn't have staff members breathing down my neck or trying to belittle us.

We were in charge in our home. Our car separated us from being outside in the rain like we had been in so many times before. Our car may have been worthless to some people, but it's all we had, and we cherished it. I hated living in there as anyone else would; but it was my home. I closed my eyes. My insides were warm and content. I hoped to feel as good in the morning when I woke up in the car all over again—minus the chicken.

16. The Suite Life: Age Sixteen

2007–2008

WE DROVE IN A HEATED FRENZY SPEEDING TOWARD the best news we had had in a while. My mom had contacted an Organization named 2-1-1 searching for any resource to help. They connected her to a church operated organization, which gave us motel vouchers for the next two weeks. The motel voucher allowed us to pick an inexpensive motel to live in. All motels didn't accept the vouchers, so we just had to find one that did. We were so excited because it would be our first time sleeping outside of the car in such a long time. The sweltering July heat made the car temperature unbearable, especially when the air conditioning didn't work.

The church gave out two vouchers in total. They used to give them both out at the same time but people would sell them, so now they issued them on a weekly basis. We just received our first voucher and we were to go back at the end of the week for the second. We couldn't wait to sleep on a mattress for a change.

We checked into a small motel downtown by the San Diego Bay. We entered a nice little room with double queen-sized beds. I flicked on the outdated television. A miniature fridge sat on the floor under the microwave. I entered the bathroom and turned on the shower. It beautifully fell into the tub and down the drain. The water felt warm, much warmer than the wipes I had become accustomed to. My mom followed me into the bathroom.

"Boy, what are you doing?"

"I'm about to take a shower."

"Nah uh, I called first."

"What? When?"

"And I called second!" yelled Pooh from inside the room.

"I'm the only boy! I should be able to take one shower first," I said.

"What happened to 'ladies first'?"

"Yeah, yeah." I exited the bathroom. Pooh sat at the foot of our queen-sized bed on the right side. We were sharing a bed and would give my mom her own. I sat next to her and grabbed the remote, flipping through basic cable channels. She rolled her eyes at me, annoyed.

"Pick one!"

"I'm seeing what's on."

"Turn to the guide channel."

"It takes too long."

My mom took her shower, followed by my sister, and then finally I stepped in. The warm beads of water ran down my skin. The hot steam filled the bathroom, making me sweat. I lathered my washcloth with soap and washed myself thoroughly from head to toe. I rinsed off, lathered my washcloth, and rinsed off again, making sure I cleaned everything. I let the water hit my head and roll down my back. Each trickling bead massaged my skin, I didn't want to get out, but I heard the bed calling for me. We didn't have anything to eat for dinner, but nothing could ruin the night for us. I finally laid down and closed my eyes. I had been sleeping upright for so long lying down straight felt a little uncomfortable. I didn't care though because the bed felt incomparably softer than the stubborn car seats. My mom and sister were already fast asleep. We were fortunate my mom found a voucher, we needed a break from the car. We needed a vacation away from home.

The next day, my mom entered the motel room door with groceries in her hand. She had picked up some bread, lunchmeat, slices of cheese, and a half-gallon of water. It would be our dinner for the next couple of days. A nice break from all the canned food and salads we had been forced to consume and we had the motel room refrigerator to keep the perishables. We made our sandwiches and laid across our bed at ease with our bellies full in good comfort.

"Did you get quarters to wash?" Pooh asked.

"Oh, no, I forgot," my mom teased.

"Dang, Mom, we really need to clean our clothes," Pooh said.

"Of course I didn't forget," Mom said.

"Where's the laundromat?" I asked.

"I think there's one around the corner," Pooh said.

"When do y'all want to go?" my mom asked.

"We can go now," Pooh said. "These clothes really need to be washed. How long has it been?"

"Too long if you have to ask," I said. "This is my fourth time wearing this shirt, and I only have five shirts to cover seven days."

Our clothes still sat in the car. I had my two pairs of jeans, four T-shirts excluding the one I wore, underwear and my socks. Every piece of clothing I had to my name. We piled inside the car and drove to the laundromat around the corner. Laundromats were usually emptier at night but cars filled the parking lot so we parked around the corner on the street. We had half of a tank of gas. My mom didn't get paid for another week and a half so gas would have to stretch. The quarter money came straight from the last of the gas money, but we had to wash our clothes. We couldn't put it off any longer.

Because of the cramped and full laundromat, it took us three hours to wash all of our clothes. After we finished, we grabbed our laundry bags and carried them to the car. A group of older Latino boys sat on the hood of our car drinking forty- and thirty-two-ounce beer bottles concealed in brown paper bags. There were about eight of them altogether and out of all the cars around, they chose ours to drink on. Maybe because to them ours ranked the most raggedy, or the cheapest, but to us our home had been made of gold.

"Hey, excuse me!" my mom said. We approached the car. "Can you please get off my car?"

One of the boys stared at my mom and spat on the ground. He and two others sat on the car as the other five hovered around.

"This is public property," the boy said. "I can sit where I want."

"The sidewalk is public property, not my car," my mom said.

"Nobody's bothering you old lady, we don't want any trouble. I'm just kicking it."

"I don't care what you're doing, just please move away from my car."

I sat my laundry bag down and stepped in front of the boy. "Hey man, we just need to go. You can have this spot. We're just asking you to get off our car so we can leave."

"Get off your car? I'm comfortable here, homes."

"Hey, Rush, just move fool." One of the boys stood off the car.

"Shut up, fool!" Rush said. "They come over and disrespect me and you want me to move? I'm not going anywhere until I feel like it and I put that on the barrio."

I had ran into types like Rush all my life. His branded tattoos made it obvious he belonged to a Latino gang. To me, there were no Latino gangs; there were no black gangs, not even white gangs. To me, there were only gangs and gang members. They all wanted the same thing, which always amounted to nothing. They all desired nothing. They aspire to be nothing more in life. Confronting us must have been the highlight of his day, to refuse to move away from our car. He wanted trouble; he lived for it. What every gang member lived for. If he had been so tough, why not go sit on the car of someone in a rival gang. Tell them you weren't going to move and then he might be considered gangster. What he did right then wasn't gangster. We were non-affiliates, you didn't gain street credit for bothering a mother and her kids. We just wanted to get back to the motel and go to sleep.

We could leave if he simply just moved. My sister had this fiery glare in her eyes, a flame which spread to my eyes, the same fire emitting from my mother.

"I'm going to ask you one more time to move," my mom said. Her and my sister were always fearless in the face of disaster. I counted eight of them and only three of us, really one of us because they were girls and we were surrounded by boys. The odds were against us but they were always against us. Bad odds had made us become fearless or stupid, sometimes it's hard to decipher between the two.

"My man, my mom is sick, we just want to leave." I tried to reason, but men like Rush had no reason. Reasoning or trying to be rational turned them on like a dog smelling fear. They only comprehend violence, drugs, and prison. In the jungle, sometimes you have to speak their language or you will get eaten.

Rush abruptly jumped up off the hood of our car and grabbed me by the collar. A little bigger than me, he seemed about five years older and his breath smelled like he had been licking piles of shit. "How 'bout you and that ugly bitch make me!"

The grabbing of my collar didn't outrage me. The fact he called my mother a bitch outraged me. My mom was one of the sweetest people I have ever encountered. Now she was a bitch? After everything we had been through, she was a bitch? The way he called my mom a bitch made me fear for her life. I quickly swung upright with a massive uppercut knocking him stumbling back. He threw a haymaker, but I countered it and connected two quick jabs to his chin. We traded blows from the shoulders until I caught him with another uppercut sending him falling on to the hood of our car. The blow caught him by surprise as he scrambled up to react. I thrust upon him madly swinging with everything I had. I knew his friends would jump to his aid in only a matter of time. I hit him all over his face as he tried to cover up. I grabbed him in a headlock and punched him over and over again on his head. I felt someone tugging violently at the back of my shirt and then I felt my shirt released. My mom had charged one of his friends who had tried to intervene. She had grabbed him and used his own weight to flip him to the ground. My sister had jumped on one of their backs holding him in a chokehold. They all began setting down their mostly empty beer bottles. They were about to accept their invitation to rumble.

I punched Rush in his ear and someone screamed, "Police are coming!" I let him go and took a step back. There were no police around. Rush quickly jabbed me in my right eye. I backed up, holding my eye and then speared him back onto the hood. I threw overhead jab after jab and finally backed up ready to get in my striking position. Suddenly, my legs gave from under me and I crashed hard onto the ground.

"Freeze, don't move!" yelled a police officer standing over me so I froze and didn't move. Rush had been tackled on the ground as well, but he struggled to get free, sending two more police officers over to contain him. All of his friends had already fled, leaving just us four with the police. The police officer standing over me tightened his cold metal handcuffs around my wrists and stuck me into the back of his car. Officers forcefully pushed Rush into the back of another car, screaming and trying to spit at them.

As a gangbanger, Rush had a lot of pride and refused to cooperate with police. He abided rules of the street code in which he dedicated his entire life to. He didn't even comprehend outside his little hood, outside the ghetto, nobody cared about street code, nobody cared about the ghetto. If he got shot and died the same day, nobody outside of his gang life would even be notified. And even then, libation wouldn't bring him back.

Being belligerent won't get you anywhere except jail. I already knew. I had seen my friends act belligerent, and how everything drastically went worse right after. One time, my friend Marcus had punched an officer in the face during an attempted arrest. This allowed the police to beat him up pretty bad and then still charge him with assaulting an officer, receiving extra jail time.

My mom stood outside of the car talking to an officer and he turned and trailed over to me. My arms rested uncomfortably behind me as I sat on the hard back seat of the police vehicle. He opened the door with a pen and a piece of paper in his hand.

"What's your name?"

"Michael Gaulden."

"Spell it."

"Michael G-A-U-L-D-E-N."

"Are you on probation or parole?"

"No, sir."

"What happened?"

"My mom, sister, and I were coming from washing our clothes when the guy refused to move away from our car. He attacked me, his friends attacked my mom and sister and we got into a fight."

"They attacked your mother and sister?"

"Yes, sir."

"You don't look like you were in a fight."

"My right eye didn't swell up?"

"Not as of yet—" A glass bottle shattered on the ground outside and the police officer quickly shut me inside of the car. His comrades huddled around my mom and sister with their hands on their holsters. The officers waited for a brief moment checking to see if the area had been secured. The officer I talked to jogged to the other police car and began trying to talk to Rush who still tried to spit on them.

He returned to my door. "How old are you?"

"I'm sixteen."

"And what's your address?"

"I don't have one."

"Excuse me?"

"I don't have one." I sighed not really wanting to explain. "Right now, we're in a motel, but we're sleeping in and out of our car."

The officer stared at me square in my eyes, checking for the truth, and through my eyes the truth became more than evident. He stood me out of the car, removed the handcuffs, and released me free to go.

"What's happening to him?" I nudged my head toward Rush. "He's twenty-two, fighting a minor, on parole, and drunk in public. He's going in."

The officer told me to stay out of trouble and he let us drive away after we loaded the trunk with our laundry. We only sat in the car for about fifty seconds when Pooh uncontrollably blurted, "What the hell was that?"

"Nonsense," my mom said. "People always want to mess with us."

"Mom, are y'all crazy?" I said. "What's wrong with y'all jumping in like that? They could have hurt you."

"They could have hurt you!" Pooh said.

"Sun, you didn't see because your back was turned, but all of those little boys were about to jump on you."

"Yeah, Mom, but still, you can't be reckless like that. What if they all jumped on us? Then what? You and Pooh would have had to go straight to the hospital."

"And I'm fine with that," Pooh said. "If they're going to jump us, they're going to jump us together."

"You guys are crazy," I said.

"You have to think about it this way," my mom said. "You're my only son, you're your sister's only brother, and we'd go insane if anything happened to you. We're all each other has, so we either stand together or we fall together. It's that simple."

"All of a sudden mama can judo flip people." Pooh laughed.

"Right?" I said. "Mama turned all thuggish ruggish on us."

"That's right, nobody messes with my babies," she said. We pulled back up to the motel. Evidently exhausted from the fight, she slowly exited her seat. She tried to head toward the trunk to grab her bag, but I knew she couldn't carry it.

"I got it, Mom." I beat her to the trunk. "Just go open the room door so it's already open for me."

"You sure, Sun? I can grab it."

"Yeah, I'm sure. I just want to go straight inside."

"Can you grab mine, too?" Pooh said.

"Oh my God, did you just see that flying pig?" I pointed at the night sky.

"What? No?" Pooh glanced up.

"Yeah, me neither."

"Shut up, stupid."

Our last day of the first week in the motel arrived. I had to admit it I had long since forgotten about that type of bliss: the bed, the warm showers, and the space to move about. I could use another week of heaven. I needed a nice long break from the car. We pulled up to the organization issuing the vouchers. Pooh and I sat in the car as my mom went inside. She had told us it wouldn't take more than fifteen minutes, but after thirty minutes had passed, we were beginning to worry. After about an hour, my mom reemerged from the building with a discomforted expression on her face. She sat into the car without saying anything to us and abruptly pulled away. She drove with an extra ferocity, so I knew something had gone wrong.

"What happened?" I asked, but she didn't respond, she just focused on the road. "Mom, what happened? What did they say?"

She squinted her eyes at the road. She glanced at me through her rearview mirror and then over at Pooh.

"Mom?" Pooh asked.

"They ran out of funding," my mom said, really low and in a monotone voice.

"How can they run out of funds? They owe us another week," Pooh said.

"They're telling me all of their resources are used up for the rest of this fiscal year."

"Weren't they supposed to hold it for us? What happened? They just gave our voucher away?" I said.

"I don't understand how this happened."

"Well what did they suggest we do?"

"Nothing."

"Nothing?" Pooh said. "They gave away our voucher and suggested nothing?"

"They made a few phone calls but in the end, there was nothing they could do, according to them."

"That's messed up," I said. "They might as well have said, 'May the force be with you.' What are we going to do now?"

"We have to go get our stuff."

"There has to be something we can do," Pooh said. "I'm not ready to go back to the car just yet."

I stared out of the window as we continued down the road. "You think if we talked to the manager he'd give us at least a day extension?" I asked.

"Nope," Mom said. "I called them before I came back to the car. It's a business. If you can't make the payment, you have to leave."

"So our family vacation is really over?" I said. "We're back in the car tonight?"

"Shit," Pooh said.

"Yeah, it's over," my mom said.

"Well, it was fun while it lasted," I said.

"Is that supposed to make us feel better?" Pooh said.

"No . . . no, it's not," I said. Losing that motel broke my back. I couldn't take it anymore.

17. Like Father Like Son

W E'RE GOING TO GET ALL ELECTRONICS AND BE OUT of there quick," Romel's brother, Mathew said. It had been a while since I had talked to Romel, but I knew he no longer worked for Subway. Mathew's three years younger than me, but to my dismay, far taller.

"I have a bad feeling about this one," Kirk, my step-cousin through marriage, said. A few months younger than me, he and Mathew were both from the 4/9 Southside Blood Gang. He stared at the house as we began putting on gloves we had stored in our backpacks.

Losing the motel vouchers set me on a downward spiral. I had spent my life trying to be decent for no reason. Decency rewarded me with being ridiculed and starving. I couldn't sit back helplessly anymore. I had been burglarizing a few houses lately; sometimes by myself, sometimes with others. I finally acquired the PlayStation I always wanted—but I sold it. Burglary carried me through August, and mid-way through September. I got by decent enough. Stealing's not right, but whatever I stole and pawned, it gave me money I used to buy underwear and food for my mom and sister. Especially since they cut off our EBT again.

"Where'd this come from?" asked my mom when I had first handed her eighty dollars, keeping the other thirty for myself. Most of the revenue came from some jewelry I had a stranger pawn for me since I wasn't eighteen, the legal age required to pawn.

"I found it," I replied.

"You found it?" my sister repeated. "Eighty dollars? Just lying around?"

"People find money all the time. Do y'all want to eat or not, huh? C'mon, Mom, let's go get some pizza . . . and gas."

"Well, all right," she replied. They looked so happy eating pizza. It revitalized their spirits. Most bad actions really do stem from good intentions, it didn't make it right, but it sure as hell beat starving or going without. I knew my fourteen-year-old self wouldn't have approved, but I wasn't fourteen anymore. Two years might as well be eons ago.

Usually we would hit the houses with no problem, but I agreed with Kirk, trouble brewed in the air. I kept seeing an abnormally large amount of neighborhood watch signs everywhere on our way there to the Emerald Park neighborhood. We had already hit two houses. Pure greed motivated Mathew.

"We're good," Mathew said. "Let's just get this money real fast."

"Something feels off," I said. The theft already seemed risky. When most kids burglarized homes, they had getaway cars. We were all on foot. "Something feels off."

"Mike G, I know you're not talking. How're you even saying anything? You need this the most."

"Shut the hell up." I knew he was right.

"Stop acting like two little bitches," he replied, pushing Kirk in his chest. "We're not shooting anybody. Calm down."

"Whatever." I placed my hood on. "Let's hurry up then."

Kirk sighed, but we were doing it anyway. We tiptoed toward the house. The first two houses were random, but Mathew had picked this one out. It belonged to someone he knew who wasn't home. I already had a few stolen necklaces in my backpack along with a few loose twenty-dollar bills. Mathew had an Xbox 360 game system in his backpack. Kirk had found a small, silver .38 caliber pistol in the last house and kept it tucked on his waist. They went around the back as I slithered up to the front door. I knocked on the door as if I knew someone there, for appearance's sake. When I made sure no one was home, I would give the signal for them to break in with me joining them and we would grab everything we could.

Before I could give the signal, however, a loud crash shattered through glass. I ran around the back to see a brick lying through a broken double-pane bedroom window. Kirk already went inside and Mathew had a foot in. I grabbed him.

"What the hell? That was too loud!"

"We tried to pop it open but the glass was too thick."

"I didn't even give you a signal."

"Oh, well then." Mathew led the way inside. We entered a boy's room. The room had a full-sized bed with posters of naked girls hanging on the walls. Kirk had dispersed through the house and Mathew quickly followed, leaving me in the room alone. A leather belt laid on the light-brown carpet. I picked it up and placed it in my backpack. A silver watch glimmered on the brown wooden dresser and I grabbed it as well.

"Mike G, what are you doing?" Kirk came back into the room holding a laptop. He had some jewelry wrapped around his hands. "You're supposed to be the lookout. Go lookout!"

"All right, calm down." I tucked the watch into my backpack. "You shouldn't have used a brick to smash through the window like an idiot."

"Whatever, man. I got in here, right?"

I climbed through the window and out of the house.

"Wait, take this." He handed me the laptop from inside. I returned toward the front of the house but not directly in front. I hid from the sight of one of the next-door neighbors standing on his porch with a wooden bat. He hadn't seen me. My eyes zoomed across the street to a woman peeking through her blinds, talking timidly on the telephone. She definitely saw me. She stared directly at me. She yelled into the phone, then let go of the blinds as soon as she noticed me notice her. Damn!

I ran back around. I leaped through the window and ran through the room and into the hallway. I found Mathew, in another room, stuffing some rings in his pocket.

"Let's go! Police are coming!"

"You heard them?"

"No, I saw this lady calling them."

"Fuck!" Kirk ran past the hallway, and into the boy's room carrying a few cell phones. "I heard neighbors knocking on the door."

"Mike said police are coming," Mathew said, as the three of us congregated in the room.

"Screw this, I'm gone." I jumped back out the window with them following behind me. We ran from the back of the house. The man with the bat grabbed me from out of nowhere, trying to tackle me. Mathew punched him in his jaw, making him fall as we took off in a sprint. I tossed the backpack behind some nearby bushes as police sirens filled my ears, a lot of police sirens. Down the street, two of them approached from in front of us. We stopped and turned back around, running so fast I wished I had grew wings. We cut behind a few houses. Mathew led the way in front toward his group home just up ahead where we could hide out.

We emerged from behind the houses.

"Freeze! Police!"

"Don't move!"

"Police, freeze!"

Three officers ran toward us with their guns drawn. I bounced around in a panic with nowhere for me to go. We were surrounded as the other cops caught up. Shit.

"Freeze!"

Shit! I stopped moving and threw my hands up as two officers forced me to the ground along with Mathew and Kirk. They pressed my face against the pavement, tightening the handcuffs around me. I shook my head at Mathew. Damn. I should have listened to my bad feeling. Now I had a feeling this would be worse. The cops dug into my pockets but they didn't find anything, no ID, no money, no gloves, nothing they could use to convict me. Mathew had discarded everything he had, too, but Kirk, I guess he thought we would escape because he held onto everything he stole. Lucky for him, he had tossed the gun. He didn't want to risk receiving a gun charge. They took everything else from him and sat us up. They stood us one by one as another police car silently pulled up from a distance with the lady who had called them inside to identify us. We couldn't see her face through car, which enabled witnesses to view criminals without placing them in harm's way. Two officers stood me up. They made me face the car, showing them a side and back profile as well. They sat me back down and did the same thing to my cousins.

"Positive confirmations on all three," one of the officers said to another.

I was pissed. Those idiots should have waited for my signal. They put us in the back of separate vehicles and we were gone. They took us to the local precinct and put us in cells until they decided they had enough information to process us. The brick through the window would be vandalism and they would let us go. We would have to go to court, but nothing too serious. But because we stepped one toe across the threshold, it turned into breaking and entering. They threw us back into the police cars and drove us to Juvenile Hall.

Mathew, being thirteen, had been sent to a different division than us. He and Kirk seemed calm, they had both been locked up before. My first time in Juvenile Hall scared me. Yeah, I would have shelter, but I would prefer the streets to a cage any day. I moved through the cold, narrow hallways with two guards right behind me. The handcuffs were removed, but I had to keep my hands tucked in under my armpits. I went straight to booking and sat on the cold chair. The woman across from me stared at me with dull eyes through the thick glass separating us. To her, I was just another minority in trouble. It didn't matter why I had gotten in trouble, it didn't matter what just cause I believed I had, it didn't matter I lived homeless. I was now a statistic.

They fingerprinted me. I stared at the camera in front of me with grief and anger fixated on my face as they took my mugshot. I never imagined having one. The guards lifted me out of the room as another kid sat to be booked. They brought me to a guy in an office and left me there.

The guy didn't acknowledge me at first as he read continuously through paperwork.

"You're being charged with vandalism and breaking and entering," he said. "You have the right to remain silent. Anything you say can and will be used against you in a court of law. You have the right to an attorney. If you cannot afford an attorney, one will be provided for you. Do you understand the rights I have just read to you? With these rights in mind, do you wish to speak to me?"

"Sir, I'm not a bad kid."

"Why'd you do it?" he asked, not bothering to look at me.

"Honestly? Sir, I'm homeless."

He stopped shuffling through the papers and raised his gaze. "Homeless?"

"I thought if I pawned some things, I could get money to feed my family. That's why I did it. We've been homeless for years."

"And did this help your family?"

"No, sir."

"'No, sir' is correct. Now you have to drag your family through legal fees, you'll go on probation, and all sorts of things. In trying to help, you've really set your family back."

I lowered my head. He had been right, of course.

"You get one phone call. Call your mother."

"Who?" I said. "I'm not calling my mom. This would kill her."

"Well, you have to. Someone has to pick you up. Luckily, this is your first offense. He slid a piece of paper my way. This is a promise to appear in court. You sign, you get to go home," he paused, thinking about his unfortunate word choice. "You get to leave here. If you don't appear in court, a warrant will be issued and we will find you, homeless or not."

"The hell with that. I'm not calling my mom. I never told her what I've been doing when I'm away from her. It'll break her heart. I can't do this to her."

"You already did." He slid the phone my way. "Now it's time to man up."

I hesitantly picked it up and slowly dialed her cheap prepaid cell phone number. Last time I checked, her minutes were low and she awaited a call from a new family shelter. She didn't get paid for two more weeks, so she couldn't buy any extra minutes.

"Hello?" She didn't recognize the strange number calling her. I didn't respond. "Hello?" she repeated.

"Mom?" My voice quivered.

"Michael? Boy, where are you at? The car is getting lonely without you," she joked.

"I'm . . . I'm in jail."

"Jail?" She couldn't tell if I joked with her or not. "Sun, where are you?"

"I'm. . . ." I couldn't finish. I could not strip away all her dreams and aspirations for me. I just couldn't. I handed the phone to the man and allowed him to. He told her everything on the papers in front of him. I overheard her mention how good my school grades were, but he assured her it didn't matter. I was in real trouble. He then handed me back the phone.

"Hello?" I said.

"How dare you!" she said in tears. I could hear the heart break. I could hear the disappointment. "How dare you! Is this what I've been struggling for? So you can fuck around and end up just like your father?"

Her words echoed in my head. They made me angry. I was nothing like my father! I glanced around my imprisoned surroundings. Actually, it seemed like I was everything like him.

"Mom, I'm sorry."

"Now I have to miss work and come all the way there to get you! I can't afford to miss work. Damn it, Michael!"

"Mom . . . I'm—" I heard the dial tone and placed the phone on the desk. She didn't hang up on me, she wouldn't hang up on me, but I had just wasted the last of her prepaid minutes.

"It's not the end of the world," the man said, but I didn't want to keep talking. "I never want to see you in here again." Two guards came in and escorted me to the shower.

The cold water and rough soap made the shower unpleasant. It seemed like as soon as I stepped in the guards were banging on the door for me to step out.

"All right, hold on." I wasn't done, so, I stayed in the shower. To my surprise, they opened the door and came in, shutting off the water. They gave me a towel and shipped me to a cell with four cots in it. It resembled a shelter room. My cousin, Kirk, along with another boy, were already inside. Kirk smiled.

"Don't worry," he said. "I'll show you all around. I feel like I'm back at home. I'm excited."

He could tell I didn't share his enthusiasm. I lied down on my cot, trapped within those cold walls, caged like the animal society deemed me to be. I didn't understand how people kept getting locked up. I had barely been there and already dove into a depression. The only thing worse than being homeless was being a homeless criminal. I wasn't a criminal. I just wanted to survive. I just wanted to take care of my family and Juvenile Hall was where I ended up. The street life is no life, just a timer for death or incarceration.

The fast money wasn't worth it. Criminality itself just wasn't worth it; my forefather's history showed me. My father's side of the family were all troubled and growing up I only talked to his youngest sister, my Aunt Kay. On my dad's side of my family tree, I came from a line of troubled men. History preached about my destined path to follow in their footsteps because I lived under the same impoverished environment. My great grandfather had been murdered; someone stabbed him in the center of his heart. My grandfather had also been killed, except his death happened in prison. My father currently served a fifteen to life imprisonment sentence for murder. History showed I would be no different. Statistics depicted my only two options were death or jail. And, with the confines of my cage, it appeared like the statistics were right.

Kirk came and sat next to me on my cot. "Lighten up, bro. This is nothing. You'll be out of here in no time. It's about time you get some street credibility."

"Screw street credibility. And I'll be out of here tomorrow."

"Tomorrow?" He lost enthusiasm as his smile slowly drooped into a frown as if I had just insulted him.

"Yeah, it's my first offense."

"Lucky for you." He stood and returned to his cot.

"When do you think you'll be out?"

"Six months, minimum." He turned on his side, ending the conversation.

I retracted back into my thoughts, listening to my mom's voice, *"and end up just like your father"* as it replayed over and over again.

No, Mom, I wouldn't end up like Dad, you raised me better than his sins. My life would be better. Although it didn't appear to be the case, my life would be more than what it was currently. Someday, my name would matter.

Being a drug lord or criminal would put me right back in jail. I needed a different way to succeed. I could already tell the street life wasn't going to work for me. I needed an alternative; a path my forefathers had not traversed. The opposite of street life is school life. I always thought of myself as a pretty smart guy. I still had good grades. Maybe school could work.

18. Where Homeless Kids Learn

(Pre-Reconstruction)

EARLY IN THE MORNING, MY SISTER AND I READIED ourselves for school. The beginning of October started off to a great start. We didn't talk about me being on probation much. We were afraid what would happen if the shelters found out, so we hid it as much as possible. The new shelter we somehow lucked our way into said we had to switch from our high school to another school they claimed to be "more suited for our needs." We were so happy to get in the shelter and quickly complied with all rules.

My mom had signed up for this waiting list months ago and they just now had open space. One of the staff members had strolled by us sleeping in the car and recognized my mom, tapping on the car window. She said they had been trying to call us a few weeks prior, but the number had been out of service. With me being sixteen, it would probably be the last shelter we could get accepted into and then we would all have to split up. Staff confirmed I was too old during our intake. They tried to send me to a shelter/group home for boys down the street, but it didn't have room. Another problem I faced, the older I became, the fewer places there were for me to go.

The new shelter gave everyone a three-month time limit, sometimes four in extreme circumstances—like death or childbirth (which happened a lot). Our tiny room lacked space but anything was bigger than the car. We were one of four families there with cars so we seemed extra cool whenever we pulled up. They all had raggedy cars too, except this one family had a Camry, but no one really saw them because they came back late at night right before curfew.

The small school they had sent us to resembled a charter. Its founders called it the Monarch School, where students transformed and flew away toward success. It had grades K–12 and everyone ate together in the miniature outside courtyard which consisted of three or four bench tables. The staff at the shelter told us how good the school used to be. Before budget cuts, it used to have a small restaurant where it would employ its students, the teachers tried to really educate and reach out to the students, the counselors took the time to help sort through life problems, and it seemed like a great school. The institute operated under the juvenile court systems, which ironically seemed like a prediction of where homeless and most inner-city kids were supposed to end up: inside the juvenile court system.

Two weeks had passed since our enrollment. The school year started in August but we were used to starting and leaving schools at odd times. Being around other kids like me for a while relieved me from acting "normal." We all came from different backgrounds, different upbringings, but we were all brought up under the same homeless umbrella. Some kids had both parents, some kids had no parents, but we all struggled. I knew it may have been bad to like to see other people in my situation, but it wasn't for the reasons people would think. I didn't enjoy knowing other people were living life as bad as me, but it comforted me knowing we weren't the only ones. Our case might have been a little worse given my mom and sister's health, but we weren't alone, and there's strength in numbers, or at least there's supposed to be.

We only had one classroom for all twenty of us high school students whose grades ranged from ninth to twelfth grade. One teacher, Mr. English or English as I called him, taught all grade levels with all coursework all at the same time, and I could have bet a million dollars he wasn't qualified to teach every subject. Neither I nor my sister liked the way he taught. The other students never said anything, but we noticed it right from our first day. Instead of periods, we had allotted time for each subject, usually an hour to an hour and a half. Every day, English would introduce new course material and spend more than half of the allotted time explaining it, most times rather poorly and opinionated. After he explained, he assigned massive amounts of classwork, which Mr. English wanted to be completed the same day for the same subject. For such a workload, we only had an average of thirty minutes to complete it. Then he forced us to stop working and switch subjects, introducing a new topic and new course material, repeating the cycle. At the end of the day, he allowed fifteen minutes for everyone to catch up on his or her work, and then we had to turn everything in, which mostly consisted of incomplete work. One day, he addressed the class, telling us how disappointed we made him because no one finished their work. He proclaimed we lacked a work ethic. He said he didn't want to give out bad grades, but we had left him no choice.

Pooh and I had claimed a desk at the back of the small classroom, perpendicular to English's. We sat and stared at him as he lectured the class. Some of them were disheartened; others gazed out into space because they could care less about the classroom. Pooh stared at me and raised her eyebrow, annoyed.

English had the type of voice, which seemed to nag and drag, lingering in the air long after he had stopped speaking. His voice had a mellow whine to it, which accompanied his self-proclaimed sense of superiority. In his eyes I could see he looked down on us, not in a discriminatory way, but he simply had no belief in us. When he spoke, he liked to jam a lot of big words into the conversation for no real reason. I guess his own vocabulary impressed him, but he didn't realize my sister and I could comprehend him better than the others. We'd spent many homeless days in libraries. He grew upset when we corrected him. His big words were supposed to be a display of his vast intellect, but they seemed rather forced and used with a struggle. When he spoke, I didn't get the impression of someone very knowledgeable, just he spent a lot of time reading dictionaries, and it could come off as being a little dickish, especially because a lot of the other kids couldn't comprehend and he would talk to them as if he was better. Every day he came to class in a crisp suit and tie as if he was so much grander than we were. If he he'd been so grand, why wasn't he teaching at some university somewhere, why waste his intellect on us?

I slowly raised my hand as English continued to speak. I watched as he watched my hand rise. He kept talking, but I didn't relent. We started off on a good foot my first couple of days in class until he asked my sister a question and then said her opinion was wrong. I understand if he disagreed, it's perfectly fine to disagree, but to tell her she had been flat out wrong was what was wrong: everyone is entitled to their own opinion. It told me he didn't care about what we thought which bothered me. Pretty much my whole life no one cared what we thought. We were told the classroom is where you could express yourself, where you could share and develop ideas, but my classrooms were never like those.

"English, my brother has a question." Pooh stared at him. The whole class turned and stared at me in one big dramatic move.

"Let me finish," English said.

"Well how long are you going to talk? He's been holding his hand up for a while now."

"Yup, he has," Brandon, another student in the classroom, said.

"Yes? Michael?" English tried to hold back his frustration.

"You don't give us enough time to finish our assignments."

"That is not a question."

"Well, I mean you're wondering why nobody finishes their assignments, and it's because we don't have enough time. It's not our work ethic, we do the work right here in front of you."

"You have a copious amount of time to complete all allocated assignments."

"No, we don't. You use up most of it. If the whole entire class has incomplete assignments, that should tell you we need more time, or a more evenly dispersed workload. We can't even take it home because you give us so much homework."

"This is school, no one said that it would not be demanding."

"This isn't demanding, this just isn't feasible. It's clearly a flawed system. Plus, Cherish is your only TA, and I don't like the way she grades."

"There's nothing wrong with my system. Shannon's an exemplary example. Shannon gets all of her work done on time and presents high quality work."

Shannon was the school's golden child. She had spent most of her life growing up within the school and so did her brother. She was the only one they believed could become something and they treated her accordingly. She didn't have to sit in class most of the time with the rest of us; she could do activities such as use class time to go on a school-sponsored trip to the movies. No, I hadn't read the *Twilight* books (the last time I checked they weren't course material), but when she came back to class with a shirt from seeing the movie, well, it just wasn't fair. She met all of the school's donors, and universally held in higher regards than the rest of us. I had nothing against Shannon; she's smart and displayed real potential. I just didn't like the fact everyone blatantly treated her superior to the rest of us. I didn't fault Shannon, anyone in her shoes would have continued to enjoy the benefits of favoritism, and rightfully so, but even she became aware of the unfairness.

"Shannon's barely in class and even then, you give her extensions on all of her work." Shannon, who glanced at me and my sister, blinked heavily a few times. She didn't want to be dragged into our conversation. I didn't drag her into it; English did, but either way she was in it. I didn't like being subordinated under her. Although it seemed like everyone else had been convinced, I wasn't entirely sure Shannon was more intellectually gifted than my sister and me. Not saying she's dumber than they thought, but we were smarter than they could imagine.

English's face began to turn red. The classroom light reflected off the lens in his square spectacles. He brushed his right hand through his dull and flat brown hair. He glanced around the class at the other student faces.

"No one else is cantankerous about how my class operates."

The student faces were all bland besides the blatant intrigue by the dispute between me and English. "Well, I mean, it doesn't seem like anyone else cares."

"I don't care." Another student named Daniel, raised his hand in admittance.

"If my other students do not care about the way in which I am operating my grading system, why disrupt my class with your offensive comportment?"

"If they don't care, that's up to them, it's their life. I care about my life. You have one teacher's assistant to grade all subjects, you don't thoroughly explain the work and just give your opinion of it. I thought you had to present the material in the course books you assigned, not go on tangents about the president all day—and then assign an essay about the Gettysburg Address. You taught us nothing about Gettysburg; you didn't even address it."

"I am furnishing you with an interactive learning experience that'll—"

"Interactive?" I gasped dramatically. "You monologue the entire time. You don't give us enough time to complete our work, and you're taking even more class time to monologue about how disappointed you are because we don't complete the work we don't have enough time to finish. That doesn't make sense. This is a big time management problem. And I'm a junior; I don't think I'm fulfilling any of the class requirements required for college. We're getting heavy workloads about monologues that won't help us pass any standardized tests. This education system here is clearly flawed. It's setting us up to fail."

"Nonsense! If you fail, it is of your own accord brought forth by a lack of student willpower to become educated."

"Who else is passing in here besides Shannon?" Pooh said.

"You two are also passing," Cherish said, sitting behind her teacher's assistant desk. Cherish seemed a sweet person, I could tell her and my sister's personalities meshed, but the situation wasn't personal; it's academic.

"Exactly, it's just us three," I said. "And we just got here. Unless we get exemptions and extensions like Shannon, the way this system is designed, it's only a matter of time before we'll be failing, too."

"All right, since my degrees and credentials on how to operate a class clearly doesn't mean anything in your brain, use your own system. Do it yourself if you think you can do my job better than me."

"Fine, I will." I refused to back down. English had become defensive. His usual vampiric pale face flushed with red. His breathing grew heavier and heavier as the classroom eagerly watched. I wasn't trying to attack him as a person, he seemed like a half-decent guy outside the classroom, but inside of the classroom I had to do what I thought right. I wasn't completely sure what good school would do for me in the future, but my own pride couldn't watch myself fail. Right then, all I had was school and I wasn't going to let anyone take it away from me.

I waited for my sister to comment. We were a tag team duo. My mom taught us to defend one another in the face of any and all adversaries because if we didn't, nobody would. And as I sat in my chair, I awaited her as she thoroughly assessed the situation in her mind. She would be the one to correct me if I stepped out of line. If she said we needed to follow his class structure, I would have listened.

"Yeah fine, we will." She stared at English as he had tiptoed to our desk and hovered over us.

A thin man, scrawny by anyone's terms, he's the furthest thing away from being intimidating. And even if he tried to intimidate us intellectually as he hovered, with the class as an audience, I knew no fear. No, I didn't have as many degrees as he did. No one in my family had ever gone to college, or any fancy trade school. And yes, I grew up a homeless, poor, inner-city kid, but my circumstance didn't make me afraid. If anything, it made me fearless, for I literally had nothing to lose.

"Then it is agreed," he said, reluctantly. "Class, please pull out your English textbooks and turn to page one ninety-two, the section about Winston Churchill. I remember when I first learned about Churchill in high school. I remember that day because that same morning I had broken my glasses. . . ."

He still hovered over us. He still hovered over me. His beady eyes glared at me through his frames as if to say, "You may have won the battle, but not the war." But why did it have to be a battle? Why did he remain so reluctant to acknowledge the fact he might have to tweak his teaching structure if student learning concerned him so much? If student learning even really concerned him—not just a paycheck. I heard university professors were required to have their students submit teacher and course evaluations, anyway. It made sense; it allowed them the opportunity to improve as instructors.

I wasn't trying to fight, only enlighten. Teaching's his job, and I comprehended his occupation, but he needed to understand that school was my life. I didn't go home and rinse my troubles down the shower drain. Most times there had been no home, no shower drain. I couldn't just allow my intellect to waste away in his system because if anyone checked, they would not see his flawed system, they would only see bad grades and those bad grades would define me as a person. Maybe I was wrong? Maybe as a student, challenging English to give me a better education had been out of line. Or, maybe I was right. Maybe as a student, I had the right to demand a better education.

I turned to page one ninety-two and began reading the short autobiography of Winston Churchill and the World War English forgot to mention. I then began reading his speech, "Blood, Sweat, and Tears." Pooh and I read ahead silently amongst ourselves and began answering the questions following the excerpt. English always assigned mostly all of the questions so we didn't need any guidance on how to begin. There were about twenty-one questions and they were all short-answer. I reached question twelve when English said, "Please stop and put your government work away. Please open your math textbooks to page sixty-three."

Everyone ruffled through their work, filing it away, and then pulled out their tattered math book. I didn't switch subjects and neither did my sister. I wrote down the math textbook page number and all corresponding assignments and continued doing my government work. Halfway through English's designated math time, I switched to the math assignments and went over the material, sometimes raising my hand for clarification on certain points; which he hesitantly provided.

When English switched to history, I stayed in math and continued that trend throughout the rest of the day. During the last fifteen minutes of the day designated for study time, I finished up the remainder of my science work with about ten minutes to spare. My sister finished about five minutes after I did. We stapled our pages together and turned them into Cherish. I sat back down and laid my head on the desk to take a quick nap before school let out. English never took his eyes off me. He watched as I stood and stapled my paper, he watched as I smiled while handing my work into Cherish. He sat with his chin over his folded hands perched atop of his desk. I could almost feel laser beams shooting from his eyes burning through the side of my face.

I could almost read his mind. He rendered the day as an anomaly and I couldn't possibly maintain the progress long term. He thought he would get the satisfaction of putting me in my place. He could almost read my mind, as well. He knew I believed in my newly-created system. He wanted me to fail, to send a message to anyone else who dared question his supremacy. He knew I welcomed the challenge. Pooh and I laid with our heads curled up in our arms as we waited for class to end. I could still feel English staring at me. I stared him square in his eyes and raised my hand.

"Yes?" He raised his right eyebrow.

"Can I go to the bathroom?"

One week later, I stood in line at lunch. The younger grades ate right before us, but toward the end of the meal period, we were all outside together. The small, outside courtyard in front of the school came equipped with a chalked hopscotch and two lunch table benches. The area also served as the cafeteria, which explained the table benches. On the right side was a miniature "kitchen" where the cafeteria workers served our food. They said the tiny space used to be the restaurant, which may have been true, but only led me to believe tales of the restaurant's grandeur may have been delusional.

I stood adjacent to the kitchen, complacent in the food line. They said the former restaurant had been comprised of Mexican cuisines, which led to great school lunches for us students. I wish I had come then because the food being slopped on my tray reminded me of bad shelter food. All of it, bland. No matter what I ate: bean and cheese burrito, "chicken" patty, small semispherical cheeseburgers, it all tasted the same.

The lunch people served the chicken patty. The breaded patty seemed lighter than I thought it should have. The dry meat, although still partially frozen, somehow appeared a little burnt. I hastily consumed it, along with the thick, seasonless potato wedges, and went back trying to get seconds. The food didn't look appetizing, but I became beyond used to it. I didn't eat anything for the taste, just to stay full.

Lunch concluded and instead of returning to English's classroom, I wandered to the academic counselor's office. At the Monarch school, there were two counselor types of people we had to talk to. The first, of course, was the academic counselor, Mr. Robertson, and the second, the therapist, Ms. Ryan, Mr. Robertson's ex-wife. I liked Ms. Ryan. She's a sweet lady and she used expressive arts as therapy sometimes. She helped issue everyone toiletries and such with Ms. Jennifer. Mr. Robertson, on the other hand, wasn't my favorite person in the world.

I entered his cramped office and sat in the chair in front of his desk. In the portrait placed on top of his desk stood an energetic, clean-shaven young man with a big smile and styled hair. His vibrant brown eyes even smiled and he exerted this confidence about him. A far cry from the man sitting in front of me. The man in front of me had his hair hanging loosely off his head. His mustache and beard had grown in so thick he resembled a wolf man. His once vibrant eyes had lost their luster and he stared at me uninterested, although his smile tried to convince me otherwise.

"Good afternoon, Michael."

"Good afternoon, Mr. Robertson."

"How's your day going?"

"It's all right, can't complain. Well I can, but I don't see the point."

"Same here. Sometimes you have to take in the good with the bad."

"Yeah. . . ."

"I was going over your transcripts and I was wondering what your plan is after you graduate. You're a senior right?"

"I'm a junior."

"Your sister's a senior?"

"Yes."

"Right, right." He scribbled in his notepad. "Still, it's never too late to start planning for your future."

"Yeah, I agree."

"It seems here that you've been to a few different high schools, and unfortunately every credit doesn't always transfer over from school to school. For example, a lot of your credits from your last high school didn't transfer here or they aren't part of our curriculum. This has placed you a little behind on course credits needed for graduation. It's very important for you to catch up."

"Catch up? I was caught up until I switched here."

"And now you need to catch up."

"Doesn't this school help me quickly make up credits?"

"Yes, it does." He leaned back in his seat.

"Then I'll catch up." I reclined in mine.

"You'll need to hurry up if you want to graduate this year."

"I have another year left."

"Not necessarily. You can graduate ahead of time if you work hard enough. We actually urge you to."

"Why?"

"Excuse me?"

"Why do you want me to graduate early? For what?"

"So you can get out there in the real world and start earning some real money. Maybe even move beyond your circumstances. You have real opportunities, exciting opportunities, eagerly waiting for you. With your grades and work ethic, you wouldn't have any problem getting into the military, or maybe even construction. Your future is bright and the sooner you access it, the better."

"That doesn't seem too bright." I scratched my head in disapproval.

"What do you mean?"

"Why can't I be a lawyer, or a doctor? A politician? I like business, why not a CEO?"

"Michael, it is very important for us as human beings to set realistic goals for ourselves."

"Those sound realistic. People become CEOs all the time."

"It's an unrealistic goal . . . for you . . . for students in your position. Don't get me wrong; I think setting the bar high is great. I never want students to limit their options, but you're looking in the wrong direction. I think that's because of where you are in life; it would be wise to first stabilize before venturing into other endeavors. Join the military; it's a stable check . . . if you can pass the ASVAB. Or construction, you're young and strong, now is the time."

"Is that what you tell Shannon? To join construction?"

Mr. Robertson narrowed his eyes. "Shannon is a little different."

"Oh, yeah?" I leaned forward. "How so?"

"For one, she's not on probation."

I narrowed my eyes at him. I never told them I was on probation.

"See, we've helped mold Shannon into an ideal student, a great candidate for secondary learning institutions. Her grade point average is through the roof, so is her citizenship, and because of our guidance, she is set to go on and do wonderful things. You didn't have our help to prepare you to be the best candidate for higher education possibilities."

"My GPA is pretty high. I process information quickly."

"Yes, you see, but Shannon's naturally smart as well, but she wouldn't be where she is without our guidance. It takes more than being smarter than your underachieving peers, it's a lifetime of preparation."

"You're saying I'm too dumb to go to college?"

"Not dumb, you're very intellectual. More like unfit. Like I said, it is very unrealistic, highly unlikely. Shannon is an anomaly and even then, her pickings are slim. If she, with all our help, can only hope for so much, other students must find more feasible opportunities."

"I've done fine on my own without your help. What if I don't think I need your help? It doesn't seem like you're helping that much anyway."

"I don't mean to discourage, but there are some factors you must take into account."

"Like what?"

"Well, for starters, how would you pay for college? And even with financial aid, you have to first get in. And to be frank, no university like Harvard, Berkeley, UCLA, Columbia or even SDSU is lining up to take in homeless kids when they have students applying from schools in La Jolla or Torrey Pines who don't require financial aid, who have GPAs of 4.5, and who have been prepared to go to college for their entire academic careers. It's a part of their culture . . . *their* culture. I applaud your efforts on wanting to go to college or enhancing your education. The best I'd say to shoot for is a community college, but you'll more than likely just be wasting two years there before going to the military anyway. Hardly anyone ever transfers, especially inner-city students. It's a good thought, but it's not for your type of student."

I sat back in my seat watching Mr. Robertson scratch his wolf-like beard. His eyes fell upon me, uninterested in my entire being. I wasn't sure I wanted to go to college, I didn't even comprehend much about college, but the fact Mr. Robertson told me as honest as he could it wasn't for me angered me. I never met anyone who had ever gone to college or talked about it. But if I wanted to go, why couldn't I? Who was Mr. Robertson, or anyone, to tell me I couldn't go?

"Now the military has wonderful options: Army, Marines, Navy," continued Mr. Robertson.

"What about the Air Force?"

"The other three might be a lot more feasible. They don't just let anyone in the Air Force, you have to score real high on the aptitude test."

"No, I don't think I want to go to the military. For what? To end up like the homeless veterans? I'll be right back where I started. And why do you seem so against me going to college? Aren't you supposed to be telling me I can be all I can be? Aren't you supposed to tell me to shoot for the moon, and if I miss I'll land among the stars or something?"

"It sounds ideal, but you have to be practical." Mr. Robertson leaned in toward me. "I don't personally have a problem with trying to get you to college. It's extra effort on my part, but I mainly don't want to waste viable resources on something that will more than likely fall through."

"What do you mean, 'fall through'?"

"First, you have to get accepted and you're a junior who has never taken the SAT, the SAT practice test, or even any prep courses. And then *if* you get accepted, getting to college is only half of it, then you have to actually graduate, which is another thing altogether. Your sister has better odds of getting accepted than you—than male students in your position. I could tell you to shoot for the moon, but the truth is if you miss, you don't land among the stars, you come crashing down to the ground and you land with a bang."

"Why not at least try? I mean, what do I have to lose?"

"Your life. You could lose your life. Say you succeed and everything is great. No problem. But say you fail, statistics show that you're more at risk for gangs, drugs, crime, and in a state of desperation and succumb to social pressures. I don't want you to get your hopes up and then when reality sets in, you turn to drugs or crime and end up incarcerated . . . again."

"So that's my only reality? If I don't join the military or construction, I'm fated for drugs, crime, and death?"

"You have a single-parent household right? You're with your mother?"

"Yeah and yeah."

"Where's your father?"

"In prison."

"Exactly. This isn't my opinion, these are statistics, facts. This is the grim reality in which we all are forced to live in."

"Well, I don't like that reality."

"I don't like it either, but what can you do?"

"I can change it."

"How?"

"I'm not sure, yet. But I'm not going to let you or anybody else tell me what I can and can't do. If I come crashing down, let me come crashing down, but at least I reached for the moon. That at least I dreamed of being among the stars."

"Do you think you're Liz Murray?"

"No, but she beat the odds. I see that and think why can't I beat the odds?"

"When you look in the mirror do you see a homeless white girl or a homeless black boy? And you've been homeless far longer than her. You think you're going to Harvard? I wouldn't lie to you. I've seen so many students sit in that same seat, with ambition, until real life slams into them. You mean well. This, you, your life is just unfortunate. It sounds poetic, but dreaming like that can leave you homeless on the street."

"I'm already homeless on the street."

Mr. Robertson frowned and glanced at the time on his thin wristwatch. "I think that's all the time we have today."

The clock on the wall read we still had fifteen minutes left. "Yeah, I think it is."

"Thanks for coming and meeting with me. We'll inform Mr. English once we've set up your next appointment."

"Can't wait." I stood.

The much taller and huskier Mr. Robertson stood as well. "And I've heard you've had some minor quarrels with Mr. English. I heard you don't want to follow his lesson plans."

"I don't like his lessons plans. His class structure is setting us up to fail and it's like nobody else can see that."

"This may be so, but he spends valuable time setting up his lectures, and when you don't listen, you influence other students not to listen." He reached out to shake my hand. "I need you to start following Mr. English's lesson structure and keep up with his pacing."

"Did you hear me? It's making everyone fail."

"Did you hear me?" He still had his hand sticking out. "Start following his lesson structure immediately."

I shook his hand with my own and he squeezed it as hard as he could. I returned the gripping gesture empowering my confidence as his grip lessened. "Try and make me."

Mid-November, I sat at my desk reviewing my graded essay during the last fifteen minutes of class. English made it a point to grade it himself. My lesson structure seemed to be working quite fine, so fine he wanted to assign me extra work because I began finishing earlier and earlier, but I told him I had no interest in extra credit. The last few days had been a little rough. The school staff had all been a little meaner to me and my sister. English didn't let us use the bathroom in class, we were held up to eat lunch last, and everyone including the principal had an attitude with us.

Relations had worsened six days before when school donors came by for a site visit. Before they came, the principal prepped the class and told us to tell the donors how great we thought the school to be, how much staff cared about our education, and to show extreme gratitude. My sister told her if she asked, she wasn't going to lie. The school wasn't great at all and it didn't seem like anyone cared about anybody other than Shannon. I told the principal I wouldn't lie, as well. I told her I would tell donors they gave us toiletries. I had more than enough small tubes of toothpaste. But if they asked me about the curriculum, staff, or the environment, I would be forced to tell the truth; and her face tensed up.

Needless to say, we didn't get to meet the donors. Shannon did though, along with anyone else who willed to participate. I couldn't force myself to lie for the school's benefit and my own dissatisfaction. Let Shannon tell them, she wouldn't be lying. The school had been great to her. But after then, we were sort of blacklisted within the school.

Before English even handed me back my paper, I could see the red correction lines marked through it. The biggest "C –" I'd ever seen in my life sat perched in the top right corner. I had a hard time hiding my facial expression, so he knew I became instantly dissatisfied, to his pleasure. He had handed my paper back first and, as he sat down, asked if I in particular had any questions. He didn't ask if the class had questions, so I knew he tried to single me out.

"Can you re-grade my paper? I'm going through it right now and Cherish did the worst job possible. Like, this is bad."

Cherish glanced at me, knowing full well we all knew who graded my paper. No one explicitly specified who graded the papers, usually the task was split between English and Cherish, but I saw English reach into Cherish's pile and grab my paper; just as he saw me purposefully place it in her grading box.

"Actually, it was me who corrected your essay."

"Really?" I said. "Well, we have to talk about this after class."

"Come on over, let's chat right now. Bring your paper."

I zoomed over to his desk and laid down my paper. I wrote about the bombings Germany did on London and how Winston Churchill managed to keep his nation for the most part calm and collected and I compared him with some of the US presidents who led with grace in the time of war or who had seen war.

"Like that right there," I said. "You disagreed with me."

"I think that that is a preposterous, pompous, peculiar statement to make about anyone."

"Yeah, but you can't dock me off points just because you disagreed with me. You see that quote? That's my support and how I analyzed it."

"And I completely disagree with it."

"Which is fine, but it's my opinion. We're supposed to provide an argument, a thesis, and support it right? That's what I did. You're not supposed to grade it based off of whether you agree or not."

"Plus, that's not even the topic I wanted you to address in your essay."

"What do you mean it's not the topic? You said write about Winston Churchill and I wrote about Winston Churchill."

"I wanted you to write about his pre-prime minister endeavors."

"You wanted only *me* to write about it or the class to write about it? And how was I supposed to know? I can't read your mind. Next time give me a prompt."

"Mr. English, you told me that it could be about anything as long as it was about Winston Churchill," said Brandon. I had grown to like Brandon and Daniel. They were for the most part joking around all the time, but they made me laugh. Maybe they weren't actually funny, but the fact they could get under English's skin provided me with great amusement. The class bell rang and English dismissed the class without acknowledging Brandon's comment. Pooh didn't get out of her seat. She silently watched us. Cherish, who had originally stood, sat back down when she saw my sister didn't move.

"Class is dismissed," said English to my sister.

"I'm waiting for my brother."

"You can wait for him outside."

Pooh folded her arms and reclined in her seat, stagnant. I gave her a head nod, telling her I could handle English, and she reluctantly left followed by Cherish.

"And another example," continued Mr. English. "You clearly plagiarized."

"Plagiarized? I've never plagiarized a day in my life!"

"You wrote 'henceforth.'"

"So?"

"Use it in a sentence."

"The lunch here is nasty. Henceforth, I'm not going to eat it. What about it?"

"Well, you don't use it in your everyday vernacular, so clearly this comes from an outside source."

"Wait, what? Are you serious? You're saying I'm supposed to be too *dumb* to use the word 'henceforth,' so the only explanation is plagiarism?"

"I didn't say you were dumb—"

"I thought you're not supposed to write academic essays in colloquial vernacular anyway."

"You're not."

"And because I didn't, you say I plagiarized? Oh yeah, I'm supposed to be too stupid to write a paper, is that it?"

"You also have a lot of spelling and grammatical errors."

"Maybe a few but definitely not a lot. No way a C– worth of errors. I'd have to insist that you re-grade this."

"No."

"No? What do you mean no?"

"I graded your work. If you would like a better grade, put forth more effort. Maybe pay attention to my lectures in class."

"Oh, so because I don't pay attention to your meaningless monologues—"

"Lectures!"

"—That only take up class time, you give me a C–?"

"Some students failed completely. The C– is one of the higher grades behind—"

"Whose? Shannon's? Shannon wasn't in class all week. I'm in class, I do the work. You don't have to like me, just grade me fair."

"Do you have any more questions about the essay?"

"Yeah, what *online* school graduated the dumb ass who graded it?"

"That is enough! You are not going to disrespect me inside my classroom! I will not tolerate any more of your blatant disrespect!"

The principal came running inside of the classroom ready to attack me. "What is the problem, Nicholas?"

"I will not have a student curse at me in my own classroom!"

"You cursed at your teacher? That is unacceptable!"

"I didn't mean to. My paper, he—"

"Under no circumstances will cursing be tolerated! You are to apologize at once and you will be disciplined."

"Apologize? Disciplined? You didn't even see what happened? Aren't you supposed to listen to both sides?"

"You see, he is rude and blatantly disrespectful," English said. "He doesn't understand his place."

"Understand this, Michael. You and your sister need to start showing some gratitude and appreciation to this school as well as to every single member of our staff! Do you think you can just come in, disobey our rules and class structure, even worse create your own rules and class structure, and not speak to the donors who fund our jobs?" the principal said.

"Who said anything about donors? I'm talking about my ess—"

"You need to hush up, stop complaining, and follow my class rules and structure," interjected English.

"I do follow the class rules. What are you—yeah, see there was nothing wrong with my essay; it was never about my essay. You don't like I defied you and I was right."

"It's not about being right or wrong," the principal said, "It's about respect. You cursed at your teacher unprovoked and until you can get some respect you will be suspended at once."

"You can't suspend me."

"I can, I just did, and you will not be allowed to return unless your mother comes with you and sets up a meeting for you, her, and Nicholas to sit down."

"She can't. She works security. She needs every hour she can get. We need to save money. You know where we live."

"You should have thought of where you lived beforehand. You are not to return without her. If you do not return, we will fail you. Do you understand me? Those donors give us money. Now apologize at once!"

"Apologize? I'm not apologizing for shit."

"Michael Gaulden!"

"Mrs. Sanchez!" Pooh said, marching inside of the classroom.

"You were instructed to wait outside of my classroom," English said.

"So y'all can gang up on my little brother? It's two of us now. Try it now."

"Watch your step," the principal said. My sister knew the principal a little better than I did. She's a senior, and besides Shannon, the only other one they saw some potential in. They had begun to try and place my sister on a mini-pedestal as well since she's statistically destined as the next likely to succeed. My sister told me they were going to try and get her into a small college under the Guardian Scholars program, a program designed to get foster kids into college, even though it wasn't for homeless kids.

Pooh's refusal to speak to the donors slapped the principal in her face. How dare she refuse when they tried to offer her special privilege? But my sister understood how they viewed the rest of us. She told me about conversations she's had with the principal and how she didn't believe in anyone else. The principal didn't believe in my sister until Mr. Robertson finally thoroughly went through her transcripts and realized she's indeed intellectually gifted. My sister especially didn't like the fact they had no belief in me, her brother, even though my transcripts matched hers. The principal had started telling donors my sister did so well because of the school, assuming my sister would play along. People shouldn't assume. Everyone's not a liar.

I snatched my essay off English's table, grabbed my backpack, and headed toward the door.

"You have not been dismissed!" We stormed out of the classroom.

I stepped silently behind my mom as we approached the school. My sister went back to the shelter to wait for us because she wasn't feeling well. My mom's demeanor frightened me a little. She didn't speak too much and had frustration resting on her eyebrow. We found ourselves in December. It took her two weeks of asking and shift swapping to be able to call off work, and each day of work she missed reflected a drastic dip in her wages. During our last month in the shelter, we really couldn't afford for her to miss work in order to be there with me. Being homeless was expensive. Saving money is hard when you are homeless. You constantly have to buy things to adjust to new situations and places with new sets of rules and regulations, which don't accommodate you. Amidst it all, people somehow expect you to move right into a house as soon as you leave a shelter. My mom really wanted to be at work. She knew she had to be at work, but she sat there with me.

We stepped through the small school entrance and straight into English's class. School had dismissed an hour ago and he had already been informed we were coming. He had set up a student table with two chairs behind it for me and my mom, and one in front for himself. He sat with his complacent arrogance emitting from his face. His hands were folded and he tried to appear as serious as possible.

"Mr. Gaulden, Ms. King, please take a seat." He tried to display a sense of authority.

I laughed. "I'll stand."

"Take a seat." My mom sat. Without any hesitation, I quickly dropped into my chair.

Usually, she was a happy person, but she's not to be messed with. The tone in her voice told me something's wrong with her; something else had upset her. It must've been something with work, she probably had been written up for having to force a last-minute shift swap for me to continue school. She had mentioned something about her supervisors telling her no one could cover her shifts, but she couldn't leave me out of school, which possibly forced the supervisor to work her position. Most supervisors didn't want to work. When her voice sounded low and direct as it just did, I had learned a wise son quickly obeys her orders.

"This meeting has been set up so we could discuss your son's recent misbehavior in class," began English. I opened my mouth to speak, but my mom shot me a glare killing anything I wanted to utter.

"I've raised my son better. What has he been doing?"

"Michael is a bright kid, but his repudiation to participate in class and follow my class configuration has become too much of a disruptive problem. He blatantly disregards everything we tell him, and even the student counselor, Mr. Robertson, has commented on his refusal to cooperate or listen. All I want to do is help him flourish in my class and his antics are making it very difficult."

"So is he failing?"

"No ma'am, but—"

"So he's not failing? Okay, so how's he not participating and following the structure of your class?"

"He just does his own thing in class regardless of what I've instructed. He does not listen or do the assignments as I assign them. Then he curses at me when he does not get the grade he wants and disrespects the principal. This behavior will not be tolerated under any circumstances here at this school. He has issues with authoritative figures and does not care who he has offended. Now we have created a punishing guide—"

"What's going on, Sun?"

"Mom, he's trying to spin the story, he's only telling one side. He's a liar."

"You see, Ms. King, he's very disresp—"

"What's your side?" my mom said to me.

"I worked within his class system for a while, when I first got here. It doesn't work. Why do you think everybody else is failing? But I'm not failing. Tell her my grades, English, I have all A's now because of *my* system. You're complaining I don't use your system, but you gave me permission to use mine. And it works! You say you want to help me flourish, but now all you want is to help me fail. I'm flourishing on my own. You can't teach. This school isn't a real school, we're not being educated here."

"Well, if your class structure doesn't work, and my son has found a way to pass the class using a different one, which you approved him to do, what is the problem?"

"The problem is you do not pompously waltz in to someone else's classroom and try to start changing things. I've had numerous students, and not one, *not one*, has ever complained about how I teach."

"I don't care what those other students did or didn't do," I said. "I'm talking about me and my life. And you're going to bring up Mr. Robertson like he has any credibility. Mom, they're just trying to make me graduate early so they can ship me off to the military and tell their donors how much they've changed my life. The hell with that, the hell with this school."

"No higher education options?" my mom said.

"I can't really speak on higher education, that's between Michael and the student counselor."

"Well, I can speak on it. They said that, statistically speaking, I wouldn't make it to college, I'll end up dead, in jail, or drugged out somewhere. What kind of shit is that to say to a student?"

"I will not tolerate the use of profanity within the parameters of this school!"

"Yeah, well, I don't care what you will or won't tolerate," I replied, and my mom nudged me again.

"Mr. English," she said, "It seems to me my son only wants to better his education. Why is this a problem? How is this threatening your class hierarchy?"

"Well, because he—"

"Is he disruptive? Does he speak out of turn profusely?"

"No, but—"

"Does he arrive late every day?"

"No."

"Does he turn in his homework?"

"Yes." English began to show signs of frustration.

"Does he complete all assignments?"

"That was the problem," I said. "Me and Pooh are the only ones who do and it's only because we do things our way. And I'm the only one he's mad at. He doesn't care what Pooh or Shannon does. Like, I don't get it, why are you so mad I'm succeeding? You'd rather me fail by doing things your way than me succeed by doing things my way?"

"It is a matter of principle and respect. I am your instructor. It is my profession to teach you, not you teach yourself." He wagged his index finger at me as stern as he could.

"Well, if you taught me, I wouldn't have to teach myself. Do you think I want to come to class and do your job for you? Hell no, but it's my only option."

"That is a lie. It is not your only option."

"You and Mr. Robertson, I don't like you guys. You're supposed to be my teacher and my counselor, but you two are the main ones marginalizing me. What am I supposed to do? Sit by with a smile and let you run me into the ground? I been at the ground and I'm trying to go up."

"Now, Ms. King, the principal and I have created a set of disciplinary actions to deal with Michael's recent misbehavior."

"Disciplinary actions?" I said.

"He will be given a week of after-school detention, he will have to write myself and Principal Sanchez an apology letter, he—"

"Let me stop you right there Mr. English," Mom said. "My son will not be writing anything to anyone."

"Let alone after-school detention," I said. "When the bell rings, I'm gone. You can't stop me from leaving."

My mom nudged me once more and continued speaking, "And he won't be in any detention. My son has done nothing I consider wrong."

"So you are saying it is right to use profanity toward his teachers? Preposterous!"

"Mr. English, today I've missed work. Work that I could not afford to miss because you would not allow my son back in school due to your ego. He is not failing, not disruptive, on time, completes his assignments, yet he is being treated like he is a delinquent. He told me about the essay, he told me why he cursed. He also told me about the donors and the rudeness being shown to him and his sister. I taught my son to stand up for himself, and stand up for his beliefs."

"I know what's best. I have two degrees and I will not take any orders from or become subordinated by some little—"

"Homeless kid?" I said. English sat back in his seat. "Yeah, I'm homeless. . . . But I don't care. This is my life and even if it doesn't mean anything to anyone else, it means something to me. I'm not going to let Robertson tell me I'm incapable of becoming anything. I've read the statistics, screw the statistics, I don't care what they say. And I'm not going to allow you to hinder me in the classroom, either. I'm not an idiot. To you, this is about egos. Well, I don't care about an ego. This is my life, my real life, my academic life and it's an ego game to you. No one's going to take away my future."

"What future?" English adjusted his glasses. His cold words jolted through my body. "This is your future. This school is the best chance you or any of you students have to become something else in life."

My anger already seeped into my tone of voice. "This school can burn in hell for all I care. I can promise you I won't be going to detention, I won't be writing any letters, I won't be doing any of that."

"Those are the conditions in order for you to return here."

"I don't need to return here. I'm better off on my own than to go through this every day. This school was supposed to help me."

"Which is why we provide toiletries and other necessities."

"Which would make the perfect shelter," my mom said. "But this is a school. The kids are still supposed to learn."

"Where else can your children go more suited for your needs? The fact is, you, Michael, need this school. Now you will serve detention, you will write those apology letters, and you will start following me in class, do I make myself clear?"

"As clear as mud," I said.

"You will not be allowed to re-enter these premises otherwise, which will ultimately cause your grades to suffer. I would not want to, but if you leave me without a choice in the matter, I do have the power to fail you, which would be horrendous for your junior year. I am fully backed by the principal and counselor."

"Look into my eyes, English," I said, "Do you see fear?"

English thought he had trapped me in a corner. He knew the shelter told us to enroll there. He also knew no other school provided the hygienic supplies the Monarch School distributed. However, my mom taught me never to surrender on my beliefs. If I surrendered to English, I would forever be locked in a subordination in which I wouldn't be able to escape both physically and academically.

I believed I could become more than what their statistics believed I could. I also knew, outside of my mom and sister, no one else believed I could beat the statistics. But there comes a time where you have to follow your heart, where you have to make your own decisions to better yourself, even if everyone else calls you crazy. I knew to Mr. Robertson and English, I sounded crazy, naïve . . . a little homeless boy trying to dream big. I was being overlooked. I knew there were other non-homeless students in better schools who were given an opportunity. Wanting the same opportunity shouldn't be a crime. How could they expect me to look around at my life and just accept it, and just roll over and die? Why couldn't I have more? I didn't choose the life I lived. But I could choose to opt out for a better life for myself since I was the only one who had to live it.

"What do you want to do, Sun?" my mom asked. I stared at English, who sat with his arms crossed, assuming he had already won. He knew I didn't have any other options. He believed without them, my future would end up where my past started. He thought he had me cornered on top of a cliff staring down at the drugs and poverty beneath.

"Withdraw me." I leapt off the cliff hoping I would hit water instead of all those rocks I saw. "I'll go somewhere else."

19. The Inner City

TWO MONTHS LATER, IN EARLY FEBRUARY, MY MOM called me and told me she wanted to meet up at the Twelfth and Imperial transit station. My friend, Jason, had given me a prepaid cell phone and I bought minutes whenever I could, which hadn't been too often. If I made five dollars panhandling, I would buy five minutes' worth of time. Luckily, I had made twenty dollars panhandling and used half to buy ten minutes. Of course, I couldn't afford the cell phone, it spent most it's time out of service, but it was for aesthetic purposes. It made me seem a hell of a lot cooler. From the transit station, we were to meet up and find somewhere to sleep. Our time at the shelter would be over at the end of December. However, according to our file we were considered an extreme circumstance and they let us stay until January. But now, we were back in the car nonetheless.

With my mother at work and my sister at school, I had time to kill. I visited some friends of mine down on Thirty-Third Street and Oceanview Boulevard and we hung out outside, passing time. Too much time had suddenly passed and I rushed toward the Thirty-Second and Commercial trolley station, the closest to me. I saw the trolley coming, slowing in order to pull into the station. I didn't want my mom to be stuck waiting for me so I ran for it.

As I ran, I suddenly had this bad feeling I should miss the trolley, but I had to meet my mother so we could find somewhere to park and sleep. I raced toward the trolley station at full speed and managed to catch the tail cart of the trolley. The doors opened up and I stepped inside, breathing heavily and glad I made it. I abruptly stopped dead in my tracks as the doors closed behind me. Standing in front of me were five older black men with a permanent scowl stamped on their faces, with bad intentions emitting from their tensed up brows. I briefly glanced at them and then quickly tried to make my way toward the other direction, but the tallest one cut me off. I took a step back.

"Where you from, cuz?" he asked.

"I don't gang bang," I said, but I knew it didn't matter. They had already made up their minds about me. I had learned growing up in Southeast San Diego sometimes people were going to not like you without a reason, as in most hoods. Being homeless, I'd been exposed to a lot of things. When my mom worked, and I had nowhere to go, I ended up around other people who didn't have anywhere to go and who were angry about it. I had always been a good kid at heart, I had just always been forced into a lot of unfortunate situations. I lived the typical story of young men growing up in the inner city.

"You don't bang? How you don't bang with that green shirt?"

They were Crips and green notably the color of the Washington Park Blood faction there in the Southeast. I noticed my shirt and shook my head. Even though it's my first favorite color, I didn't realize it had been green until he had said something. I just knew it had been my last clean shirt. But telling them any of my plight wouldn't help me at all, it would have made things worse.

"I'm just wearing a shirt. I don't bang."

He glared at me but he didn't say anything as the trolley pulled off and I stepped past him to find a seat. The crowded trolley had only one seat available, a few seats from them, and it faced them. I took the seat and stared out the window. The guy who first approached me watched me the entire time as I sat and he marched toward me.

"Where you from? Whatchu lying fo', cuz?"

His eyes were fixated on me. His four friends laced up their Chuck Taylor shoes and tightened their belts. I wasn't scared. I'd been in fights before. He's by far bigger than me but one person is a fair fight. However, two people is jumping someone. No one should ever fight three people, and there had been five of them altogether.

"I'm not lying. I don't bang."

One of the other four rushed past me. Another stood beside the first guy. The second guy who passed me now paced back and forth. All three of them were standing up around me as I sat entrapped by the seat. The other two kept inching closer and closer. I peered out the window as they all glared at me. I sat defenseless, a real bad position. If my life turned into a movie, I could almost hear the sad song playing in the background just as a catastrophe happened. Only I had no song, it wasn't a movie and I was in real danger.

The two girls sitting next to me were nervous. The younger Latino boy sitting across from me emitted remorse. He had a bruise under his right eye and he silently sympathized knowing the exact same thing I knew. I didn't blame those boys. I didn't excuse them, but I didn't blame them. They had nothing personal against me. I understood their minds were entrapped in the savage cycle of impoverishment. A cycle I could see beyond, but a cycle I hadn't escaped from yet.

Although mentally above it, physically the inner city still submersed me and subjected me to it. I should have stood and ran to the other end of the trolley, but I wouldn't have made it. If I tried to stand up quickly, I would be immediately assaulted. I just had to sit and wait for it. I searched for somewhere to escape as they all crowded around me ensuring I had no exit. Damn.

Suddenly, a haymaker abruptly hit on my right cheekbone and, as my head swiveled from the force, another haymaker punched my left cheekbone and slumped me over as they all rushed on top of me like a pack of savage wolves. The girls next to me started shrieking as my face absorbed blow after blow getting pummeled into the seat. I started wildly swinging my arms, kicking my feet trying to get them off of me. I landed blow after blow, but there was too many of them for me to impact any significant damage.

They climbed over me, pushing the boy across from me out of the way, madly swinging at me. The boy across from me scrambled away from his seat and they knocked me onto the floor. I curled up in the fetal position to shield myself. I could not move under their weight. Too many of them surrounded me. I had nowhere to go. Feet stomped on my rib cage as someone grabbed my arms, prying them apart and exposing my face. My left eyesight went black from a punch and then came back in to focus. My eyesight went out and back once more and I twisted and jerked my body trying to break free.

Fist and feet came flying toward me in every direction. My nose took one punch too many and it started running with blood like a faucet. My eyes watered as the soles of their shoes scraped against the side of my head, banging it into the trolley floor like a drum. They swung their arms and stomped their feet, dancing to the sound of their rhythm. It must have sounded so beautiful to their ears.

Blood spilled everywhere, my blood. They yelled, cursing at me, screaming fuck a gang I wasn't even from. Although bloody and beat, they didn't stop. They lived for brutality, the senseless violence. The rush made their lives feel meaningful. I felt more kicks to my ribs and the side of my head. Never-ending blows obliterated my body. I broke my arms free and used them to shield my face once more. Two hands gripped each of my arms and yanked them from protecting my face. I coughed up blood as my head jerked back from the force behind someone's foot, and then—nothing.

I awoke with a pounding headache. I had a trolley cop under my left arm and another cop under my right as they dragged me away from my blood-drenched seat. In my hands were a pile of bloody tissue papers. I couldn't feel my face but my ribs felt like they had been cracked. Everyone on the trolley watched in horror as they dragged me toward the door. A few young children were crying and some women held their hands over their mouths. My blood-soaked green shirt stuck to my flesh and blood-splattered all over my blue denim jeans. The trolley cops dragged me off and sat me down on a bench at the Twenty-Fifth and Commercial trolley station. One stop before the Twelfth and Imperial transit, and one stop after the Thirty-Second and Commercial station.

Police officers surrounded me with drawn weapons pointed at my head. I sat, blinking my eyes, discombobulated. My hands sat raised above my head praying to God I didn't get shot. The guns had me motionless. An officer waved off the trolley and it drove away. The other officers holstered their weapons and began to disperse. Another officer stood right in front of me, blankly staring as he handed me more tissues.

"What's your name?" he asked.

I thought about his question, but I had a hard time processing information. Thick gray clouds drifted through my head. I closed my eyes trying to sort through the bleak fog clouding my mind. I searched for an answer, but I couldn't find one. "I—I can't remember," I said. My mind wasn't working right. My vision looked off and I couldn't quite pinpoint what exactly happened yet.

"Why'd they hit you?"

"Hit me? They hit me?"

"What do they call you?"

I thought hard. I couldn't make sense of what he talked about. Information had just stopped processing. "Who's 'they'?"

"Are you on probation or parole?"

"I . . . shouldn't be."

Another officer strolled up and asked me what happened.

"It's gang related," the officer who questioned me said.

"I'm not in a gang." They kept talking like I didn't speak.

"He's being evasive and uncooperative," the officer continued.

The cheap blue flip prepaid cell phone in my pocket rang and the caller ID said "Mom." I hesitantly answered the phone. "Mom?"

"Boy, where are you at?"

"I'm not sure."

"You're not sure? Why do you sound like that? What's wrong?"

"You're my mom?"

"Sun, its mama, what's wrong with you? Michael? Who's around you?"

"These men. They said I got hit."

"You got hit? What the hell do they mean you got hit? Put one of them on the phone." I held the phone out to the officer.

"Who's that?"

"It's my mom?" I said, unsure.

He took the phone and I could hear the lady going off on the other side of the line. He gave her our location and hung up, handing me back the phone. The two officers hovered around me talking to each other. After a few minutes, a car door slammed.

"Sun!" A woman ran over to me. "Oh my God!" she said upon seeing me. She turned to the officers, "Where's the paramedics?"

"Is this your son?"

"Yes, this is my son! Where's the paramedics?"

"He doesn't need the paramedics."

"That's not your decision to make. I work security and understand it is protocol for you to call the paramedics."

"What's his name?"

"His name is Michael."

"He is being evasive and wouldn't tell us his name. It's a part of the street code. He doesn't want to 'snitch.' He's fine. He's probably sustained worse injuries playing football."

"You've never met my son before! He doesn't even play football. Do you see his face? Does he appear to be fine to you? He probably can't remember his name, they did my baby so bad. Where are they?"

"They got off right here and ran away."

"You didn't go after them? Why is my baby sitting here like this and you just let them *get away?*" My mom emotionally waved her arms around.

"Ma'am, we had got a phone call saying someone had been shot so we made sure no one was shot."

"There was so much blood somebody thought he was shot? And you didn't call the paramedics!"

"He doesn't need them, I'm sure he's fine. It was a gang-related incident. He just didn't have any of his homies with him."

"My son isn't in a gang! I'll take him to the hospital myself!" Infuriated at the officer, my mother grabbed me and brought me to the car. I sat in the passenger seat and she sped off crying and periodically glancing over at me.

"I'm so sorry they did you like that, Sun. What happened?"

The fog in my head became thicker than ever. "I'm not really sure. I can't recall. It doesn't feel too bad though."

She glanced back at me. "You can't see your face. Can you recognize me now? You didn't recognize who I was when you saw me."

"I didn't. I don't. . . ."

"I think they gave you a concussion. We're going to the hospital."

We arrived and rushed through the front door of the emergency room of the Vacation Valley Hospital. We stepped to the front desk and the nurse did a double take when she saw me. She eyed my mother suspiciously and said, "What happened?"

"My son got jumped on the trolley."

The nurse eyed me suspiciously as I somberly nodded my head in accordance. We filled out some paper work and sat.

Everyone in the lobby stared at me. Being homeless people stared at me all the time, but those stares were different. A mirror outlined the wall above and I stood to see my reflection. I jumped at the sudden sight of the grotesque image reflecting back at me. I didn't recognize the face I saw. I had swollen up like a balloon with black and blue bruises all over me. Both of my lips sat on my face like they had a bad allergic reaction to fists. Dried blood imprinted under my nose and around my chin. My left eye had closed and I couldn't open it no matter how hard I tried. I lifted up my shirt to see bruises along my abdomen and ribs which reminded me I had been stomped on.

As I sat and waited to be seen, it became harder and harder to open my mouth and speak as my face kept swelling. Now I could feel the pain in my face, it felt like they cracked my skull. My head throbbed as I leaned forward in my seat. They called my name pretty quickly and took me to a room. They hooked me up to an IV and started giving me morphine as they talked to my mom outside my door. I had never taken morphine before, so I wasn't sure how it would affect me. After a few minutes, my body felt warm and numb. Soon, my pain subsided and I could focus my thoughts a little better. I began remembering more and more.

A doctor came into the room and closed the door behind him. He pulled up a chair and made gentle conversation.

"How are you feeling?"

"I can't really feel anything."

"Which is perfectly normal, it's the morphine taking effect. So Michael, before we start doing anything, I need to ask you a few questions about your incident. I need you to answer as honest as possible. Can you be honest with me?"

"Yeah, sure."

"How did this happen to you?"

"I got jumped."

"Do you recognize the guys who assaulted you?"

"Nope."

"Random act of violence?"

"Yeah."

"Does your mother have any type of violent background?"

"My mom? Nope."

"Has she ever beat you before?"

"Hahaha, no my mom didn't do this to me. I really got jumped."

"If she did, would you be afraid to tell us? We can protect you. You're safe here."

"Haha, I'm pretty sure I could beat my mom up. She's a sweetheart to me, though. I really got jumped in a random act of violence. That's how it goes."

"Okay." The doctor stood. "I'll be right back."

He left the room and I rested my head against the hospital pillow. After two hours had passed, my mother finally came into the room and sat next to me.

"How are you feeling?" she asked.

"I'm good. I feel all weird and numb. I remember you now, Mom."

"Oh, my poor baby. Sorry it took me so long to get in here. They thought I did this to you."

"The doctor came in all like, 'Is your mother violent?' and 'You can tell us, we'll keep you safe.' I thought it was funny."

My mom gently traced over the bruises on my face, "This isn't funny."

"How long are we going to be in here? Don't we have to go get Pooh Bear from the Monarch School? She's probably mad because it's taking too long to pick her up."

"They say they're going to take some X-rays of you. I'm not sure how long it will take. Your sister's fine, she called me from the school phone."

The doctor re-entered the room this time accompanied by a few nurses. They wheeled me away to the X-ray machine and began X-raying me. They wheeled me back to the room and told me they would be back once the results came in.

I laid still with my eyes closed. The morphine made me really sleepy. My mother sat beside me still as frightened as when she first saw me bleeding at the trolley station. She took a warm cloth and wiped the dry blood off my face. I could tell the incident had hurt her as much as it had hurt me. To see me in pain broke her heart.

"Knock, knock." The doctor reentered the room holding a folder. He slid some X-ray photos out of it and put them on a fluorescent white board. "How're you feeling?"

"Fine," I said.

"I have your X-rays." He pointed at a photo of my skull. "Needless to say, you have a concussion. This is your face. You see these little dark slits, those are fractures. You can see these three fractures, one on your forehead, one under your left eye and one under your right eye."

"Oh, no." My mom grimaced at the picture.

"Also, you see this dark spot under you're left eye, it is a gas bubble. I also noticed right eye's movement seems to be restricted. We're going to have to refer you to an eye specialist. The fractures should heal over a stretch of time, and the gas bubble should eventually go away, so your only concern will most likely be your right eye. We're going to write you a referral, a prescription for pain meds as well as a few antibiotics. I'm also giving you a doctor's note to keep you out of school for at least a week. You need to recover, which means no sports, no physical activities, and nothing too physical. You'll have to miss PE."

"I'm sure that won't be a problem," I said.

"Great. Because all it takes is an elbow to the face or a bad fall to crack open your face and you're in serious trouble. A nurse will come by with everything you need shortly and you can be on your way. Any questions for me?"

"How long will it take him to heal?"

"It really depends on him. He should heal fine. Like I said, the only thing is his eye. He's going to have to get it checked out. Maybe surgery."

"*Surgery?*" Mom said.

"Possibly, but we'll have to see what the eye specialist has to say. The left eye appears worse because it's swollen shut. However, the right eye, it's not functioning, and rotating properly. Something is hindering its movement."

"Dear, God." My mom teared up.

"The good news is he'll live," the doctor said. "He's one of the lucky ones. Most kids I see coming in here are usually filled with bullets."

"Thanks, doc," I said.

He firmly shook my hand and told me to, "Hang in there" before he exited the room.

"This is crazy." I gently touched my face. I knew I shouldn't have caught the trolley. If only I didn't catch it. Now I suffered the consequences.

I couldn't believe I was laying in a hospital bed. First the Monarch School marginalized me, now an assault. It just wasn't fair.

"This nurse needs to hurry up." My mom stared at the time on her phone. Pooh waited for us. We still needed to go pick her up so we could go find a place to park and sleep.

After my discharge, we met up with my sister who went hysterical once she saw me. She couldn't stop crying, which didn't help my self-esteem. I sat in the cramped cars back seat with a wall of bags and dirty laundry covering the left seat and the middle seat leaving me pressed up against the window. The back of the passenger seat in which my sister sat pressed against my knees. She had as almost as many items up there as I did in the back. My surroundings stiffly locked me in an upright position.

Pain pulsated through my body every time I blinked. I swore I slowly died, probably internal bleeding the doctors somehow missed. I shifted about an inch on my side, which wasn't really on my side, but I told myself otherwise. I closed my eyes and leaned my head against the hard cold window. All I could do was try and get a good night's sleep.

20. Breakdown: Part III

ONE WEEK LATER LANDED US IN MID-FEBRUARY. WE sat at a park bench early Saturday morning. The sun gently warmed our skin as we ate cold turkey sandwiches with no condiments or cheese. I sat on one side of the bench and my mom and Pooh sat on the other. We ate in silence. I hadn't been talking much lately. I hadn't really had much to say. My body felt beat up, face cracked open like a dropped egg. I exhausted my mind preparing to adjust from a specialized school for homeless kids, to a public school. The Monarch School had limited expectations for me, so they pushed me in an obscure direction. However, in my experiences with public education, no one had any expectations for students at all. No one pushed you in any direction.

Most kids I knew were dropping out. I knew I would have to fight the public school system with everything I had if I wanted to come out college ready. If, and only if, living on the streets didn't kill me first. I gently touched my still heavily bruised face. We had Medi-Cal so the medicine the doctor prescribed had me feeling numb like the morphine did. I could tell I still hadn't healed yet because my mom and Pooh tried to over compensate it by forcefully staring at me whenever possible to try and make me feel normal. I tried to overcompensate by not looking at myself so I could forget my reflection. I thought for the first time in a long time, I personally felt ill. Not just my situation, but me, I didn't feel good. Not the sick type of not feeling good. But the sickening type of not feeling good which occurs when you've done all you can do, tried as hard as you can try, and life still beats the crap out of you. As I sat and quietly ate, I could feel my mom watching me. She could tell something saddened me. Her spirit could feel my ambitious fire dimming.

"You'll be all right, Sun." She smiled, showing confidence.

I didn't respond.

"You'll be quite all right."

"Will I?" I stared at my sandwich.

"Yeah, you will," Pooh said.

"Not going like this," I said. "This is what makes people say 'screw it' and start hustling or something."

"You can't start hustling," my mom said. "Or join a gang. You've seen the end result for all hustlers, all gangbangers, ask your father."

"Mom, what am I supposed to do? It's like I can't win! I can't catch a break. Out here, they want to eat me up. If I don't gang bang, I don't have any backup. I'm alone when I'm attacked. These kids out here don't care if I'm homeless, they'll rob me or kill me just as fast as they'll rob or kill the next guy. All I can do is fight back like a cornered cat, but I'm outnumbered by thousands of angry dogs. Here they constantly try to prove how you're a punk. They try to make you seem soft and make you feel like you don't belong in the neighborhood."

"Sun. . . ."

"Then outside the ghetto, people try to make you feel like that is exactly where you belong and they criminalize you for it but marginalize you toward it. And then school, my counselors, my teachers, they don't expect anything of me. They barely want to help me. They don't see anything when they glance at kids like me. They just want to force us into the military. Maybe they're right. Maybe I should just go."

"Sun, I'm sorry those boys did this to you. If I could have had it be me, I would have. And if you decide that you want to go into the military, I will support you. I respect the troops, and of course, you do, too. But I want you to be happy. I want you to follow your aspirations."

"I don't . . . think I can. This is hard. Really hard."

"Sun, I—"

"Like really, really hard. It's not a coincidence no one we've met has ever achieved more. I don't think it's from a lack of trying. America's societal system is designed for us to fail. I'm juggling being a homeless minority in the streets, while also being a homeless minority in mainstream society. It's two completely different worlds. It's a game of what Du Bois called 'double-consciousness,' and I'm losing badly."

"Yes, Sun, but if you don't succeed, if you don't push through, who will? You say America is designed for you to fail. What greater satisfaction then would it be to succeed?"

"Michael, we can't quit," Pooh said. "If you quit now you'd just be proving everyone right. The Monarch School asks me all the time how you're doing. They want to see you fail. You're like a test subject, someone they'll compare other kids to. You want them to say, 'If Michael did it, you can too,' not 'You see what happened to Michael? You better just run along to construction like a good little inner-city kid.' People don't think we can make it at all." She bit into her sandwich, one bite away from finishing it completely.

"I see why. I mean all of this keep moving forward, this keep going, it's for what? I'll probably get killed before I turn eighteen. You see where we are. I hate where we live. Everybody else is sleeping in comfortably on a Saturday morning. We're spending the day at a park bench because the car grew too claustrophobic. We need money fast. I have to get some. We can't keep doing this."

"And how do you expect to get money fast?" Pooh said. "Selling drugs? Or hit the lottery? Or are you going rob some more houses, and end up back in Juvenile Hall? That's the only three options."

"Those options are better than this option. Mom, your feet look like my face. They're so swollen they're about to burst open. I have to do something."

"Those options will land you straight to prison. You are doing something, Sun. More than you know. Everyone is thinking like you, why do you think so many people sell drugs? Why do you think so many people end up dead? To achieve what others have not achieved, you have to be willing to do the things that others can't do. Anybody can sell drugs. Anybody can gangbang and shoot people. Anybody can be homeless, Sun. But not too many people can maintain good grades in school while sleeping in the car. When life gets this bad, anyone can quit. But it takes someone special to keep going, to keep fighting. It takes someone special to not sell drugs, to not gangbang, to not succumb to the social pressures all around. Michael, you are my sun, my star, my pride and joy. You are from the ghetto, but you are not of the ghetto."

"Homelessness, gangs, drugs, violence, these teachers and counselors, how can I win?" I said. "They stomped on my face! No one expects me to win and how could they with all these odds stacked against me? Can't you see my face! How am I supposed to win? We're all destined to lose." A few tear droplets trickled from my right eye burning my flesh as they rolled down my cheek.

"Homelessness, gangs, drugs, violence, you don't win playing that game. It's a game that everyone loses," my mom said.

"Exactly." I lowered my head. "Exactly."

"So play a different game," Pooh said. "School, hard work, use your mind, that's the game we have to play. It's the only game we can win. Other than that, we're doomed. We have it worse than most poor people. But we can cry about it, or we can change it."

"I'm not crying about it."

"Looks like you're crying to me. You're supposed to be Michael Gaulden, my fearless little brother. Are you going to let some worthless hoodlums stop you from reaching your goals?"

"I mean, you can see me just fine. It feels like they already did."

"Yeah, I see you. You're beat up right now, but you'll heal."

"I wish I was Superman."

"No, you're more like, what's the guy with the claws? Wolverine! You're more like Wolverine. You take the bangs and bruises, you get the crap literally beat out of you, but you'll heal and you'll keep coming back and keep fighting. Incidents like these don't stop you, they piss you off. You don't want the Superman mentality, realistically no one is invincible. Being Superman only works until you run into kryptonite. But being like Wolverine will get you through anything."

"You don't even like superheroes." I finished my sandwich.

"I like Wolverine."

"It's just so hard."

"So bring out your claws—make it a little easier."

"What's my claws?"

My mom reached over and tapped the side of her head. "That brain of yours. Fight with your mind."

"I wish there was someone to help guide me, anyone, someone who's been to college, or owns a business, or something. Someone who could show me their trail so I can follow."

"But there's no one, Sun. Just you. You have to be strong and trail blaze now to make it easier for someone else. Everyone wants the easy way out, but someone has to be strong and take the hard way out."

"I'm limited at the Monarch School," my sister said, "But you, you're limitless right now. It's all on you. Is that too much for *the* Michael Gaulden to bear? You seem timid."

"Nobody's scared."

"Oh lord, I think those boys beat the Gaulden out of my poor baby." My mom took the last bite of her sandwich.

"I'm Gaulden all the way."

"Well, stop feeling sorry for yourself and act like a Gaulden," Pooh said.

"That's easy for you to say, but no one is walking in my shoes. Nobody is stomping their shoes all over your face, either, okay. Y'all didn't get stomped on like rats. Y'all don't get what it's like, you don't understand how I feel."

"We didn't get jumped," my mom said, "But every night, we're right there in the car with you. Every night, we eat or don't eat the same food you do. Our clothes are dirty, too, and we're sick of washing ourselves with just wipes. I'm busting my ass every day at this security job, a job I hate, just to keep us alive. I've almost died, had two different surgeries, and your sister had illnesses and surgery so young, pain you can't imagine. And yes, I can see my feet. The doctor said I can't stand on them for more than an hour at a time. One hour, and every day I roam around for eight. They gave me a cane to use like I'm an old lady. We're just as hungry as you, just as tired as you, our bodies have been bruised and beaten just like yours, so no, we're not walking in your shoes, but our burden is just as heavy."

"Like you said before," Pooh said. "Keep moving forward. It's all we can do. We have to keep going until we can climb out of this hole."

"What if we never escape?"

"I don't believe that," my mom said. "Hard work always pays off."

"You've been working hard your whole life, Mom, and it hasn't paid off."

"Oh, but it has. I'm watching my children choose a different route. You're not perfect and I don't expect you to be. But I'm watching my children aspire for greater things out of life than what impoverishment offers. You didn't accept these conditions, you dare to defy them. That is all the payoff I need."

"You want to keep being homeless and living like dogs?" Pooh pointed her index finger at me.

I dropped my head. "No, of course not."

"You want to keep barely eating?"

"No, but—"

"Mom, my brother must like not taking showers and stuff."

"Hell no."

"All the girls can't wait to find them a homeless poor guy to hook up with . . . Oh, wait . . . that's never true."

"Sun." My mom took the last two pieces of bread from the bag, creating herself another sandwich. I watched as she stacked it high with the last of our lunchmeat. We were all still hungry, but she deserved to eat it. She's the only one who could get a job and the only one working. "I honestly believe that you can become anything you want to become. And if you feel like you want to go to college," she placed the sandwich in front of me, "I believe you can do it. I have your back no matter what happens."

I stared at the sandwich. I knew my mom was just as hungry as we were. Just like a true mother, she believed in self-sacrifice for her kids. To sacrifice was a noble gesture, but I didn't agree with it. I picked up the sandwich and split it into three parts and disbursed them among us. They were right, I couldn't quit. Those homeless people I saw on the streets smelling like dumpsters, eating out of garbage cans, most of them were what quitting embodied. A lot of people asked me where my pride came from. I spent my life homeless, poor, wore soiled clothes, barely ate, and honestly, I had no idea. Something within me refused to be degraded.

I knew how the world viewed me, but I didn't need to view myself the same way. I think pride itself kept us going for so long, the refusal to believe we were destined to live homeless. I did want out of homelessness; I had to get out, somehow, someway. I had to get out. I decided to choose something else. The tears I had just shed weren't because I was lost in grief, consumed by defeat and mortification. Those tears were my constrained ambition, leaking through my eyes.

"Mom, you're the first person to say that to me. And . . . I choose to believe you. You've never lied to me. I guess if I've been through all of this, I owe it to myself to at least try, or it'll all be for nothing."

"But if you did make it to college and get a big fancy job, I would like a house."

"Mom, if I get to college, or get a good job, I'll get you two. Pooh can get you the cars and stuff, it's a collective effort. Or maybe she'll get the houses. Whichever's more expensive."

"You're so cheap!" my mom said.

"She's the first one getting her high school diploma, even if it's from a school for homeless kids. She has a head start."

"Cheap, cheap, cheap," Pooh said.

"Hey, whatever, man. So wait, be honest. How bad is my face still?"

"Honestly?" Pooh said.

"Yeah, honestly."

"Every time I see you I want to scream."

"What?"

"Yeah, Sun, they got you pretty bad, boy."

"Hahaha, yeah, I was in the car mirror this morning like *daaaaaannnnggg.*"

"Yeah, the next time you start back-talking me, I'm going to call Tyrone and the gang to keep you in line."

"Man, they caught me while I was sitting down."

"And if you were standing?" Pooh chuckled, enjoying her piece of the sandwich.

"Well, obviously my Wolverine claws would have shot out of my fists. . . ."

21. School for Everyone Else

THREE MONTHS AGO, I HAD LEFT THE MONARCH SCHOOL with prejudice but being a senior, my sister was forced to stay. She only needed a few credits to graduate so she couldn't afford to keep bouncing around schools during her last year. She had told Mr. Robertson she wanted to pursue higher education. They told her about community colleges but Pooh insisted on shooting for San Diego State University and tried to get in under the Guardian Scholars Program, the program designed to admit and aid foster care students. I didn't think it was fair SDSU had a special program for foster kids and not homeless students, but when they said they might accommodate my sister, I didn't mind as much.

Pooh Bear just had to work hard for it. She was currently off doing work and studying trying to complete all of her A-G requirements. She'd been to four different high schools in three different states in the last three and a half years which had caused her to lose some credits. They wanted to make an example out of her and how they transformed a homeless girl to an exemplary student while her brother, who left the school, failed miserably. Mr. Robertson even printed out the SDSU application for her. They were going to take all the credit for her success although she had always been exemplary.

They wanted to proclaim they guided her to SDSU to throw it in our faces. It didn't matter to me, though. I wanted to see if my sister could actually get in to a big-time university like San Diego State. To be honest, I did sound like a boy dreaming when

I talked with Mr. Robertson. To tell the truth, it seemed impossible for kids like us to get into college. From my point of view, such a world seemed unattainable. No one I knew and no one they knew ever attended college or did anything other than go to prison, join the military, or get killed. I needed to find out if it was in fact possible and who else better to show me besides my sister.

March had come. I sat in the middle of biology class with my head laid against my desk, eyes heavily closed shut, in deep sleep. Mr. Bollen woke me up twice already, but I couldn't stay awake. All of the students thought of me as a rebel the way I blatantly slept mid-lecture, but it wasn't on purpose. I hadn't been getting much sleep lately. Police and security guards kept waking us, making us move and re-park the car from place to place. Everywhere we went, someone said we couldn't park there. And we were sleeping on high alert every night. People kept trying to bother us, flicking things at the car, making loud noises just outside of it. We hadn't been getting any peace of mind.

School had been the only time I'd been able to really sleep, which became a clear problem. My teachers didn't like it; none of them did, but especially Mr. Bollen. Most students fell into trouble for sleeping in class and not paying attention. Then when they took their tests, they failed. I, however, aced most of my tests which put the teacher in an awkward position. He couldn't really say anything about my sleep because I kept acing his exams. He had even given me Student of the Month twice even though he really didn't want to. I knew it frustrated Mr. Bollen, he had asked me time and time again not to sleep but I couldn't help it. He took it personal, but I slept in all my classes. And it wasn't just class, I slept at lunch, too. I slept whenever I could.

A classmate nudged me and told me to wake up because Mr. Bollen passed out last week's quiz. I sat up and wiped out my tired eyes yawning.

"You're so rude!" a girl behind me said. I acted like I didn't hear anything.

Mr. Bollen strolled around class handing students their quiz papers face down. He placed mine on my desk without acknowledging me and kept moving. I turned it over and saw 95% circled at the top in red.

"How do you get high scores when you sleep all day in class? You're a cheater!" the girl peeked over my shoulder.

I didn't respond and did my best to tune out her negativity.

Mr. Bollen returned to the front of the class and began going over the quiz. I slowly felt my head uncontrollably lowering toward my desk again as if connected through some sort of magnetic pull. My eyelids felt as if someone tied anchors to the bottom of them. Exhaustion overtook me and I fell fast back asleep.

The class bell woke me up and I hoisted my backpack over my shoulder. Mr. Bollen stared at me as I stepped out of the classroom door, but I didn't return a glance or acknowledge his. I made it to my homeroom class and sat near the back. Mr. Oakley's a little more outspoken than Mr. Bollen. I couldn't just fall asleep because he would turn it into a class scene. I remember one time he smacked a yardstick ruler right next to this one girl's head when she fell asleep in class and made her fall out of her chair. Being on edge, a yardstick smacked by my head wouldn't process well like it did for her. It would have turned into a problem.

Mr. Oakley stood and told us to hand in our essays. I had been dreading turning them in all day. I reached into my backpack and pulled out my five-page essay hand written on lined paper. He patrolled around collecting the essays and stopped when he reached mine.

"What is this trash?" he said.

". . . It's my essay."

"An essay would be typed, doubled spaced, with 12-point font and one-inch margins."

"I . . . ran into some complications."

"Complications? You just didn't do it. Then half-assed it last night and came in here with garbage."

"No, the library's been—"

"I'm not accepting it."

"It's still an essay. I just couldn't type it."

"You're full of shit, Gaulden." He passed me, leaving my essay behind. The entire class stared at me. The "good" students who turned in their essays shook their heads. The ones who didn't silently cheered me on. I leaned back in my chair crossing my arms and waited for the end of class.

After the bell rang, I marched up to Mr. Oakley sitting at his desk and handed him my essay.

"I don't need full credit, I just need some credit. I did the work."

"Why isn't it typed? You have the audacity to slither into my classroom and hand me a handwritten essay on some wrinkled pieces of paper?"

"No. I tried to type it. The computer lab after school is closed for renovation or something. The library's been closing early before school's out and when I was in there this weekend, I could only get an hour on the computer each day and they charge to print."

"And you couldn't have used a laptop or your parent's computer? I see kids like you all the time. You sleep in class, don't pay attention, and turn in half-ass assignments."

I took a deep breath. The essay was worth a lot of points toward my final grade. I couldn't afford to fail. "I'm not doing it on purpose. I'm in between places right now. We don't have computers, we don't have lights, we don't have anything. I wrote that essay outside under a streetlight."

"There are no excuses! It is your responsibility to complete all assignments or your grade will suffer accordingly. Take your paper and please exit my classroom."

I stared at him in disbelief. I grabbed my paper and headed to Physical Education. I could do nothing else besides go to my next class. I had always enjoyed PE. I loved sports. However, being my last class of the day, I tried to avoid as much exercise as possible. If I became sweaty and musty, I couldn't go home and wash it away like everyone else. The sweat and stench would stay with me until I could find a shower; which wasn't too often. Wipes could only do so much.

My PE teacher, Mr. Matthews, would let me jog the track field, throw a football around, or shoot a basketball; real laid-back activities. He knew I was homeless. He understood. He sat me down one day without me telling him anything, and started asking questions. He knew something was off. He's a real good guy. His concern really caught me by surprise. I wished I had more teachers like him, but I didn't. After class, he sat me down and checked up on me again.

"How are you doing?"

"I'm fine."

"How's your mother and sister?"

"They're doing good. My mom's working, my sister's working on graduating high school."

"If you need anything, tell me. There's not much I can do, but I'll do what I can."

"Thanks, Mr. Matthews."

I knew he couldn't really do anything for us, but at least he wanted to help. Mr. Robertson couldn't have cared less so it refreshed me. After school, I went straight to the rendezvous point upon which my sister and I had agreed earlier in the day. Since we were at different schools, we were on two different schedules. I mostly always released first, except for her early day.

As I waited, I pulled out my math book. I had to get my work done before math class the following day. My math teacher, Mrs. Madison, had a much harsher attitude than Mr. Oakley. She had harder homework, math usually was, but it actually wasn't too bad, just tedious. It's just very time consuming. She thought I didn't do her assignments, but her assignments took the longest time to do and when I ran out of daylight, I couldn't finish them. And if I spent too much time on it, it would not leave time to do anything else.

She thought I did the bare minimum just to pass. There wasn't any talking to her, I had tried. I began doing as many questions as possible. My sister snuck up on me and then started doing her homework as well. I paused halfway through my math homework and switched to biology. From biology, I switched to my homeroom readings and skimmed through them. By then, the sun had already begun to set and I stopped reading and switched back to math. I answered as many questions as possible before I had to meet up with my mom.

We packed up and moved to the next rendezvous point and I sat on the curb pulling out the rest of my math homework. The sun faded and the streetlight above us dimly illuminated the pages of my textbook. I sat and did what I could until my mother drove up honking the horn. We piled into the car, picked up our salads, and found a place to park. My mother heard me scribbling and turned around.

"Boy, don't read in the dark, you'll hurt your eyes."

"I have to get this done. Can we repark next to a streetlight again?"

"If you can find a parking spot next to one, sure."

"We barely found this one," Pooh said.

I closed my textbook. I couldn't make out a single number in the pitch-black car. I scratched my head trying to think. Mrs. Madison's homework concerned me so much I didn't finish any other assignments. I could still wake up and do them before class, but I'd rather have partial credit in all my classes than full credit in one and zero in the others. Even with Mr. Oakley's attitude, I should get by in my classes on partial credit. I paused then reached back through the darkness for my mathematics textbook. It's in my best interest to finish the math homework, I could get by on partial credit for my other courses. Math, however, was a completely different subject, a subject which just happened to be my first class the next day.

"Your grade is suffering because of your laziness," Mrs. Madison said after math class.

"I did as much as I could."

"No, you did as much as you wanted to. You are to complete all given assignments."

"I'm trying to, but it's not as easy as you're thinking it is."

"Stop making excuses for yourself. Own up to it. You're not stupid, Michael. You're just lazy. It's not going to be easy. If you study the book and do the assignments, if you pay attention instead of falling asleep in class, if you spend less time on your ass watching television, it'll get easier. You just have to do the work. You're lazy and you just transferred back to school, so you're already behind."

"I do the work. It's just hard because I live in my—"

"You do half the work. You'll get some points for turning it in but your grade is definitely decreasing because of homework and participation."

"Can I have extra credit?"

"Why would I give you extra credit to make up work when you don't try to do your regular work?"

"I do try."

"The lunch bell has rung."

I grabbed my backpack and headed to the school courtyard. I waited in line and grabbed my lunch. I had leaned on free lunch for most of my life to offer meals. I asked for extra juice and left shamelessly. I stashed the extra juices in my backpack. I ate my bean and cheese burrito and stepped into an empty hallway. I slid down against the hallway wall and rested my head against my knees, falling into a quick sleep. Sleeping in the car officially took its toll on my exhausted body. The lunch bell rang and I slowly rose. Time for biology.

I sat up in class. I wanted to fall asleep, but I didn't. Three others were already asleep. Mr. Bollen marched by their desks and abruptly woke them up.

"If you're going to sleep in my class, you better get A's on my tests!" shouted Mr. Bollen. He didn't acknowledge me, but the rest of the class did.

"You never yell at Michael!" a girl whom had been startled said. I didn't mind being singled out. I had bigger problems to worry about. I reclined in my seat and let them debate. Every one waited for me to respond, but I remained silent. I just didn't have the energy and it didn't really matter anyway.

I had been starting to feel really exhausted as of late. I could only imagine how my mother felt. We never had a break. We couldn't relax when we sat in our car. All of our belongings piled inside forced us to constantly sleep sitting up. My body wasn't adapting as well as it used to.

The class bell rang and I sped to my homeroom. I left without acknowledging Mr. Bollen or the girl. I sat in my homeroom class barely able to keep my eyes open. At my rate, I'd never be able to stay awake and do all of my homework. I thought about not doing it at all anymore. It was too stressful to handle.

"Gaulden! Wake up!" Mr. Oakley shouted. "Get out of my classroom. Go fall asleep in the principal's office."

Mr. Oakley had actually suggested a good idea. I didn't argue as I stood and exited the room. I entered the principal's office and waved at the receptionist, Ms. Baker. She's a nice lady who knew of my homelessness too. She helped Mr. Matthews get my bus pass. She waved and I headed to the table and laid my head down.

"Gaulden!" The school counselor, Victoria Garcia, walked up beside me no less than thirty seconds from when I sat. She's a small round woman with pointy glasses. "Why aren't you in class?"

"I got kicked out." I didn't bother to lift my head.

"Mm-hm, come into my office." She strolled to the end of the school office and into her own.

"Yes?" I sat across from her at her desk.

"I'm seeing you waste away, Gaulden. You need to start thinking about the next step."

"I've been thinking about the next step."

"Oh, and what is your next step?" She raised a brow.

"I've been thinking about college."

"Well, great! You'd need to stop getting kicked out of class, but I think you can do it. Unlike most of your class, you're a bright kid, shouldn't have any problem getting into City College or Southwestern."

"No, I'm not talking about a junior college, I'm talking about big boy college."

"A four-year university?"

"Yeah."

"You're kidding?" She had a condescending change in her tone.

"Nope." I crossed my arms with the same tone.

"Is dreaming of a four-year university why you've been stealing books out of teacher's classrooms?"

"I haven't been stealing, I've been borrowing. You have to write college essays and if nobody's going to teach me how to write at that level, I'll teach myself. If no one is going to help me study for the SAT, I'll teach myself."

"Michael, I admire your determination, but you have to be realistic. The odds of you making it into a four-year university are—"

"I don't care what the odds say, they're always saying something against me. The odds need to shut the hell up."

"Do you even comprehend how to make it to college?"

"No, but I'm trying to learn. And aren't you supposed to be helping me?"

"I am trying to help you. I'm trying to get you to be practical. You can apply to these universities and don't get in, then what? Minimum wage for the rest of your life? The college application process is extensive. I can help you aim for something far more feasible. We can take it one step at a time and see where we land."

I stood out of my seat and gave a courteous smile. Our meeting had concluded. Despite what anyone said, I would make it to a university. My determination would change the life I forcibly grew up living. If I failed, if I didn't get in, I would still figure it out. A junior college wasn't a bad option if I failed. However, my plan wasn't to fail, and the only way to make sure I didn't, was to succeed. All success required was hard work; hard work was the formula.

To me, my goal had been plain and simple. My homeless world had shaped my dreams and forced me to aspire for greatness in life. She called for me to sit back down but I returned to the main office and laid my head against the table. I slept until the bell rang and began PE a little refreshed. I partook in a couple of three-point shootouts until school ended.

After school, I walked to the rendezvous spot, a few small tables lined up outside a small pizzeria. During my early days, I had about three hours until my sister came to meet me. I used to stay around and linger after school, but I ran into problems after school so I just journeyed to the rendezvous to be alone. I pulled out my math homework and strained to keep my eyes open as I finished it. I put my homework away and laid my head on my backpack.

A felt a nudge against my shoulder to see Jason standing in front of me.

"Where've you been?" he asked.

"I've been around."

"You barely chill with us anymore."

"My bad, bro. I've been handling life man."

"I heard you got jumped not too long ago."

"Shit, it happens."

"I feel it. You trying to roll with me right now?"

"To where?"

"Meet up with Husky and Ray and them."

"Nah, I'm good, I have to finish up this homework."

"Haha, check you out being a good little school boy. You turning into a square-bear on us?"

"Haha, something like that."

"I feel it, though. I say the hell with homework, though. Screw school, bro. I'm trying to get paid." He pulled out a small wad of cash from his right pocket. "You can make some money with me if you want, bro. I got you. We all have to watch out for each other."

"Thanks, bro. But I'm good."

"You're not good, bro. That's why I'm offering to help you. Why not take the opportunity?"

"I mean that's quick money, but how long can it last? I want the type of money the police can't kick in my door and take from me."

"You talk funny, bro."

"I'm just saying people expect us to sell drugs. I don't want to do what's expected of me."

"I mean, I don't want to, but I have to eat. I have a daughter I need to feed. Nobody's hiring, I have to get money somehow. I'm not going to go without."

"You have to do what you have to, I get that. Just stay safe and out of the way from any bullets."

"What do you want to do?"

"In life?"

"Yeah, well, right now, high school is almost over. I walked by y'all, sleeping in the car, like last week."

"Oh, for real?"

"Yeah, I didn't want to wake y'all up plus I had transactions to make. I left twenty dollars outside of your window, though."

"Oh, for real? I think I do remember my sister finding twenty dollars."

"Yeah, so, I figured you out of all people would be trying to sell something. I couldn't sleep in the car like that."

"Yeah, man, but I want a stable life. Prison isn't for me, bro. I wouldn't make it. Drug money isn't stable and it almost always ends up bad."

"That's the allure of it, bro. Death, jail, shooting people, getting shot at, it's a thrill," he said, revealing a thirty-two ounce bottle of Olde English beer from under his black sweatshirt.

"It's stupid, bro. Think about all the friends we lost, Taylor Michaels, Ronnie, and Little Gerald was only twelve, think about all the people we heard about dying. The sad truth is outside of our friends and family, nobody else knows or cares. When people hear of San Diego, they don't even realize the Southeast is there. They think of La Jolla or somewhere. They think of Sea-World and the San Diego Zoo."

"No, a lot of gangbangers in LA and Sacramento heard about the Southeast." He swigged some of his beverage.

"Yeah, but gangbangers don't matter. None of them matter outside of their gangs. They're all dispensable. Same here in the Southeast, we're all dispensable. These streets, these neighborhoods we claim, aren't ours and we don't matter. That's nothing for me to die for."

"This is just our life, Mike G. We didn't ask to be here, but shit, we're here, so let's raise hell." He took a longer swig of the beer. "Let's meet some of these ghetto expectations."

"I have a different idea. It might sound crazy."

"What?"

"We were born here, but what if we leave?"

"Leave? And go where?"

"To college."

"College? With all of the goodie goods and expensive tuition? Nah, I'm good. We're not meant for college. Well, I'm not. I guess you're the dreamer out of everyone. If you go to college, I'll stop slanging and enroll into a junior college or something."

"Yeah?"

"Hahaha, hell no. But my homegirl tried to go to college three years ago and she couldn't get in anywhere. She ended up working at the strip club. I hear getting accepted to college is hard as hell, but that those strip clubs accept any girl with a pretty face or slim waist. "

"Yeah, I hear the same thing."

"Well, good luck, bro. If you change your mind, I'll put you on. I'm going to go make some money." He shook my hand, slipping me a twenty-dollar bill. He took another long swig. He offered me some, but I denied it.

"All right, bro. Stay safe."

"Always." He walked away.

My sister finally showed up and sat next to me. "How's your face feeling?" She observed me. My face had healed a while ago, but she used it to poke fun at me.

"Better than yours."

"Shut up, stupid."

"It looks better, too."

"Who lied to you?"

We wandered around downtown trying to kill time. The deeper into downtown we went, the more homeless people we encountered. The more homeless people we recognized.

"Screw them," I blurted.

"These homeless people?"

"No . . . just like . . . everyone. They never met us before. It's hard, but college *is* our way out."

"College would be cool. It would be a quick way out of this shithole."

"Right? Sleep in a warm dorm every night."

"I hear they're not even that big of rooms. They're like shelter rooms, maybe a little bigger."

"I'll take it. It comes with a meal plan, too. That's food, a place to sleep . . . sounds good."

"Amen," she said.

"How the State application going?"

"It's okay."

"Well, if you get in, I'll be convinced it's possible. Then leave the rest to me whether you finish it or not. And we'll do what they think is impossible for two homeless kids from the Southeast. Nobody's expecting college."

"Hell, yeah," she said. "Plus, anything beats this life."

"Hallelujah."

We arrived at our rendezvous point and waited for our mom to pull up.

"How was your day at school?" she asked, as we entered the car.

"Fine," we answered simultaneously.

"How was work?" I asked, initiating another one of her loveable stories taking us all the way to the spot we would be calling home that evening. I yawned as we settled in. I turned off my imaginary television I had drawn on a piece of paper and taped to the back of the passenger seat's headrest. I wanted to go to sleep early. I had to wake up early for school the next day.

22. The Road Less Traveled

MARCH TURNED INTO MID-APRIL. MY MOTHER'S health had completely deteriorated. She had tried to cope with it as best she could, but it quickly failed. We were finally out of the car again and into another place. It wasn't a traditional shelter. Fondly named "Project: Homebound," it was a three-bedroom house typically used for women who were in between places. A nice aspect about shelters like those were they had a smaller capacity for occupants, you can stay longer, and people on the outside just think they were regular homes. I called them "House Shelters." The appearance of being a regular home was a reassuring aspect, the best part in my opinion. Being constantly reminded you lived in a shelter can be depressing. At least in house shelters, we had the illusion of having a home. If I could have chosen my preferred shelter to live in, it would have been in house shelters. They were harder to get into, but worth it.

Our current house shelter had mostly elderly women who were there before we went there. Project: Homebound didn't usually accept families but they made an exception for us because we couldn't go anywhere else and they personally pitied us. We just had less time than everyone else there, since we weren't supposed to be there at all. As the only boy in the house, the elderly women were a little jumpy around me. I had to be particularly careful to not intimidate them so I made sure to keep a low profile and stay out of the way.

The government cut our food stamps off and I wasn't sure exactly why. The women in the house graciously shared some of their food with us, but they barely had enough food to feed themselves. Something about taking the last bagel from an elderly lady didn't set too well with me; so, although we had a nicer roof at this point, it came at the cost of being a little more hungry than usual. We were going to get our food stamps turned back on soon, we just had to hold out until we made it to the social services office.

We were used to the government shutting off our food stamps, or cutting our food stamp budget to a few mere dollars, so we knew how to get by. By then, we were professionals at the homeless business. We knew how to survive. We knew how to maneuver around the homeless system downtown, we knew which food lines to go to, and we knew to stay away from traveling circuses—especially since we heard about this one woman getting sexually assaulted. A few years ago, I'd be worried about not having any more food stamps, but now we just kept moving, kept going, until something better revealed itself. It wasn't our mantra, anymore. It happened subconsciously.

The house shelter had a counselor come visit the second day of our stay. To make sure there weren't any psychos moving in the house shelter, counseling was standard protocol. All three of us had to individually meet with her and we took turns using the room, as the other two waited in the living room. I sat on the bottom bunk. The counselor had pulled up a chair next to me. My mom and sister had already met with her. I didn't take my anger out on counselors, anymore. Whether they actually cared or not, they were just doing their jobs. I would just pretend they were some paparazzo interviewing me about something grand I did.

"I'm not sure which is worse, to be in a bad situation and be in despair, or to be in a bad situation and not be in despair." She sat, intently watching me. She had a pen in her hand and furiously scribbled in her notebook.

"What do you think?" she asked.

"I ask myself what keeps me going. I wonder what kept us all going all these years. Is it just blind faith? Hope? Are we hopeful there's light at the end of the tunnel? Or is it anger? Are we angry because there is no light at the end of the tunnel and pressed forward from spite?"

"What do you think?" she asked me again.

"Well, something keeps us from despair, maybe a mixture of both hope and anger. Maybe it is that mixture of hope and anger that drives us ambitiously forward. After all this time, we can no longer be sad. Sadness for ourselves changed nothing. But hope and anger does."

"Are you angry about losing your food stamps?"

I scratched my chin in contemplation. "Nah, not really." She continued to scribble. "Losing things like food stamps don't affect us anymore. We're only attached to each other. My sister and I learned to cope with loss at an early age, over time we became immune to it. Now when we lose things like food stamps, there's no panic, we keep moving, and go and get something else."

"Mm-hm," she said. She stopped writing and folded her hands. "School's coming to an end soon. What will you do? You'll be out of here by then."

"Well, the summer is always interesting because there's no school food to rely on and there's no school during the day. Those free food programs really help. The summer is usually the dark days for us. This time, however, is going to be a little different."

"Oh," she continued scribbling, "How so?

"I'm older now."

"Care to elaborate?"

"When I was younger, all I could do was watch as my mother try everything she knew how to keep our heads floating above water. Now I can swim on my own. I understand that nobody's going to help us. I understand that society thinks that those unfortunate to be born in my impoverished situation should stay here, but I want out. I'm determined to do everything I can to bring our homelessness to an end. If I don't do it, it won't happen."

"Sounds like you want to be your family's superhero. Who were your childhood heroes?"

"Well, growing up, I did want a hero . . . but there aren't any heroes. At least not for us. There are never real heroes for many kids just like us. Many kids who give up and get caught in a cycle of drugs, poverty, gangs, and violence. I'm supposed to get trapped in that same cycle. But I want out of this lifestyle completely."

"Do you think you can achieve your goal?" She observed me with intrigue.

"I mean, I'm not entitled to anything, and I understand that. I won't be getting any handouts. I don't expect it to be easy but I refuse to be deterred. I'll do it all by myself if I have to. I'm so done being homeless. I'll do whatever it takes. I don't want to be the one who gave up. I don't want to accept this fate. I won't accept this fate. I see nothing but obstacles ahead of me. Obstacles that appear mightier than me. Obstacles that have been around longer than I've been born. The same obstacles so many before me have fallen to, become addicted to, and impoverished by."

"And how do these obstacles make you feel? More angry?"

"Hell, yeah it makes me angry. I'm not an idiot. I realize my chances are beyond slim. The world is too big and mean of a place to care about the life of one little homeless boy. I grew up with a voice that never counted. My opinion always went unheard." I stopped and gazed out of the window. A few birds had moved into a large tree. I watched as they gathered twigs and other material they required to make themselves a nest. They constantly flew back and forth carrying more and more material. I would have to create my own nest the same way, piece-by-piece, step-by-step.

"Michael?"

"I'm aware how unreal my aspirations seem," I continued, refocusing my thoughts. "I'm constantly reminded every day. There's no one I can talk to, and no, assigned counselors don't count. Most of my friends can't see life beyond what's in front of them."

"What is it they cannot see?"

"Beyond the ghetto, beyond the perils of poverty, is the American dream of a better life. However, generations of impoverishment have made that dream feel unattainable to the point it is not even discussed. This is why I understand how irrational I sound to everyone around me, you probably have 'crazy' written all in your notes, but I don't care. We don't have an example of how to succeed. I never met anyone who has legally succeeded. There's no one there to guide me, no light to show the way, like I said before I have no heroes. I'll just have to be my own hero. I'll be my mother's hero. But first I'm going to have to claw my way out of the bottom of this crab barrel one step at a time."

"You mentioned 'crazy,'" she read from her notes, "Do you think your mother is crazy?"

"My mom? Yup."

"You do?" she said, in almost a surprise.

"Yup."

"Do you think your sister is crazy?"

"My sister's like twice as crazy as my mom."

"What about yourself, do you think you're crazy?"

"Nah, not really," I said. "I used to be crazy. Now I'm just borderline insane."

Two days later, I sat in class and I overheard my friends talking about a program. I barely heard the gist of it because they were two rows behind me but one of them mentioned something about a job. I stood and pulled up a chair next to them.

"What are you talking about?" I asked.

"Jobs," my friend Marcos said.

"What jobs? There aren't any. I've put in like a thousand applications."

"I've put in two thousand applications," my other friend Tyson said.

"I saw this flyer," began Marcos. "It's a program called Hire-A-Youth or something like that. They're talking about money. They'll give you a summer job if you qualify."

"How do you qualify?" I asked.

"You have to fill out some paper work. I turned it in yesterday."

"You said Hire-A-Youth?"

"Yeah. It makes sense."

"Yeah, it does," I said. "I'm going to look into it after school." I scratched my head in deep thought. It could be exactly what I needed.

"Yeah, me, too," Tyson said.

"For real, Tyson, you should really do it," Marcos said.

"I will." Tyson said, avoiding eye contact.

"You always say that, but never go through with things."

"Gaulden! Return to your seat!" Mr. Oakley stood in front of the class staring at me. I gave an unapologetic-apologetic smile and returned to my desk.

After school, I made way to the resource office, or our version of a resource office, which consisted of "outside" counselors temporarily hired by the school to assist with certain programs. The office wasn't big, partially a computer lab, as well as another office for something else. The Hire-A-Youth flyer hanging outside the boy's bathroom instructed interested students to go to the resource office. I saw a lady and began talking to her about the program and how I could apply.

"The funds allocated for this program comes from the American Reinvestment and Recovery Act. Local business partners have agreed to take on students as interns. We technically hire you, but you'll be working for them at their locations. Before you are hired by them, you have to undergo our work readiness training. No matter what job you end up with, we'll pay you the Hire-A-Youth pay rate. You'll get more details later once we go over paperwork. Does this seem like something of interest?"

"Yeah, definitely! But it doesn't start until the summer? I need a job like now."

"Yes. Well the training is toward the end of the school year as well as the job placements, but you don't technically start until the summer time. Another thing is paperwork." She went into a file cabinet and pulled out a packet of paper. "You and your parents have to fill this out and return it with your two forms of identification and tax returns. To qualify you have to make under a certain amount of income. It's mainly geared for low-income, inner-city students."

"I'm a no-income, inner-city student. Last year, my mother made only like five thousand dollars in wages."

"Five thousand a month? You might not qualify. It's for low-income students. Think twenty thousand dollars a year type of low income."

"No, she made five thousand dollars last year, altogether."

"What? Are you kidding? How do you survive on five thousand dollars throughout the entire year?"

"Hmm . . . well, when you do it, you don't think about how you're doing it, you just do it."

"Well, you definitely qualify. Bring the material back to me. I'll help personally oversee your paperwork."

"Thanks. I'll bring them tomorrow."

"It doesn't have to be tomorrow."

"I'd prefer tomorrow."

"You have over a month until it's due. You want to take time and make sure you gather all of the proper documents, especially your parents' tax returns."

"I'd just rather bring them in tomorrow. The sooner the better, right?"

"Proactivity is a great attitude to keep. Sounds good. If you have any friends, spread the word."

"Will do," I stuffed the papers into my backpack and exited the office.

"Hey, Mom, I think I found a job." We sat in our enclosed shelter room, later that night.

"Doing what?" she asked.

"Not sure yet. It's a summer program. We have to fill out these papers."

"What program?"

"Hire-A-Youth. They say it's a program to give jobs to low-income students if they qualify. We just have to fill out this packet. I need two forms of identity and last year's tax returns."

"Why do you need all of my private information?"

"It's government funded, so they want every detail."

"How do they decide who qualifies?"

"It goes by income."

"Oh, well, you should beyond qualify. Pass me my bag so I can find these tax returns."

I passed the bag to her and began filling out the packet. The paperwork turned out to be pretty extensive but I figured it should all be worth it in the end. It asked for the basic details: name, date of birth, address; although the address question stumped me. I didn't have one. I thought maybe I should use the house shelter's, but we were about to be out of there soon.

"What should I put for an address?"

"Put not applicable," Pooh said.

"Use the school address," my mom said.

I continued filling out the application as my mom took a nap and my sister did her daily chores. The application had a magic box you could check if you were in foster care. I had seen those types of boxes before. It usually meant if you were in foster care, you automatically qualified, how nice for them. I made my way to the short essay part of the application, which had a two-part prompt. The first:

Why do you want to work for Hire-A-Youth?

Maybe telling them I was homeless wouldn't help my case. They might see it as a liability. How could you expect or even trust a homeless person to show up to work well-groomed, in proper attire, good hygiene, on time and be there every day? Such a normal expectation may be considered too unrealistic. When people hear the word homeless, they automatically, subconsciously, think of dirty, stinky, lazy, alcoholic, and drug addicted among other things. Those are the connotations associated with homelessness. I didn't fit the homeless image, but they could not see me through the application. They could not stare into my eyes and see my determination. They could not feel my ambition; they could not hear my hunger. Especially, when there were hundreds of other low-income students who arguably wanted a job just as much as I did who were not homeless.

How will you use the skills obtained during the internship?

I wasn't too worried about getting skills right then. My mom groaned in pain as she rested. I hated how that kept happening to her. As for my sister, at the start of summer she would be going off to college. She had just found out two and a half weeks ago. SDSU initially rejected her, but she appealed the decision and they let her in under the Guardian Scholars Program. She's supposed to initially apply under the program in the first place, but Mr. Robertson, of course, dropped the ball.

"I got in!" she had yelled, bursting through the room door.

"In where?" my mom asked.

"The circus isn't that selective," I said, annoyed she had woke me up from my nap.

"San Diego State! See for yourself!" Pooh handed my mom an envelope. "They just mailed it to the school today. This is crazy!"

"What?" I leapt off of the top bunk, landing with a thud. I snatched the envelope away from my mom and zoomed in with my eyes reading, "Congratulations." We started cheering as if she had made the game winning shot.

I embraced her, squeezing her with all of my might. We started jumping up and down and my mom soon joined in hugging the both of us. She didn't jump though, she couldn't, but her tears of joy rolled down her face. She stepped back with her hands over her mouth, beaming with pride. I tossed my arm around my sister, "Pooh Bear, this is amazing. You're the first person to get accepted to college! I'm so proud of you! They said it was impossible."

"I guess not." She admired the letter as if made of gold. "It feels so good. It's like a colossal weight was lifted off of my shoulders." She exhaled deeply. She couldn't stop smiling. "You'll be next, little brother, trust me."

The day of her acceptance seemed surreal. I'd never seen my sister smile so big. It made my heart happy. Her hard work had indeed paid off. The thought of it was crazy. To think she would be leaving our world, our life. To think college could actually be accessible. Pooh made me so proud. She did it. Now I would do it, too. College was a different world, a foreign world, but I eagerly wanted to embrace it. I wanted to see what life looked like when you didn't view it through homeless eyes. I wanted to experience what life's like on the other side. I wanted to feel a colossal weight lift from my shoulders, as well.

"Wow you really meant today, huh?"

"Yeah, I did. I have everything, right?"

"Let me just double check your file, social security is here, your ID card is here, application plus essay supplement, tax returns . . . yes, you have everything you need. All we have to do is set you up for intake to see if you qualify, and after you qualify you come back for orientation."

"Do I do intake with you?"

"No, but I can oversee your file along the process."

"Okay, cool. What was your name again?"

"Tori. And yours?"

"Michael."

"Sit tight, Michael, I'm going to hand your file to one of our counselors and they'll do your intake and you'll be set. Any questions?"

"How come you can't do my intake?"

"I'm a case manager. I'll be helping train and monitor students in the program."

"Can you be my case manager?"

"Of course, if you want me to be."

"Cool. Sounds good."

"Okay, sit tight."

She skipped into a side office and returned, assuring me a counselor would be right with me. She then left to aid another student. A bald, shorter man exited out of the side office and called my name.

"I'm right here." I stood and shook his hand.

"Pleasure to meet you Michael. I'm Mr. Thomas."

He led me into his cramped office space and I took a seat. He read off a checklist making sure my file had everything it needed for completion.

"All right, everything appears to be good."

"Is that all you need?"

"Appears so. Yup, Mr. Gaulden you are all set." He reached into his desk and pulled out a couple of fliers. "In about a month and a half, we'll be having our job readiness training. There's more than one session. The first session is—"

"Sign me up for that one."

"Eager man, I see. All right. These flyers should explain everything you need for now and the rest will be covered in training. I can't wait to see you there. And spread the word to all of your friends. Tell them it's real jobs and real money."

"So what do I do until training?"

"Hang tight. Your file is in order, so the next step for you is pretty much training in a little over a month."

Damn. I'd forgot we didn't go to work right away. Our time would be up in the house shelter in one month. "There's not an advanced program or something? Or like a job I can do until the other jobs start? I need a paycheck."

"No, not really, not until the training starts. You do get paid for the training."

"But there's absolutely nothing I can do until then?"

"I'm afraid not. But I like your attitude. The determined drive to work. Bring your ambition to orientation with you. For now, I'd advise you to just finish strong at school and relax at home until then."

Bad timing. We'd be in our car in a month. We wouldn't be able to get a motel or anything and my mother was too weak to sleep in a car that time around. Her ankles kept swelling up, different parts of her body kept swelling up, and she couldn't be left in certain positions too long or her muscles would spasm. She could barely stand to work but still did. We didn't have food stamps, so we couldn't get food. We were all out of options. We were out of answers.

"Sounds good. I'll see you at training." I exited his office. I told Tori goodbye and headed out the door. All I could do was wait until then.

Sure enough, a month passed and we were back in the car, and hungry. My mother's body couldn't take it. The day before, her ankles swelled up to the point where she couldn't move. She had to miss work and go to the hospital where they gave her cortisone shots. My body couldn't take it, either. My neck, back, and limbs sorely ached from not being able to stretch out in our cramped space. I could barely turn my neck without it hurting. I didn't complain about my pain. Sitting in the car, my mom went through ten times as much pain as me, it gave me no right to complain. I snuck back extra school breakfasts and lunches every afternoon to sustain us until her next paycheck, but our food supply wouldn't last for long since we were in May and school prepared to end.

My sister already left for summer school at San Diego State. She didn't want to go, though, out of concern for my mom and me. We told her we were okay. We told her we had been accepted into a new shelter we were going to transition to after she left. We didn't mean to lie to her. We had no choice. She would have tried to stay with us if she knew the truth. Even if she left with the truth, she would be too worried about us to focus on college. And school's where she needed all her focus. I slept better in the car knowing she slept comfortably in a nice warm bed. She deserved it. She earned it by herself, no matter what the Monarch School claimed. I sat in the car talking to her on my same prepaid cell phone now missing half of its buttons. I thought I had already ran out of minutes. She had called from the school phone.

"How is it there?" I asked.

"It's pretty cool. I'm a little lonely, though. The meal plan is nice. I can eat all I want. The cafeteria is like an all-you-can-eat buffet."

"A buffet? You think me and mama can eat in there with you?"

"I wish. I only get one meal swipe per meal period and they guard the entrance. I can smuggle y'all out some food though."

"Shit, I'll take it man."

"Haha, where's mama? She asleep? I tried calling her first."

"Yeah. She's tired. Her phone doesn't have any more minutes, remember? I'll make sure she calls you from somewhere tomorrow."

"How's the staff treating y'all?"

"Staff?" I glanced around the confines of the cramped car. "They're all right. It's like they're not even here."

"That's good."

"Hey, Pooh, I'm proud of you."

"You keep telling me."

"I really am, though. This is crazy. One of us in college? No way, man."

"You can make it, too."

"Seeing you there does make it seem even more possible. I still have a long way to go though."

"Just stay on track. Don't be hanging out and stuff with those bad-ass friends of yours. I'm serious! If we both go to college, we don't have to be homeless anymore. Mama wouldn't be weighed down by taking care of us, either."

"Yeah. . . ." I glanced over at my mom folded over with her head resting against the steering wheel.

"Hey, I'll talk to you tomorrow. I have class in the morning."

"Okay, I'll talk to you later."

"Love you."

"Love you, too," I said to a dial tone. I had used all of my minutes. I had hoped she heard me. I still had a real long way to go if I wanted to achieve what my sister achieved. But if she could do it, I could do it. I knew the goal I wanted to achieve. I could see my destination. Getting there's the hard part. And because I wasn't in foster care or at the Monarch School with Mr. Robertson's mediocre strings, I didn't qualify for the Guardian Scholars Program.

May had reached its last week. I sat at my desk after school. My eyes were heavy, my mood grim, but I forced myself to stay attentive. On the last day of the job-readiness training for the program, a woman stood in front of the gathered students explaining how to choose a job. In front of us lay a packet with different jobs followed by their job descriptions. On a separate piece of paper, we wrote down our top three job preferences in order from most preferred to least.

We weren't guaranteed to get our first preference so they made us put down three. The Hire-A-Youth program enlisted students from participating schools across the school district. Every student would get a job, but not every student would get the job they wanted. There were some cool jobs like being a newsroom intern, and interning for a few small businesses, but then there are some unappealing jobs like filing and urban clean up.

Some kids teased about one of the jobs—the job I had actually been considering, a custodian intern. No one wanted to be a custodian intern. The job description: hard manual labor. You get dirty, smelly, and it's just overall not appealing to students. It's unappealing description the exact reason why I considered it. I didn't want to be a custodian but the job offered the most hours per week and no one had signed up. A news intern would have been cool, but I needed more than ten hours per week. The job wouldn't be pretty, but I wasn't working for aesthetics. I worked for survival.

I put down custodian intern for all three of my preferences and turned my paper in after the end of training. What else could I do? I needed to work. Every morning I feared I would wake up in the car, lean over to talk to my mom, but then see she wouldn't respond. Every day I feared for her life. I had no choice. I chose nothing else. Like I had told the last counselor, I would save us. I would be our hero. Being homeless, people automatically thought of me as shit. People often automatically assumed custodians were shit, too, because they were cleaning up rather than watching the stock market. And as a homeless custodian, I would be shit cleaning up shit. My life. I should've been used to it, but I wasn't. I didn't think I could ever get used to it.

23. Ambition:
Age Seventeen

2008–2009

I SAT ON MY KNEES SURROUNDED BY THE FECES-SCENTED aroma of the boys' bathroom. My June gloom had nothing to do with the weather. I held a sponge in my left hand and a bottle of graffiti removal in my right. I scrubbed graffiti off the wall with the coarse part of the sponge as I tried my best not to gag. The graffiti came off hassle-free, thanks to the graffiti removal, but there's lot of graffiti and I had to clean it all. My stained blue jeans scraped against my knees as I knelt scrubbing the wall.

My uniform consisted of a mud colored T-shirt, some jeans, and some gray construction gloves. The gloves were the most important part. Without them, I wouldn't have a barrier between me and the filth I interacted with. Summer students came in and out of the bathroom, intrigued by a fellow student cleaning it. They tried to get a look at my face, but I kept my head glued toward the wall as I cleaned. I didn't want anyone to recognize me.

At first I had been assigned a custodian intern at one of the other high schools in the school district. The school was far. I rode a one and a half hour bus ride each way every day. I didn't have to try and hide as I cleaned because no one there knew me. When some of the kids saw me and laughed, I didn't care; they were strangers and I'd never see them again after the job ended. But I couldn't stay in incognito bliss for long. During the first week of work, I couldn't consistently make the trip. I ran out of bus tokens, I couldn't walk there, and the few times I managed to get bus fare, the bus arrived late. I had no choice but to request a change of venue. If I didn't, I would be forced to quit or, more likely, I'd get fired. My superiors made the importance of punctuality clear midway through my first week.

To my surprise, I had only one other alternative: to clean up for my own high school. My stomach cringed when I heard the news. Cleaning after my peers humiliated me as they watched, joked, or even worse, sympathized. I'd heard it all already:

"Michael the Janitor."

"I've left a surprise for you in the toilet."

"Can you clean my house next?"

I had to do what was necessary, which brought me there on my knees cleaning graffiti off the wall in a bathroom where I had seen kids piss right where I knelt.

I cleaned the wall; my job description said to clean it, so I cleaned it. Everyone knew the next day it would be covered with even more graffiti than it had the previous day, but still I cleaned it. The toilets were backed up with feces floating in the stalls. Someone had smeared excrement on the wall as well, but thankfully I wasn't cleaning it up. I had just been told I would be on trash duty, thank God, because a lot of feces had been smeared on the wall. Exactly what could be expected in the boys' bathroom at my school and it's still better than the girls' bathroom. Girls could sometimes be nastier than boys, like for example leaving bloody tampons on toilet seats or all over the floor I had to clean up.

I grabbed the bathroom trash bag, tied it in a knot, and carried it outside to the custodian golf cart the head custodian drove. The head custodian was a guy named Gerry. He was a big guy, easy-going, and easy to get along with. I liked custodians. They were like me in a way. People saw their job and thought of them as something inferior, something less than whole. They couldn't see a normal person behind the uniform. A person who smiled, cried, and laughed just like anyone else. Just like me.

I climbed into the passenger side of the cart and we pulled off. We rode around the school campus picking up bags of trash set outside by the other custodians.

"How do you like being a janitor?" I asked.

"I'm not a janitor. I'm a custodian."

"Same thing, right?"

"No. Janitors bounce around from building to building, like cleaners for hire. We custodians monitor the maintenance of mainly one primary location."

"Like the school?"

"Right. We have our own set of master keys here and therefore are held accountable for the entire premise. Different janitors at any given point can be assigned to clean a building whereas here it's the same custodians every day."

"So janitors are like a lower-class custodian?"

"No, it's just a different job. It has a different job description. It's similar in which we both clean, but we have a little more responsibility."

"Oh, cool. At first I thought you didn't get paid that much, but you have a nice car."

"I work hard. I deserve a nice car." He smiled.

"I deserve a nice car."

"Work hard enough and you'll get one."

"Do people ever make fun of you? Like your job?"

"Yeah, sometimes."

"Does it bother you?"

"I mean, not really." He smoothly operated the cart with one hand. "I'm making money to support my family, that's all I care about; to make sure we're all right. I understand what type of job I do. Everyone can't sit in the corporate offices. But where would they be without someone cleaning up after them? Doing the job that they refuse to do? Someone has to clean up and make sure everything is running smooth. And just because I sanitize doesn't make me less intellectual than any one of those other guys."

"Yeah, I agree with you."

"Why'd you choose this internship out of all the other ones? Believe it or not, the ladies don't leap for joy when they hear you're a custodian."

"I didn't want to. No offense but who really wants to."

"So why'd you take this job?"

"Because of the hours being offered."

"Yeah, exactly. So you did want to because of the hours. I wanted to in order to provide for my family. We all have our reasons for doing the things we do. Believe me back in high school, I didn't sit around dreaming about being a custodian. I was even in the military for a little, too."

"The military, huh?"

"You're thinking about enlisting? It's not a bad option."

"No, not really. I feel like it would be too expected of me. It's either dead, jail, or the military. But there's nothing wrong with the military."

"Nothing wrong at all. It's a good alternative to the drugs and gangs."

"Yeah, I agree. What's funny, though, at first black men couldn't even join the military, now it's all they try to force on us. Like you said, there's nothing wrong with it; it's just too expected of me in particular. It's all everyone's told me since I was little. 'When you get old enough, go to the military.' 'It's the only way out.' I want to do something unexpected of me. I want a different way out."

"Like what?"

"Well, my sister got accepted into college, and I'm going to go, too."

"College, huh? I think that's great. College is where young black men's minds should be focused. I thought you were going to say the NBA like everyone else."

"Haha, nope. College. I mean, the military or prison shouldn't be the only options. I think education is the means toward upward mobility. Let's be real, everyone's not going to the NBA or NFL. I mean, if you can, that's great. I would if I could. But for the rest of us, we need a real plan."

"What made you decide to stay in school? I'm sure you know some knuckleheads running around in gangs and selling dope. Why aren't you?"

"Let's be even realer. Every gangbanger isn't going to be a rap star and every drug dealer isn't going to be Nino Brown. Most of them are going to end up in prison if they're not killed first. And I'm allergic to prison and I like living way too much to die."

"You don't want to be a famous rap star?"

"Who wouldn't? I'd golf, too. But I'm homeless and need a real way out right now."

"I wish more young men can see it like that. How'd you come out a saint growing up in hell?"

"I'm not a saint. There aren't any saints out on the street, only villains, martyrs, and survivors. I've been through things, just like the next knucklehead who grew up in the inner city. It's just a dead end. I'm thinking beyond the hood, beyond the streets. I don't want to slang on the corner. I want to own corporations."

We continued going around the school piling trash bags into the cart and drove them to the larger dumpsters at the back of the school. We started tossing the trash bags into the already overstuffed dumpsters. The putrid smell made me want to plug my nose, but I couldn't because of the dirty gloves on my hand. One of the bags suddenly ripped and a half carton of milk spilled on my jeans. I reacted quick enough to save my shoes but the damage to my jeans couldn't be undone. Out of all things to spill, it had to be milk. I hoped I could wash it out in the bathroom because we had no quarters to wash clothes. If left in my jeans, the milk would to start to reek.

Gerry laughed at me and shrugged. "It happens."

I rolled my eyes and tried to use my gloves to wipe away the soaking milk. I could already feel it seeping through my jeans. It smelled sour, spoiled from sitting in the sun all day; just my luck.

We went back around the campus picking up more and more trash bags. I wanted to drive the cart but Gerry kept telling me it's a liability.

I arrived at the main custodian's office, a medium-sized room equipped with a table and a mini fridge. I tried to clean the milk off of my jeans with some cleaning solution and then graffiti removal when all else failed.

"You pissed your pants?" Gustavo said, another full-time custodian. He entered with another intern named Jacob behind him. Gustavo thought of himself as a funny guy, always cracking jokes, always picking on Bob. Bob, another custodian, wore thick glasses and went bald at the top of his head, making him common fodder when it came time for jokes.

"He spilled milk on his pants," Gerry said.

"Did you forget how to drink?"

"The bag ripped. Why would somebody just drop a full carton of milk in the trash? It makes no sense. Pour it out."

"I'm sure you've dropped all kinds of cups full of shit in the trash before," Gerry said.

"I mean, yeah, but I never thought I'd have to clean it up."

"Yeah, I'll bet you'll think about that next time," Gustavo said.

"I'm thinking about it right now."

I waited for my mom to come pick me up. Tired and hungry, I just wanted to go to sleep. When she finally came, I saw she had placed a blanket to cover over all of our belongings in the back seat.

"Why'd you cover everything?"

"My supervisors don't want all of this stuff just sitting in the car in the parking lot so I had to cover it."

She handed me a foot-long Subway sandwich for me to hold until we pulled over. We had applied to go back to one of our previous shelters, but we were far back on the waitlist where we would most likely stay until they found out my age and removed us from the list altogether.

Parking downtown became more hostile, and so had the people when they passed by us sleeping. We didn't have many places to park, so we pulled up on the side of the shelter where we were currently waitlisted. A streetlight shone right in our face, so we put up some old newspapers in the front windshield.

I gave my mom her half of the sandwich and we ate together. We ate the sandwiches quick. We were still hungry, but wouldn't get any more food that night.

"Mom, this is bull-crap." I listened to my stomach rumble.

"Always is, Sun . . . I'm going to scrape some quarters together to get a loaf of bread we can snack on."

"Man, I'm so hungry and tired. I've been working all day."

"Welcome to the club. Oh my, God, my ankles. They swelled up in my shoes. The doctors told me I should go back to using my cane. I can't have it at my job though, that's the problem."

"The doctor? When'd you go back to the doctor?"

"I wasn't feeling well, so I went in and arrived to work late a few days ago."

"Why didn't you tell me? You never tell me!"

"I didn't want you to worry about me."

"Well, you hiding that you're feeling sick enough to go to the hospital isn't going to make me not worry about you."

"You're right, I'm sorry."

"This just isn't fair. I used to wonder all the time, 'why us'? Why do we have to keep living this way? All the rappers wants to rap about being from the streets. I don't want to be from the streets. I hate the streets."

"I've tried my best to take care of the family without any help."

"Exactly, and that's what makes it even worse. You—"

Our rear left window shattered and glass flew everywhere. A large rock tumbled across our back seat. We heard heavy laughter and then footsteps growing distant.

"What the hell!" my mom said. We exited the car to examine the damage. Our entire window had fragmentized. Glass shards covered our back seat and littered the ground outside. I turned around to see the group of kids running in the distance. I didn't see the point in chasing them. It wouldn't fix anything. I would just be burning energy. I could do nothing more.

"I don't want any more homeless memories. I'm done with it. I'm done with this," I slumped back in the car. The window had been completely shattered. Luckily it was June and not freezing outside.

"Me too, son. Mama, too. I was done nine years ago. But boy, as much as I love conversing, we have to go to sleep or we're not going to wake up in time for work."

"Yeah, can't wait."

"And what's that smell?"

"What smell?"

"Don't play."

"I'm not."

"Boy!"

"I spilled milk on my jeans at work today. I thought I cleaned it all out."

"Oh, uh-uh boy, that's milk. It's going to funk up the whole car. Set those pants outside."

"Aw, Mom. What if someone sees me in my boxers?"

"You're not about to stink up my whole car."

"Well, ventilation won't be a problem with our window like that."

"Boy!"

"Let me just spray them with some cologne."

"What cologne?"

"Oh, yeah, huh." I began taking off my jeans.

The next day, Jacob accidentally knocked a student desk to the ground. I helped him pick it up and properly stacked it on top of another desk. Prior to my job, I had never wondered how schools were cleaned. I knew each school year the graffiti on the desks were mostly removed, the dry-erase boards were clean, and the floors were shiny. Well, turned out, custodians came in, took all of the classroom furniture, cleaned it and stacked it to one side of the room, swept and then mopped the floors, and then waxed the first half. Then they went back, unstacked all of the furniture, transported it to the other side of the room, restacked the furniture, swept and mopped the floor, and then waxed the other half. Then they had to come back, unstack all of the furniture, and juxtapose the room to the exact specifications of the teacher.

When they finished, they went right into the adjacent classroom and did the same thing all over again. The work was as tedious and painstaking as it sounded and, unfortunately, I had been doing it all day. The task required a lot of manual labor having to lift heavy teacher desks, or move couches around. The all-day process tired me out.

We finished stacking the furniture and moved to sweeping the floor. It didn't take both of us to sweep the floor, so I told him I would mop. The other half of the floor had already been waxed and after we finished we would be done with the second of five school buildings. They didn't let us wax with the wax machine because they said it's another liability, so we were forced to do the grunt work.

I wheeled in the mop and water and began mopping the floor after he swept. Mopping's pretty easy and I often volunteered so I could have a breather before entering the next classroom. I mopped the entire floor half and I mopped it one more time to make sure I had enough rest. I turned the small portable fans on for it to dry and exited the classroom.

Jacob held a long metal scraper and talked with Javier, who held two more. Whatever he was about to do didn't look too appealing, so I turned to slip back in the classroom and re-mop the floor.

"Mike G, you done?" Gustavo asked.

"Yeah, I just finished." I reluctantly turned back around.

"Good." He handed me a metal scraper.

"What's this for?" I feared I already knew the answer.

"We're going to scrape up gum. Exciting stuff."

I had already scraped up gum before at the other school and it's arguably one of the worst things I had done being a custodian; worse than even cleaning toilets—not as dirty, but psychologically worse. The razor blades from the scrapers always dull against the cement and we always had to stop and change them after every ten minutes of just scraping. Endless scraping. Everyone spat gum out on the ground all the time, but I never considered someone had to clean it up.

He led us by the main quad and pointed to a portion of cement covered with black, hardened gum. I pushed against the grain of the cement as I scraped up the stuck pieces of gum. I scraped and scraped and scraped. I exchanged razor blades and then continued scraping. Sometimes it took ten minutes just to scrape up only three or four pieces of gum out of hundreds. After a while, my forearms began to hurt and I took a break. The outside heat didn't make my task any easier. I scraped and scraped until someone called my name.

"What's up?" Jessica rushed up to me with two of her friends. I hadn't really talked to her much since I was fourteen when she caught me sleeping outside in the tent with Rudy.

"What are you doing?"

"Nothing." I held the metal scraper. "Scraping gum."

"Why?"

"It's my job."

"So you're a janitor now?"

"A custodian, but yeah."

"Are you doing summer school?"

"No, just working."

"Why don't you get a real job?" interrupted one of her friends, the same friend from back then.

"This is a fake job?" I said.

"Don't play stupid. That's a dirty job. I'd never do that."

"I have to get paid somehow."

"Why don't you get a job somewhere else instead of doing that? It's pathetic."

"Oh, my bad. Are you hiring?"

"No." She reached into her purse and pulled out a pack of gum. She took a piece chewing it up, and spat it on the ground right in front of me. "But at least I'm not scraping that shit up, either."

"Mike G, get back to work." Gustavo to the rescue.

"Yeah, Mike G, get back to work," the girl said.

"See you around." Jessica rolled her eyes at the other girl and they left.

"Don't let them get to you." Gustavo sensed a hurtful blow to my human pride. "Come Friday, payday, you won't even remember what she said."

After work, I flew into the car to my mom's smiling face and fastened my seat belt as she pulled off.

"What's wrong with you?" she asked.

"Nothing, I'm just tired. We cleaned classrooms again. How was work?"

"You won't believe what this mofo did at work today. . . ." I engaged in her story while we searched for parking. We ended up parked behind the shelter again and talked as we ate another Subway sandwich. We couldn't afford to dream about affording to fix the window so we taped a large black trash bag where the glass used to be. It made the car ghetto, appearing cheaper than it usually did, but we didn't care. We settled down and tried to get some sleep.

My mom's prepaid cell phone beeped and she read a text from one of her friends. Each text she sent took half a minute from her phone time. I wasn't the biggest advocate for my mom's friends or her wasting precious call minutes on them. Through my short time on this planet I had realized the term "friend" had become redefined. Being a friend wasn't a deep, personal connection between you and a like-minded individual. Being a friend meant an association between two people who get along momentarily. There wasn't real depth, no real meaning to the word anymore, especially when a friend needed help.

She read the text, laughed and then snapped a picture. I opened my eye and asked her why she took the photo.

"Veronica texted me."

"Oh . . . what did she want?"

"She asked me how we were doing."

"How we are doing? We're sleeping stuffed up in the car while she's home all warm and toasty with plenty of room and she's asking you how we're doing? What did you say?"

"I took a picture of us and sent it to her saying 'What do you think?'"

"I don't like your friends."

"I don't like your bad little friends."

"Why can't she help us? At least for a night or two so we can take a full shower. What kind of a friend is that?"

"A bad one."

"That's messed up."

"Life's messed up. We're clear examples."

"Yeah, well, at least we still got each other. You remember my friend Christine?"

"She stayed with her dad and sister, right?"

"Yeah."

"I liked her dad. He was a nice guy. What about them? I haven't heard from him since we left that shelter."

"That's because he's dead."

"Are you serious?"

"Yup. He had medical problems like you do. Being homeless didn't give him a fighting chance to recover and . . . he died. The shelter reoccupied his room; and everyone just moved on without missing a beat. Life's really messed up, but sometimes death can seem even more cold-hearted."

"Wow. That even hurts my heart. He was a really nice man. What happened to Christine and her sister?"

"I don't know, Mom, I don't think anyone does. Christine's strong. Hopefully she finds a way out. Hopefully."

"I don't want to die on you and your sister, too. I remember talking to Harry, he didn't want to die on Christine, that was his biggest fear, too. It's just out of my control."

"You're not going to die, Mom. We're going to hold strong together. It's just us, me, you, and Pooh Bear. That's it."

"That's all we need. We'll get through this."

"Nothing lasts forever. We won't stay low forever. This life we had to live, bouncing around from place to place, shelter to shelter, state to state, being humiliated over and over again, and living in the places we lived, it's going to come to an end."

"Amen."

"When I was little, I watched you take so much stuff from people just so Pooh and I could have a place to sleep for a week. I saw guys disrespect you, I saw them trying to take advantage of our situation. I was trapped being a little kid. So helpless. I hated it. I remember when being out here like this used to scare us. Remember? When we were like, 'Oh no, what are we going to do?' You remember?"

"Yeah, in the very beginning."

"It's crazy we're like professionals now. I feel like I can write a book on how to be homeless."

"You're so silly, boy."

"Pooh said that one day we're going to look back on all of this and laugh."

"I hope because, right now, this sure the hell isn't funny. Actually, I don't think I will look back at this and laugh at all."

"Haha, yeah, me, neither! It just sounded good to say."

Back at work, I rode passenger in one of the carts on trash duty again. We loaded and unloaded trash as we traversed the campus. I happily picked up trash and scraped gum. I had to help clean a few classrooms but even then, I remained in a good mood. The next day would be payday, *my* payday, which meant eating something besides Subway or taquitos from a 7-11, laundry day, and gas money. If I had enough, I would try and rent a motel for a night or two so we could have a good night sleep. I couldn't wait until Friday. If I could I would just skip past Thursday. But I couldn't, so I went about my daily routine. At least I had a good mood.

After we finished trash duty I went back to the bathroom and rescrubbed the graffiti off of the wall. I still didn't understand why no one could figure out the war on graffiti's a losing battle. But as long as they paid me to clean, I cleaned it. Jacob came in and helped me scrub the wall. He's a taller, heavier, white guy with medium sandy brown hair. He was a bit goofy, soft-spoken and a little socially awkward, but cool with me. I could tell he had been teased a lot growing up. Nothing he had said admitted it, but his over-apologetic mannerisms, shyness, and passive aggressiveness told me everything.

At first, he wasn't sure how to approach and talk to me. We were completely different, and later he said he considered me "too cool" to want to talk to him. He said most blacks or Mexicans he had met have tried to harass him. I told him most blacks and Mexicans I had met have tried to harass me too. After then, he loosened up and we became good work friends.

We sat on our knees scrubbing and laughing about how we were going to go on strike the next time Javier tried to hand us a gum scraper. Gerry came in with more cleaning supplies and told us the three of us were going to clean the bathroom. Thankfully, the bathroom didn't have anything brown—or green, smeared on the walls. Just all over the toilet seats. We each picked a stall and went to work. I skipped the first two stalls because they were the worse. The stall I chose had urine on the floor and toilet seat, and feces smeared against the seat and floating in the toilet water. I put on the yellow rubber gloves Gerry gave me and began drenching the toilet with cleaner. I grabbed a yellow sponge with the green coarse scraper on its backside and started cleaning.

The excrement smeared even more across the toilet seat with the first wipe. The smell made me gag and want to throw up. Why was it so hard for people to just aim their anuses toward the toilet water? What kind of person liked to smear excrement everywhere? I'd never understand it. The next few wipes picked up most of it and, after the sponge became too dirty, I just threw it out instead of cleaning it. I wiped the urine from everywhere and cleaned the entire toilet. The putrid smell in my nose lessened with the entrance of the cleaners, but the smell from the cleaners burned my nostrils still making me uncomfortable. Bathroom duty was my last task of the day so I just finished as fast as I could.

I met up with my mom and I reminded her the next day was pay day. I asked her if she wanted anything special from the store or something and she reminded me we shouldn't buy things we didn't need.

"You deserve something nice," I insisted.

"A house would be nice."

"Until then, let me get you like a neck pillow or something. Or a booty pillow. Is it me or is this car getting smaller and smaller every night?"

"Child, it seems like it. I can't move an elbow without bumping into the steering wheel or hitting the window. Speaking of the car, it was smoking today on the freeway going to work."

"Well, that's not good."

"I got it to stop, but we don't need this car to stop running."

"I think she's given us all she's got."

"Well, she better give us some more."

24. My Way Home

DURING MY LUNCH BREAK I SAT IN THE CUSTODIAN office, peeling an orange given to me by another intern. I'd have actual lunch after payday when I had money to buy some. I ate the orange and returned to work hungrier than I had been before my lunch break. Nothing beat finishing off a hot June week of work with scraping gum all day. But nothing could break my spirit on payday. I'd been waiting for it for a while. The Hire-A-Youth program had partnered with Bank of America to give us student accounts so we could have our checks direct deposited. The beautiful thing about direct deposit was I didn't have to cash my check, it automatically showed up in my bank account.

After work, I purchased quarters to wash and put gas in the car and then I took my mom to a Mongolian fast food restaurant in Horton Plaza Mall; treating her to a nice meal. As we sat there and ate, I found myself at ease for the first time in a long time. My mom merrily ate and my sister studied off at college, away from our displaced life. Life was nice. I could become used to fine dining. Our lives were finally starting to turn around for the better. I wasn't too worried about sleeping in the car because I knew I could buy us some good food in the morning. Working as hard as I worked, when I finally received a paycheck, it rewarded my soul. I earned every penny I made and I proudly saw the fruits of my labor. I made two hundred and seventy-nine dollars plus fifty-four cents. I was like a billionaire.

"When does she need it by?" I gasped, early July.

"Sometime this week. She said she can get us in, but she needs it now. I don't get paid for another week and a half and by that time it'll be too late." And even then, her check wouldn't be enough. She hadn't been working as many hours lately being too sick to perform security tasks like patrolling.

"Can she wait until Friday? I get paid on Friday. I can pay it."

"I'm going to ask. Let's hope."

"Hell, she better wait! Did you already fill out the paper work?"

"I filled out mostly everything. We just need to pay and she'll give us our keys. We won't have any furniture or anything but—"

"Screw furniture, Mom, we just need those damn keys. We should park in front of her office every day until Friday."

"She'll let us. Ms. Bebe wants us to move in. I told her I'm not living in this car anymore. We used to stay in those apartments when you were very, very little."

"And there's nothing wrong with moving back."

We tried to get through the next few days masking our enthusiasm. I didn't get excited because I knew at any given moment, everything could come crashing down again. I stayed alert watching for anything that could go wrong. Most things were out of my control but I stayed alert anyway because it distracted me from getting too excited. We had moved into apartments for a short period of time before, but my mom always did it on her own. This time, I could move us in. I could really be our hero. I could save my mom.

Friday finally arrived and my mom took off work early, picked me up from work early, and we headed to the apartment manager's office before it closed. I had the money order in my hands, we were so close, racing against the clock and trying to bypass traffic. We parked in front of the office and rushed to the door. We knocked and knocked with each knock getting louder and louder the more we stared at the "Closed" sign hanging on the door.

"Call her." My mother already listened intently on the phone as it dialed Ms. Bebe.

"Shit!" my mother said, after leaving a voicemail.

"Doesn't she stay in the complex?"

"Yes, but I'm not positive which apartment."

"Which direction? I'll bang on every door."

"It's toward the left but also could be toward the right."

I held my head and thought to myself. I knew something could go wrong. I knew something would go wrong. It always did. But we were so close to finally getting a roof over our heads, I believed it in my soul. "Okay, well we're sleeping parked right here until the morning."

"It's closed over the weekend."

"Oh, no. I'll be back." I headed toward the left vicinity of the apartment complex. I hoped the residents wouldn't get too mad by me going around to every door, but then again, I didn't care. They weren't the ones sleeping in the car.

I sped to the first light-brown apartment building, which housed four apartments: Apartments A–D. Both A and B were downstairs and C and D were on top of them, respectively. I knocked on apartment A and waited for a response. After about thirty seconds, I knocked again. The door crept open and an old, frail African-American male stood in the doorway.

"What?" His eyes were red as if he had just awakened from a nap. He held on tightly to a metal cane.

"Does the apartment manager live here?"

"No." He immediately closed the door in my face. Undeterred, I turned and knocked on Apartment B.

"Yes?" asked a middle-aged Latina. Past her were about ten other people, children, teens and adults, moving about inside her apartment. They had far too many tenants to legally exist in that small of a space. "Yes?" she repeated.

"Wrong door." I turned and headed up the steps.

Apartments B and D were unanswered and I jogged to the adjacent second apartment building which had Apartments E–H.

"Does the manager live here?" I asked the woman in Apartment E.

"Does it look like the manager lives here?" She was a heavy-set woman with short hair and an attitude. She wasn't the manager.

My mom told me Ms. Bebe had a somewhat thin build with her hair styled in dreadlocks. My stomach rumbled and both the woman and myself glanced at my abdomen. I could smell chicken frying in the kitchen.

"Is that it?" she asked.

"Well, can I have a piece of chicken?"

She laughed and closed the door. I knocked on Apartment F but it went unanswered. Apartment G went unanswered as well. I knocked on Apartment H and a young boy, probably in elementary school, answered the door.

"Yes?" he asked. He stood shirtless and wore small basketball shorts with no shoes or socks.

"Are your parents home?"

"Momma's not back until the morning, she's at work."

"She left you by yourself?"

"No, with my brother, hold on." He disappeared then reappeared holding a three-year-old boy. "I'm watching him."

They were too young to watch themselves, but I guessed the mother couldn't afford daycare. If Child Protective Services found out, they would take the children away.

"Listen," I said. "Don't open this door anymore until your mother comes back. Not to police, not to anyone, okay?"

"Why not?"

"Just don't. If you get hungry, the lady in E has food."

"Mom left us pizza."

"What's your name?"

"Michael. What's your name?"

I had no choice but to smile at the young Michael. I saw myself at his age. "My name is Michael, too."

"Oh, cool, me too!" he said in excitement.

I reached forward and shook his hand. "Take good care of your brother, all right? Your mom's counting on you."

"Okay." He still gripped my hand. I left and he stood watching me as I headed down the stairs. "Bye, Michael!" He waved after me.

I turned and waved back, "Bye, Michael. Lock the door."

The next two buildings were hopeless. Good thing I had all the time in the world because I readied myself to annoy the entire complex if necessary. As I headed toward the fifth building, I noticed a lady wearing dreadlocks and holding a manila folder rushing in my direction. She dialed on her cell phone.

"Ms. Bebe?"

"Yes?"

"I'm Michael, Monice's son."

"Are you the one harassing my tenants?"

"Guilty." I laughed, happy I found her.

"Oh good, I was just calling your mom back right now. My phone had died. I thought you weren't going to make it. I stayed extra for a while. I figured you'd show up because your mom really wants these keys. She's been by here every day this week. You see, I kept your folder with me."

"Yeah, thanks, I really appreciate it. She's waiting up by your office."

We entered the office and Ms. Bebe sat behind her desk as she organized our folder. "Everything is good. All we need now is your remaining balance of four hundred dollars and you can have your keys."

I handed her the money order. All of my sweat, all of the spilled milk, all of the gum scraping, all of my hard work led to the point where I could hand her the money order to pay for the deposit. I handed her my determination. I handed her my motivation. I tossed my arm around my mom, kissing her on the cheek. Ms. Bebe handed us the lease to sign, accompanied with the keys of our very own apartment.

We didn't live in a house, but the hell if we cared. Right then, those metal keys were more precious to me than gold. We sped to the door, Apartment B, and almost broke it down rushing inside. My mother ran through the house screaming and crying as I leaned against the wall and then sat on the floor, taking it all in. I closed my eyes and took a deep breath. The moment seemed surreal like I would wake up any moment, but a dream I had worked for wasn't going to disappear once I opened my eyes. But, just to be sure, I opened my eyes and made sure the apartment didn't disappear. When it didn't, I fell into bliss and elation overwhelmed me. I had set a goal and accomplished it. It made me smile. It made me feel whole.

My mother went into the bathroom and turned the shower on and off. She came out with a giant smile. "Help me get the stuff out of the car."

I stood and hugged her, tossing my arm around her. I knew she would be getting another surgery soon but now we would have a place for her to recover properly, and make her feel whole, as well. "We did it Mom, we did it."

"Lord as my witness I couldn't do another night like that."

"Me, neither, Mom. Me, neither. Oh yeah, there's something I've always wanted to tell you, but I didn't want you to get offended."

"Boy, what?"

"I don't want to sound unappreciative, but . . . I've always hated that car."

25. My Way Out

W HAT'S IT CALLED?" I ASKED A YOUNG CAUCASIAN
man sitting across his desk from me. August neared its
end, right before the start of my 2009–2010 senior year in high
school. We were in his small office on the third floor of the building I did an internship with. The San Diego Workforce Partnership operated on the fourth floor and its CEO Mark Cafferty
invited me to interview with them. He'd heard me speak on the
USS Midway on behalf of the Hire-A-Youth program and how I
used my paychecks to change my living situation. At the Workforce Partnership, I met a woman named Regina Malveaux who
said I should meet a guy named Chris.

"Reality Changers," he replied with a grin.

"And it'll help me get into college?"

He chuckled. "Yes, I can guarantee it. Everyone who's been in
the program for four years has gone on to a four-year university."

"I'm about to be a senior. I don't have four years."

"You don't need four years. Our program is designed for four
years, but you're a senior so you'd go to our College Apps Acad-
emy where we have volunteers helping you with applications.
It's run by a volunteer named Debbi, she's great. There's something about you, Michael. With your resiliency, your passion,
your voice, in time you're going to do great things. But first, college. With everything you've been through, I'm sure you can
manage a little paperwork."

"I'm not worried about paperwork, anybody can fill out
applications."

"Exactly," he replied. "So what do you say?"

I leaned back in my chair examining the guy before me. He stood about 5′9″ with somewhat spiky brown hair. He had a big smile. He leaned forward in his chair, patiently awaiting my response. I prayed he could see my aspirations. I had the ambition. I had the perseverance, the grades, the determination, and the will to succeed. I knew college was my destination. My former plan had been to follow the North Star until it led me there but I didn't exactly know the way. A road map would make getting there a hell of a lot easier, and Reality Changers appeared to be one.

"I'm all for it," I said. "But I better get in."

Late September, I stood staring at the computer screen in Reality Changers' computer lab, really the computer lab for the Metro Economic Development Center Reality Changers "borrowed" after hours when the building closed to the public. I had just finished applying for my dream school of San Diego State University, a few other California State Universities, and a few private institutions. The clock read ten at night. I had been sitting in the same seat since four in the afternoon.

Every day for the last month, I'd been going there for hours, reworking my personal statement over and over again until it became suitable for me to submit as part of my applications. Wednesday came and I exhaustedly remained as one of the last few students there. I thought Reality Changers would do more than it did and the program turned out a lot harder than I thought. There wasn't any magic formula for college acceptance, just a lot of hard work. Lead tutor Debbi's support made everything a lot easier. I stretched and stood preparing to leave as Chris came in.

"How's those UC applications coming along?"

"UC?" I said. "Like the University of California?"

"Unless you heard about another one," he replied, ever trying to make a joke.

"It's not coming. I'm going to just go to SDSU like my sister."

"Just because you want to go to SDSU doesn't mean you shouldn't apply to the other ones still. You want to get in as many schools as you can get in and then try to decide from there."

"Nah, I don't want to. I mean, I probably wouldn't even get in to a UC. I'm not their typical type of student."

"Well, the worse they can tell you is no."

"Nah, I think I'm good. I know myself." I packed up my backpack, zipped it up and tossed it over my back.

"Well, don't do it for yourself, do it for me."

"Nope."

"Please?"

"No way."

"I'm going to bug you until you do it."

"Chris, I'm good."

"It's one common application you can send to multiple UC campuses. It won't take long."

"I can submit one application to every school?" I said somewhat perturbed by his persistence. "Which ones should I apply for then?"

"Not every school, but you should start off with UC San Diego, it's local, or Berkeley, Riverside, or maybe UCLA."

"UCLA? Like Kareem Abdul-Jabbar Jackie Robinson UCLA?"

"Plenty of other people have gone there, but yes."

"You really think they'd want a student like me? With my background?"

"Only one way to find out," he said. "Start on your UC app first thing tomorrow."

"I think Reggie Miller and Troy Aikman went there," I replied, lost in the possibility. I would probably get rejected and end up at SDSU as planned regardless, but still, the idea's nice to fantasize about. "See you tomorrow." I headed out toward the bus stop, which would take me home.

In mid-March of my senior year, I opened up the laptop I had purchased from my winnings of a Rotary Club Speech tournament

I participated in through Reality Changers. I had never owned a laptop before and the technology thoroughly impressed me. We didn't have Internet but I hacked into a neighbor's wireless service. I checked my email to see a new message from . . . UCLA? I had received a few acceptances already, but I still waited for SDSU and the UCs. When they send students an acceptance, it comes in the form of a big envelope in the mail. When they deny students, the envelope is small and depressing. But I couldn't tell whether I became accepted or not by just glaring at an email and not opening it.

I hadn't received anything from either my dream school of SDSU or before then, my fantasy school of UCLA.

I laid on my mattress rested directly on the floor. We had only two donated mattresses and a couch.

As I sat there trying to guess what might be inside my email from UCLA, my mom returned from work and quickly disappeared into her room. My mouse cursor lingered over the email as I deliberated whether I should open it or not. But as Chris said, the worst they could say was no. And my life wouldn't stop if they did. Still, I anxiously wanted to find out. I clicked on the email and let my gaze fall upon the black print illuminated on the screen.

Dear Michael Gaulden,

Congratulations! You've been accepted to—"

I leaped up off of my mattress screaming for joy, jumping up and down as if I turned into a little child.

"Whoo!" I exclaimed, smiling from a fulfilled elation I'd never experienced. I ran around my room screaming until my mother knocked on my door, cracking it open.

"Boy, what the hell's—"

"I got in!" I shouted, jumping in her arms as if she could carry me. We stumbled, almost falling.

"You got in?" she questioned, searching both for context and her balance.

"I got in to UCLA!" I shouted.

"*What?*" she said. I pointed her toward my laptop. She read my email and yelled louder than I did, jumping up and down on my mattress. Due to her illnesses, I hadn't seen her move so much in a while, which made me even more excited. I ran over to her and joined her as we jumped up and down celebrating together. We ran around my room, then the house, until we were tired. I sat against the bare living room wall. I called my sister on my new cell phone and my mom called everyone she ever thought she knew.

"Hello?" Pooh sounded groggy as if she had just woken from a nap.

"I got in!" I shouted over the intercom.

"Oh my God, to where?" she exclaimed.

"You'll never believe it! No one will!"

"Tell me! SDSU? Where?"

"U-C-L-A!"

"No way!" she shrieked in complete shock. "Impossible!"

"I guess not." I beamed with pride. "I guess not."

Early August, I pulled my luggage up to a large building whose elegant design appeared to be out of a movie scene. I had decided to take my sister's approach and attend the Freshman Summer Program. I mean, why wait? Especially since I wasn't even supposed to be standing on campus, at least, according to what most believed. According to statistics, I should have still been panhandling Downtown San Diego somewhere. I laughed thinking about how far I'd come. I had lost many friends along the way. Some had died, some were incarcerated, and many were still downtown entrapped in the same cycle in which I had sought to escape. I could have sat and cried, waiting for a miracle, but self-pity wouldn't have changed anything. Tears wouldn't have brought me to Westwood, to UCLA, where the air smelled different. Not because LA's air pollution was different, but the air you breathe when your hard work finally pays off. The type of air you could only smell where I was.

I faced the fact sometimes there is not an easy way out. Sometimes there is no alternative route. Sometimes you have to just hold strong and trail blaze through the hardships ahead. You have to work hard and do whatever it takes to achieve the life your heart desires. My heart wanted to shock everyone who condemned me to a life of impoverishment. My heart wanted to defy what society expected of me.

See, people thought because I grew up poor and homeless, they could project my life. They thought the path I would follow would be the path which would lead to my destruction. I couldn't blame them. After all, the history of self-destruction had repeated itself over and over again in my environment, failing to prove them otherwise. But I could now finally prove homelessness had no control over my destiny.

I stepped through the large open doors of one of the many dormitories surrounding me. I had never been in such a place before. Signs for the Freshman Summer Program directed me down the hall to where a few other students congregated. I sat my belongings down and headed over to the registration table where a bubbly girl with a big smile stood and shook my hand.

"What's your name?" she asked.

"Michael Gaulden," I replied. She searched through the paper, flicking through pages in search for my name. I anxiously waited. She took forever. I expected something to go wrong. Something always went wrong. Could my acceptance have been a mistake? She smiled and highlighted my name off the list. She handed me a welcome packet.

"There you are. We'll get you all situated once everyone has checked in. In the meantime, feel free to mingle around. We have cookies from Diddy Riese, which are the best cookies in the world. Help yourself."

"Cool, thanks," I replied, taken aback on how simple the check in process turned out to be. Everything seemed surreal.

"Welcome to UCLA!" she cheered. "Go Bruins!"

"Go Bruins!" I replied, in almost a laugh. I was no longer a homeless boy. I wasn't a criminal locked in prison. I wasn't just a kid from the inner city anymore. I was officially a Bruin.

Epilogue

IT HAS BEEN A WHILE SINCE I EXPERIENCED THE COLD sting of the night air. Or faced the everyday uncertainty homelessness brought. When I graduated UCLA I went back to San Diego to work for Reality Changers, the college prep organization which helped me apply. I had a job offer to stay in Los Angeles, but a longing in the deepness of my soul called me home. I had an obligation to give back to those students and lead them the best way I could. I served as the Director of Business and Community Relations in an effort to connect the people and be a voice of the youth.

Along my path, I found myself back in downtown San Diego on the other side of the coin. This time passing out sandwiches, playing rock–paper–scissors and performing spoken word in an effort to raise awareness for my people. All homeless people. As I pressed forward, life has a funny way of coming full circle. At Reality Changers, I helped low-income students get into college, but I wasn't touching those students who were like me. Who battled the emptiness of homelessness. The ones they said were filled with hopelessness.

I met with the talented Erin Spiewak, the new CEO of the Monarch School, and she informed me of the total reconstruction of the school. I told her the school and I weren't on the best of terms to say the least. After visiting the school I gave a keynote speech to the graduating class of 2015. Being back around my former environment convinced me I had to go back to the school. I had to be the voice I wish I had.

This is where I currently sit as the College and Career Development Coordinator. Some students are fit for college, others may be better suited for vocational school, but it is up to me to distinguish the difference. It is up to me to make them push beyond their daily grievances and work toward a better future; a future I must see even when they can't. To do so I take a trauma informed approach. I understand they have been through hell and I adhere to their trauma. But at the same time I give them no excuses. I had been given no excuses and in life we must succeed no matter the price. I hold them to the same standards I held myself: to succeed at all costs. And now I have the pleasure of helping so many young men and women find their own way home.

Acknowledgements

M Y PRAISE GOES OUT TO MY MOTHER WHO NO MAT-
ter what, always believed in me. At my lowest point, broken both physically and mentally, her undying faith in me kept
me going. I want to thank my sister who fought the good fight
right alongside me. I want to thank them for their courage. *My
Way Home* is not just my story; it is our story. Each time I tell
our story, we are forced to relive our greatest pain, our greatest
turmoil. I want to thank them for the strength to tell the story
with me and endure onward.

I want to thank the many displaced people I have met along
the way for the experiences we shared. Many who have vanished,
many who have died, many who never escaped. My story is their
story. Their story is my story.

I want to express my gratitude to the many friends who
helped make this book a reality. I received help from many community partners, colleagues, and friends along the way—Tara
Anderson, Mark Cafferty, Rebecca Smith, Nathaniel Buggs,
Dave Salisbury, Rhonda Rhyne, Professor Libby Lewis, Chris
Yanov, Jared Aaker, Erin Spiewak, Joe Wiseman, Catherine Pat-
terson, Maddy Kilkenny, Megan Collins, Gil and Gail Johnson,
Debbie and Ali Leto, John Ohanian and so many others have
impacted and helped shaped my life. It truly does take a village
to raise a child. And even more so, it takes the community to
educate and uplift its people.

About the Author

M R. MICHAEL GAULDEN RECEIVED HIS BACHELOR'S of Arts from the University of California, Los Angeles. He is a former qualitative and quantitative researcher for UCLA's Black Male Institute, a research institution whose goal is to conduct reliable research, practical interventions, and effective programs that enrich the educational experiences and life chances of minority males in the United States.

Mr. Gaulden is the former Director of Business and Community Relations for Reality Changers, a college prep organization with a focus on building first generation college students. He is experienced in business development, communications, and community relations. He is currently the Career Exploration

Coordinator and Internship Coordinator for the Monarch School Project. Monarch is the only operational school in the United States that exclusively educates K–12 students who are impacted by homelessness.

Michael also attended the school in his youth. He is an active Homeless activist, education enthusiast, poet, musician as well as an activist for all disadvantaged people. As a motivational public speaker, he has spoken to audiences ranging from 20 to 2,000. He is a Spoken Word artist and advocate for the arts. He focuses on video projects in order to shift the negative perception and connotation around homelessness and the people it impacts.